港航物流双语教学系列教材

BILINGUAL TEACHING MATERIALS OF PORT AND SHIPPING LOGISTICS

国际货运代理实务

INTERNATIONAL FREIGHT FORWARDING PRACTICE

张　敏　杨丽华　钱　芳◎编著

双语版 汉—英

BILINGUAL EDITION

中国财富出版社

图书在版编目（CIP）数据

国际货运代理实务：双语版：汉、英／张敏，杨丽华，钱芳编著．—北京：中国财富出版社，2019.12（2023.1 重印）

（港航物流双语教学系列教材）

ISBN 978－7－5047－6851－3

Ⅰ.①国…　Ⅱ.①张…　②杨…　③钱…　Ⅲ.①国际货运—货运代理—职业教育—教材—汉、英　Ⅳ.①F511.41

中国版本图书馆 CIP 数据核字（2019）第 271074 号

策划编辑　张　茜　杜　亮　　**责任编辑**　张红燕　郑晓雯

责任印制　尚立业　　**责任校对**　卓闪闪　　**责任发行**　董　倩

出版发行　中国财富出版社

社　　址　北京市丰台区南四环西路 188 号 5 区 20 楼　　**邮政编码**　100070

电　　话　010－52227588 转 2098（发行部）　　010－52227588 转 321（总编室）

010－52227566（24 小时读者服务）　　010－52227588 转 305（质检部）

网　　址　http://www.cfpress.com.cn

经　　销　新华书店

印　　刷　北京九州迅驰传媒文化有限公司

书　　号　ISBN 978－7－5047－6851－3/F·3151

开　　本　787mm×1092mm　1/16　　**版　　次**　2020 年 8 月第 1 版

印　　张　19.25　　**印　　次**　2023 年 1 月第 2 次印刷

字　　数　399 千字　　**定　　价**　52.00 元

前　言
Preface

随着市场经济的快速发展，对国际化人才的需求日益紧迫。在经济贸易全球化的国际环境下，双语教学逐步成为国内物流管理领域国际化教育的重要发展趋势。

本教材在对国际货运代理行业分析和职业岗位分析的基础上，综合考虑从业人员应掌握的基础知识和基本技能，采用任务驱动的方式，以货物出口作为主线，以中英文工作情景模拟的方式介绍了国际货运代理业认知、海上货物运输、航空货物运输、多式联运等内容。本教材内容易学、易懂、可操作性强，可帮助读者在提高专业英语水平的同时，熟悉货运代理业务内容，进而提高综合素质。同时，本教材在附录中列出了重难点词汇等资料，以便大家在学习或工作时随时查阅。

本教材由天津海运职业学院的张敏、杨丽华和青岛远洋船员职业学院的钱芳编著；由天津海运职业学院的张明齐、闫高杰，天津海运职业学院的任明雪，天津东方海诚国际货运代理有限公司的刘美一，天津誉洲国际货运代理有限公司的张杏莉，深圳广天展运物流有限公司的于华德，大连航运职业技术学院的杨凯，深圳职业技术学院的张兆民，交通运输部科学研究院的罗凯，天津电子信息职业技术学院的关剑，沧州职业技术学院的姚玉兵，福建船政交通职业学院的吴闽真，芜湖职业技术学院的孙磊，泉州海洋学院的郑小金，江苏航运职业技术学院的郭海涛等多位教师、专家共同参与研究。

本教材的出版得到天津海运职业学院的大力支持。

本教材适合高等职业教育相关专业作为教材使用，对相关自学者、企业管理人员也有一定的参考价值。

由于编写时间仓促，加之编者水平有限，凡有不妥之处，请读者批评指正。

With the rapid development of the market economy, the demand for international talents is becoming increasingly urgent. Under the international environment of economic and trade globalization, bilingual teaching has gradually become an important development trend of International Education in the field of domestic logistics management.

Based on the analysis of the international freight forwarding industry and professional positions, this textbook comprehensively considers the basic knowledge and fundamental skills that the practitioners should grasp, adopts task-driven approach, takes the export of goods as the main line, and introduces the recognition of the international freight forwarding industry, sea freight transportation, air freight transportation and multi-modal cargo transport in the way of Chinese and English work scenario simulation. Thanks to easy instruction and strong operability of this textbook, readers can improve the professional English level, familiarize with freight forwarding business content, and thus improve the overall quality. This textbook lists important & difficult vocabulary and other materials in the appendix, so that readers can consult them whenever they study or work.

This textbook is written by Zhang Min, Yang Lihua from Tianjin Maritime College and Qian Fang from Qingdao Ocean Shipping Mariners College, and participated by many other teachers or experts, such as Zhang Mingqi and Yan Gaojie from Tianjin Maritime College, Ren Mingxue from Tianjin Maritime College, Liu Meiyi from Tianjin Oriental Haicheng International Freight Forwarding Co. Ltd., Zhang Xingli from Tianjin Yuzhou International Freight Forwarders Co. Ltd., Yu Huade from Shenzhen Guangtian Exhibition Logistics Co. Ltd., Yang Kai from Dalian Shipping College, Zhang Zhaomin from Shenzhen Polytechnic, Luo Kai from China Academy of Transportation Sciences, Guan Jian from Tianjin Electronic Information College, Yao Yubing from Cangzhou Technical College, Wu Minzhen from Fujian Chuanzheng Communications College, Sun Lei from Wuhu Institute of Technology, Zheng Xiaojin from Quanzhou Ocean Institute, Guo Haitao from Jiangsu Shipping College and et cetera.

The publication of this textbook is strongly supported by Tianjin Maritime College.

This textbook is suitable for higher vocational education related majors as teaching materials, and has reference value for relevant self-learners and enterprise managers.

Due to the hasty compilation process and the limited compilers level, readers are invited to criticize and correct any inadequacies.

张敏、杨丽华、钱芳

2018 年 10 月

Zhang Min, Yang Lihua, Qian Fang

October, 2018

目　录

Contents

任务一　国际货运代理业认知
Task One：Cognition of International Freight Forwarding Industry

【知识目标】

Knowledge Goals

1. 能区分国际货运代理的相关组织协会。

   To be able to distinguish the organizations related to forwarding industry.

2. 能说明国际货运代理业务范围。

   To be able to illustrate the service scope of freight forwarder.

3. 能说明货运代理公司经营范围。

   To be able to illustrate business scope of freight forwarding company.

【技能目标】

Skill Goals

1. 能模拟货运代理公司的工作人员，进行货运代理公司的推广。

   To be able to act as the freight forwarder and carry out the promotion of the freight forwarding company.

2. 能够模拟货运代理公司的工作人员，完成公司的备案和申请工作。

   To be able to act as the freight forwarder and fulfill the task of registration and application.

子任务之一　国际货运代理相关组织协会认知
Section One：Cognition of International Freight Forwarding Organizations

任务引入
Task Introduction

小张是某职业院校集装箱运输管理专业的大一学生。本学期，他将开始学习“国际货运代理”专业课程。到底什么是国际货运代理呢？你能为他好好地诠释一下吗？

Xiao Zhang is a freshman who majors in container shipping management in a vocational college. This semester, he will begin to study a professional course called International Freight Forwarding. What is an international freight forwarder? Can you give him a good interpretation?

任务分析
Assignment Analysis

最开始，货运代理是进出口商的委托代理人，为进出口商做一些常规事务，比如装载/卸载货物，存储货物，安排地方运输……

Originally, a freight forwarder was a commission agent performing routine tasks for importers and exporters, such as loading/unloading cargo, storing goods, and arranging local transportation...

在以后的几年里，国际贸易的扩大和不同运输方式的发展扩大了货运代理的服务范围。

However, in the next few years, the expansion of international trade and the development of different modes of transport have enlarged the scope of freight forwarder services.

现在，货运代理人在国际贸易和运输中起着重要的作用。

Today, a freight forwarder plays an important role in international trade and transport.

货运代理提供的服务通常从日常基础的工作包括舱位的预定、清关等开始，到涵盖整个货物运输和分发派送过程的一揽子服务。

The services of a freight forwarder generally start from routine and basic tasks such as the booking of space and customs clearance to a comprehensive package of services covering the total transportation and distribution process.

相关知识
Relevant Knowledge

一、相关组织协会
Relevant Organizations

（一）世界贸易组织（WTO）
The World Trade Organization (WTO)

准确地说，世界贸易组织是一个联盟性的组织，联盟内的各项协定都是经乌拉圭回合多边贸易谈判共同达成的。

世界贸易组织是处理国家间贸易规则的唯一全球性国际组织。

The World Trade Organization (WTO), is best described as an umbrella organization under which the agreements that came out of the Uruguay Round of multilateral trade negotiations are gathered.

WTO is the only global international organization dealing with rules of inter-states.

（二）国际货运代理协会联合会（FIATA）
The International Federation of Freight Forwarders Associations (FIATA)

国际货运代理协会联合会是运输领域最大的非政府组织，是一个覆盖大约 4 万家转运和物流公司的行业，也被称为“运输建筑师”。

The International Federation of Freight Forwarders Associations (FIATA), the largest non-governmental organization in the field of transportation, represents an industry covering approximately 40,000 forwarding and logistics firms, also known as the “architects of transport”.

（三）中国国际货运代理协会（CIFA）
The China International Freight Forwarders Associations (CIFA)

中国国际货运代理协会（CIFA）是国际货运代理行业的国家组织。

The China International Freight Forwarders Associations (CIFA) is a national organization of international freight forwarding industry.

中国国际货运代理协会于2000年9月6日在北京成立。目前，中国国际货运代理协会拥有会员650家，全国国际货运代理企业在会数量达到6,000多家。

Founded in Sept. 6th, 2000, CIFA has 650 members including individual members and group members of the Associations at provincial and municipality level with over 6,000 members attached from each province and big city nationwide.

（四）国际航空运输协会（IATA）
The International Air Transport Association (IATA)

国际航空运输协会（IATA）是世界航空公司的贸易协会，代表约240家航空公司，占总航空运输量的84%。

The International Air Transport Association (IATA) is the trade association for the world's airlines, representing about 240 airlines and accounting for 84% of total air traffic.

（五）波罗的海国际航运公会（BIMCO）
The Baltic and International Maritime Council (BIMCO)

波罗的海国际航运公会（BIMCO）是一个航运协会，为其在航运业的全球会员（包括船东、运营商、经理、经纪人和代理）提供广泛的服务。

The Baltic and International Maritime Council (BIMCO) is a shipping association providing a wide range of services for its global members, including ship-owners, operators, managers, brokers and agents.

（六）国际海事组织（IMO）
The International Maritime Organization (IMO)

国际海事组织（IMO）是联合国专门机构，负责船舶的安全和保安以及防止船舶造成的海洋污染。

The International Maritime Organization (IMO), a specialized agency of United Nations, takes responsibility for the safety and security of shipping and the prevention of marine pollution caused by ships.

（七）国际民用航空组织（ICAO）
The International Civil Aviation Organization (ICAO)

国际民用航空组织（ICAO）是联合国的一个专门机构，目的是促进全世界安全并有秩序地发展国际民用航空。

The International Civil Aviation Organization (ICAO), a specialized agency of United Nations, aims to promote the development of international civil aviation safely and orderly in the world.

（八）世界海关组织（WCO）
The World Customs Organization (WCO)

世界海关组织（WCO）是一个独立的政府间机构，其使命是提高海关当局的效力和效率。

The World Customs Organization (WCO) is an independent intergovernmental agency whose mission is to enhance the effectiveness and efficiency of customs authorities.

（九）国际商会（ICC）
The International Chamber of Commerce (ICC)

国际商会（ICC）是世界上最大、最具代表性的商业组织。

The International Chamber of Commerce (ICC) is the largest and most representative business organization in the world.

二、全国国际货运代理行业从业人员岗位专业证书培训考试介绍
Introduction of the Training Examination

（一）国际货运代理资格考试报名条件
Registration Requirements of Qualification Examination

具有高中以上学历，或有一定的国际货运代理实践经验，或曾接受过国际货运代理业务培训并有志于从事国际货运代理业务的人员。

The people who have a high school education background, or have a certain practical experience in international freight forwarders, or have received training in international freight forwarding business and are determined to engage in international freight forwarders.

（二）国际货运代理资格考试内容

Contents of the Qualification Examination

考试分两科，即国际货运代理理论与实务和国际货运代理专业英语。

The examination consists of two sections, namely, the theory and practice of international freight forwarders, the professional English of international freight forwarders.

1. 国际货运代理理论与实务

Theory and Practice of International Freight Forwarders

国际货运代理理论与实务，内容包括：国际货运代理概论、国际贸易实务、报检与报关、班轮货物运输、租船货运实务、航空货运输、陆路货物运输、货物多式联运、仓储与物流管理、危险货物运输、货运代理市场营销、货运纠纷处理与案例。

The theory and practice of International Freight Forwarders includes the following items, such as Introduction of International Freight Forwarders, Practice of International Trade, Inspection and Customs Clearance, Liner Freight Transportation, Practice of Chartered Freight, Air Cargo Transportation, Land Cargo Transportation, Multimodal Transportation, Warehousing and Logistics Management, Dangerous Goods Transportation, Freight Marketing, Freight Dispute Handling and Cases.

2. 国际货运代理专业英语

Professional English of International Freight Forwarders

国际货运代理专业英语，内容包括：货运代理，国际贸易，进出口货物手续，海运货物保险，海上货物运输，陆路货物运输，航空货物运输，货物多式联运，供货管理和物流。

The professional English of International Freight Forwarders includes the following subjects, such as Freight Forwarding Industry, International Trade, Formalities for Import and Export Cargo, Marine Cargo Insurance, Marine Cargo Transportation, Land Freight Transportation, Air Cargo Transportation, Multimodal Transportation, Supply Management and Logistics.

各科满分均为 100 分，及格分数为 60 分。单科及格者成绩可保留至下年度有效（只允许补考一次）。两科均及格者方可获得资格证书（见图 1-1）。

The full score is 100 points and the passing score is 60. The scores of single subject passing are valid until the next year (only one make-up is allowed). Tow subjects are eligible to obtain a certificate, as shown in Figure 1-1.

图 1-1　国际货运代理从业资格证书

（三）国际货运代理资格考试内容题型介绍

Introduction of Question Types

1. 国际货代业务题型

Question Types of International Freight Forwarding

单项选择题；多项选择题；判断题；计算题；案例分析题；操作题。

Single choice questions；multiple choice questions；judgment questions；calculation questions；case analysis questions；operation questions.

2. 国际货代英语题型

Question Types of Professional English

单项选择题；多项选择题；判断题；完形填空题；英译汉；汉译英；英文单证题。

Single choice questions；multiple choice questions；judgment questions；filling in the blanks；English-Chinese translation；Chinese-English translation；English documents.

以上所有题型均采用填涂答题卡的方式答题。

All of the above questions are answered by filling in the answer sheet.

（四）CIFA 证书与 FIATA 证书对接试行方案和实施暂行办法

Trial Scheme and Implementation Measures for the Interconnection of CIFA Certificate and FIATA Certificate

2004 年 9 月，经严格审核并认定，FIATA 总部在南非太阳城召开的 2004 年 FIATA

世界代表大会上通过了中国货代协会的申办，授权中国国际货运代理协会为中国大陆唯一有资格从事 FIATA 货运代理资格证书培训和考试的组织者。

In September 2004, after strict verification and identification, FIATA World Congress, which was held by FIATA headquarters in Sun City, South Africa, passed the declaration of the China Freight Forwarders Association and authorized the China International Freight Forwarders Association as the only qualified organizer in the aspect of certificate training and examination with regard to FIATA freight forwarding.

自 2017 年起，若参加 CIFA 考试的考生，双科暨业务附加题考试成绩符合以下标准，即可申请 FIATA 证书。

Since 2017, candidates who take the CIFA exam will be able to apply for the FIATA certificate if they meet the following criteria.

（1）通过 CIFA 证书培考双科合格并取证，且业务（包括申请 FIATA 证书考生必考的有关补充培训教材内容的考试附加题）和英语笔试成绩均达到或超过 85 分的高等院校或高职院校货代物流相关专业大三以上或应届毕业生，可本着自愿的原则，在一次性缴纳取证费后，通过所在培考点向中货协申办 FIATA 证书。

Graduates who have passed the CIFA Certificate Examination and obtained evidence in both subjects, and whose business (including the additional questions on supplementary training materials required to apply for FIATA Certificate) and written English test scores have reached or exceeded 85 points, who are junior or recent graduates of freight forwarding logistics related majors in higher education institutions or higher vocational colleges, may submit FIATA certificate to the China International Freight Forwarders Association through the training and examination centers after the one-time payment on a voluntary basis.

（2）通过 CIFA 证书培考双科合格并取证，且业务（包括申请 FIATA 证书考生必考的有关补充培训教材内容的考试附加题）和英语笔试成绩均达到或超过 85 分的高等院校或高职院校非货代物流相关专业大三以上或应届毕业生，应参加所在培考点组织的 CIFA 证书考前培训，并由培考点提供培训学时证明，可本着自愿的原则，在一次性缴纳取证费后，通过所在培考点向中货协提交申办 FIATA 证书。

Graduates who have passed the CIFA Certificate Examination and obtained evidence in both subjects, and whose business (including additional questions on supplementary training materials required to apply for FIATA Certificate) and written English test scores have reached or exceeded 85 points, who are junior or recent graduates of non-freight forwarding logistics related majors in higher education institutions or higher vocational colleges, should participate in the CIFA certificate pre-examination training organized by the training center and provide the training time certificate from the training center. After that, they may submit FIATA certificate to the China International Freight Forwarders Association through the training and examination centers after the one-time payment on a voluntary basis.

(3) 社会和行业内企业从业人员申请 FIATA 证书，原则上应参加所在 FIATA 证书培训中心组织的培训且考试合格，方能获得 FIATA 证书。FIATA 证书（中国）考试中心和各 FIATA 证书培训中心，仍以社会和行业内企业从业人员为主要培训对象，此外，没有获得 CIFA 证书的高等院校或高职院校货代物流相关专业大三以上或应届毕业生也可直接报名参加所在 FIATA 证书培训中心组织的培考，不在此适用对象之列。

When applying for FIATA certificate, employees of enterprises in the society and industry should, in principle, participate in the training organized by the FIATA Diploma Freight Forwardng China Examination Center and pass the examination before they can obtain FIATA certificate. The FIATA Diploma Freight Forwarding China Examination Center and all FIATA Certificate Training Centers are still mainly trained by employees of enterprises in the society and industry. In addition, junior or recent graduates of freight forwarding logistics related majors in higher education institutions or higher vocational colleges without CIFA certificates can also sign up for the training organized by the FIATA Certification Training Center.

任务实施
Task Implementation

国际货运代理业是指接受进出口货物收货人、发货人的委托，以委托人的名义或者以自己的名义，为委托人办理国际货物运输及相关业务并收取服务报酬的行业。

The international freight forwarding business refers to the industry that accepts the entrustment of importers & exporters and consignors to deal with international cargo transportation and related businesses as well as collect service rewards in the name of the consignor or on their own behalf.

国际货运代理人是根据客户的指示，并为客户的利益而揽取货物运输的人，其本人并不是承运人。货运代理也可以依这些条件，从事与运送合同有关的活动，如储存（也含寄存）、报关、验收、收款。

An international freight forwarder, instead of a carrier, is in charge of picking up goods for transportation in accordance with the customer's instructions and benefits. Freight forwarders may also engage in activities related to shipping contracts on the basis of these conditions, such as storage (including registration), customs declaration, acceptance, and collection.

思考题
Questions

1. CIFA 证书与 FIATA 证书对接条件有哪些？

What are the conditions for connecting a CIFA certificate to a FIATA certificate?

2. 请说明获得资格证书 CIFA 考试的成绩合格标准。

Please indicate the eligibility criteria for the CIFA exam.

子任务之二　国内外知名航运企业认知
Section Two: Cognition of Renowned Shipping Enterprises at Home and Abroad

任务引入
Task Introduction

小张是某职业院校集装箱运输管理专业的学生。他今后的就业方向是成为一名国际货运代理企业的员工。请你为他介绍一下国内外知名的航运企业吧。

Xiao Zhang is a student with the major of container transportation management in a vocational college, who strives to become an employee of an international freight forwarding company. Please give him a brief introduction on well-known shipping enterprises in the world.

任务分析
Assignment Analysis

货运代理公司主要负责货物运输的业务，有内贸也有外贸。分为一级国际货运代理有限公司，还有二级、三级国际货运代理有限公司等。一级代理可以直接在空运公司、海运公司或铁路公司订舱，二级代理只能在一级代理订舱，显然国际货运代理行业的形成，是国际商品流通过程的必然产物，是国际贸易不可缺少的组成部分。

Freight forwarding companies are mainly responsible for the transportation of goods with domestic trade and foreign trade, which can be classified into Tier-One, Tier-Two, Tier-Three, etc. Tier-One agent could directly book shipments from air transport company, sea shipping company or railway freight company, and Tier-Two agent has no other choice but Tier-One agent. Obviously, the formation of the international freight forwarding industry is an inevitable product of the international commodity circulation process and an indispensable part of the international trade.

相关知识
Relevant Knowledge

一、货运代理公司经营范围
Business Scope of Freight Forwarding Company

（1）舱位预定 Booking Space

（2）装、拆集装箱 Stuffing / Destuffing Containers

（3）出示货物收据 Issuing Cargo Receipts

（4）收取运费及其他授权服务费用 Collecting Freight and Other Charges for Authorized Services

（5）集装箱及其他设备的维修保养 Repairing and Maintaining Containers and Other Equipments

（6）安排与货运公司的货运代理人签订合同 Arranging to Sign Contracts with Freight Forwarder

（7）内陆运输 Inland Transportation

（8）与有资质的报关行签订合同 Sign Contracts with Licensed Customs Broker

二、国际货运代理业务范围
Business Scope of Freight Forwarding

如果发货人或者收货人不想亲自去办理那些烦琐的手续的话，货运代理人将代表他们去处理货物运输中所涉及的各个环节。

Unless the consignor, the person sending goods, or the consignee, the person receiving goods, wants to attend to any of the procedural and documentary formalities himself, the freight forwarder could handle the various steps involved in the transportation of goods on their behalf.

货运代理人可以直接或者通过次承包商或者另外雇用代理来提供这些服务。

The freight forwarder may provide these services directly or through sub-contractors or other agencies employed by him.

（一）货运代理人代表发货人（出口商）所要做的工作
On Behalf of the Consignor (Exporter)

（1）挑选运输线路、运输方式和合适的承运人。

Choose the route, mode of transport and a suitable carrier.

（2）跟选定的承运人订舱。

Book space with the selected carrier.

（3）接收货物，并出示货运代理人收讫货物证明和货运代理人运输证书。

Take delivery of the goods and issue relevant documents such as the Forwarders' Certificate of Receipt, the Forwarders' Certificate of Transport, etc.

（4）研究适用于货物出口国家和进口国家，以及中转国家运输的信用证条款和政府所有相关规定，并准备所有必须提供的单证文件。

Study the provisions of the letter of credit and all government regulations applicable to the shipment of goods in the country of export, the country of import, as well as any transit country and prepare all the necessary documents.

（5）货物的包装（在货物包装时）要考虑运输路线、运输方式、货物特性，还要适用于出口国、中转国和目的地国家的规定。

The route, the mode of transport, the nature of the goods and applicable regulations in the country of export, transit countries and the country of destination need to be taken into account when packing goods.

（6）如果必要的话，要安排货物的仓储。

Arrange warehousing of the goods, if necessary.

（7）测定货物的重量和尺寸。

Weigh and measure the goods.

（8）提醒发货人注意货物的投保，如果发货人需要投保，则须办理货物的保险。

Draw the consignor's attention to the need for insurance and arrange for the insurance of goods, if required by the consignor.

（9）将货物运往港口，安排清关，办理相关手续并将货物交付给承运人。

Transport the goods to the port, arrange for customs clearance, related documentation formalities and deliver the goods to the carrier.

（10）关注外汇交易。

Attend to foreign exchange transactions.

（11）支付手续费和其他包括运费在内的费用。

Pay fees and other charges including freight.

（12）从承运人处取得已签署的提单，并将提单转交给发货人。

Obtain the signed bills of lading from the carrier and arrange delivery to the consignor.

（13）如果必要的话，安排转运路线。

Arrange for transshipment route if necessary.

(14) 通过联系承运人和海外的货运代理，监控货物的运输直至货物交付给收货人。

Monitor the movement of goods all the way to the consignee through contacts with the carrier and the forwarders' agents abroad.

(15) 记录货损货失。

Record damages or losses of the goods.

(16) 如果货物有损失，需要帮助发货人向承运人提出索赔。

Assist the consignor in pursuing claims, if any, against the carrier for loss of the goods or for damage to them.

(二) 货运代理人代表收货人（进口商）所要做的工作

On Behalf of the Consignee (Importer)

(1) 当收货人支付运费时，即由收货人负责货物运输，货运代理人应替收货人监控货物的运输。

Monitor the transport of goods on behalf of the consignee when the consignee controls freight, that is, the cargo.

(2) 接受并审查所有与货物运输有关的单证。

Receive and check all relevant documents relating to the transport of the goods.

(3) 从承运人处提货物，必要时支付运费。

Take delivery of the goods from the carrier and, if necessary, pay the freight costs.

(4) 安排货物的清关，并向海关和相关部门支付关税、手续费及其他费用。

Arrange customs clearance and pay duties, fees and other charges to the customs and other relevant departments.

(5) 如果必要的话，安排中转仓库。

Arrange transit warehousing, if necessary.

(6) 将清关后的货物交付给收货人。

Deliver the cleared goods to the consignee.

(7) 必要时，帮助收货人向承运人就货物的丢失或者任何损坏提出索赔。

Assist the consignee, if necessary, in pursuing claims against the carrier for the loss of the goods or any damage to them.

(8) 必要时，帮助收货人安排货物入仓和配送。

Assist the consignee, if necessary, in warehousing and distribution.

任务实施
Task Implementation

一、马士基航运公司
Maersk Line

从 1928 年开始，马士基航运公司一直在提供可靠、灵活、高效节能环保的运输和物流服务。今天，该公司提供通过海运和陆运实现全球各地的点对点运输。作为全球领先的航运公司，每天都会运送数百万吨货物。公司拥有庞大的货运网络，覆盖全球逾 120 个国家或地区的 300 多个港口，帮助客户实现与全球各地之间快速、可靠且定期的连通。

Maersk Line has been known for reliable, flexible and eco-efficient transportation and logistics services since 1928. Today, it provides end-to-end transportation to every corner of the world, both by sea and by land. As the world's leading shipping line, it carries millions of tons of cargo every single day. Its vast network covers over 300 ports in more than 120 countries or regions, giving customers a fast, reliable and regular connection to all corners of the world.

公司的 33,000 名员工全身心地帮助客户优化供应链和实现业务目标。通过遍布 114 个国家或地区的 306 个办事处以及 630 艘船舶为客户提供服务，确保完美履行对客户的承诺。

33,000 employees are dedicated to helping customers optimize supply chains and realize business ambitions. By providing services to customers through 306 offices and 630 vessels throughout 114 countries or regions, Maersk Line succeeds in ensuring the perfect fulfillment of their commitment to customers.

马士基航运公司致力于成为可持续航运领域的领导者。已经实现了业内最低的二氧化碳航运排放。

Maersk Line is committed to being the leader in sustainable shipping, having already achieved the lowest emissions of carbon dioxide in the industry.

二、中国远洋海运集团
China COSCO Shipping Corporation Limited

中国远洋海运集团完善的全球化服务铸就了网络服务优势与品牌优势。以全球航运、综合物流和航运金融服务为核心业务，发展多元化产业集群，构建成为一家提供综合物流和供应链服务的世界领先企业。

The perfect global service of COSCO Shipping has built the advantages of network service and brand. Taking global shipping, integrated logistics, and shipping related financial services as core business, and developing diversified industrial clusters, so as to build a world-leading business entity that provides integrated logistics and supply chain services.

集团在全球集装箱码头超过 52 个，泊位数超过 218 个，集装箱年处理能力 11800 万 TEU，集装箱码头吞吐量居世界第一。全球船舶燃料销量超过 2500 万吨，居世界第一。集装箱租赁规模超过 270 万传输扩展单元（TEU），居世界第三。海洋工程装备制造接单规模以及船舶代理业务也稳居世界前列。

The Company owns over 52 container terminals in the world, with over 218 berthing spaces. The throughput of its container terminals worldwide amounts to 118 million TEU, taking the first place in the world; the preferred global sales volume for its ship bunker fuel exceeds 25 million tons, topping the world's list; the container leasing business scale surpasses 2.7 million TEU, which is the third-largest in the world. In addition, the scale of marine engineering equipment manufacturing and the business of shipping agency are also in the forefront of the world.

该集团的物流产业集群包括工程物流、货运代理、仓储网络、多式联运、船舶代理等业务。定位于全球领先的综合性第三方物流服务商，将成为中国企业走向海外市场优先选择的全球物流合作伙伴。

The logistics industrial cluster includes project logistics, freight forwarding, warehouses, multi-modal transport, vessel agency, etc. As the world's leading comprehensive third-party logistics service provider, it will become the preferred global logistics partner for Chinese enterprises to choose in overseas markets.

思考题
Questions

1. 通过上网搜索调研，请列举出一个国际货运代理企业，填写表 1-1。

Through Internet search research, please list out an international freight forwarding company and fill in the Table 1-1.

表 1-1　　国际货运代理企业信息

	中文	英文
公司名称		
公司信息		
商业代码		

Table 1-1　The Information of International Freight Forwarding Company

	Chinese	English
Company Name		
Company Profile		
Business Scope		

2. 假如你在××国际货运代理公司 INTERNATIONAL SHIPPING & TRADING COMPANY 担任货代销售，请根据以下要点编订中英文公司介绍，从而为公司拓展业务。

If you work as a forwarder for an international shipping and trading company, please compile the introduction in Chinese and English according to the following points, so as to expand the business of the company.

（1）公司业务主要包括集装箱运输等全方位物流服务。

The company's business mainly covers container transportation and other logistics services at full range.

（2）公司能够提供海上出口和航空出口服务。

The company is able to provide ocean export and air export services.

（3）在某些航线上具有优势。

The company has advantages on certain routes.

（4）具备强大的海外代理网络。

The company has a strong network on overseas agents.

（5）能够为客户提供优质的服务和有竞争力的价格。

The company is able to provide customers with quality service and competitive prices.

子任务之三　国际货运代理企业的设立
Section Three: Establishment of International Freight Forwarding Enterprise

任务引入
Task Introduction

请你以××国际货运代理企业法人代表的身份，根据以下资料，完成该企业的备案和申请工作。

As a legal representative of an international freight forwarding enterprise, you're required to complete the filing and application of the company based on the following information.

企业名称：

Enterprise Name:

住所与经营场所：天津市×××路×××号（邮编：300350）

Address: No. ×××, ××× Road, Tianjin (Zip Code: 300350)

电话：022-2877××××，传真：022-2877××××

Telephone Number: 022-2877××××, Fax: 022-2877××××

企业网址：www. ××. com. cn

Enterprise Website: www. ××. com. cn

邮箱：××@ ××. com

E-mail: ××@ ××. com

法人代表：

Legal Representative:

企业代码：

Enterprise Code:

组织机构代码：JD×××××××

Organization Code:

工商登记注册号：GS9 ×××××××

Business Registration Number: GS9 ×××××××

登记日期：

Registration Date:

注册资金：800 万元

Registered Capital: 8 million yuan

取得职业资格证书人数：10 人

Number of People Who Obtained Vocational Qualification Certificates: 10

运输方式：海运

Transportation Mode: Sea Transportation

货物类型：一般货物、集装箱、散杂货

Type of Goods: General Cargo, Container Cargo and Bulk Cargo

服务项目：订舱，分销，仓储，中转，集装箱的整合、报关、检疫、保险，船舶服务，运费率以及海事信息咨询服务

Service Items: space booking, distribution, warehousing, transshipment, containers' consolidation, customs declaration, quarantine and insurance, ship movement service, freight rate, maritime information as well as consultation service

经营方式：国际货运代理业务

Operation Mode: International Freight Forwarding Business

保险公司：××保险公司

Insurance Company:

保险合同号：×××××××××（9 位数字）

Insurance Contract Number: ×××××××××

任务分析
Assignment Analysis

国际货运代理业务的申请人应当是与进出口贸易或国际货物运输有关，并有稳定货源的单位。符合以上条件的投资者应当在申请项目中占大股。

The applicant for the international freight forwarding business should be the one that is related to import and export trade or international cargo transportation and has stable sources of supply. Investors who meet the above conditions should occupy large shares in the application projects.

国际货运代理企业应当依法取得中华人民共和国企业法人资格。企业组织形式为有限责任公司或股份有限公司。经营海上国际运输代理业务的企业，注册资本最低 500 万元；经营航空国际运输代理业务的，注册资本最低 300 万元；经营陆路国际运输代理业务的，注册资本最低 200 万元。每设立一个从事国际货物运输代理业务的分支机构，应当增加 50 万元注册资本。

International freight forwarding companies shall obtain the qualifications of legal enterprise of the People's Republic of China in accordance with law. The organizational form of the company is a limited liability company or a company limited by shares. Enterprises that engage in international maritime transport agency business have a minimum registeredcapital of 5 million yuan; those that operate aviation international transport agency business have a minimum registered capital of 3 million yuan; and those that engage in land international transport agency business have a minimum registered capital of 2 million yuan. Each time the company establishes a branch engaged in international cargo transportation agency business, it shall increase its registered capital by 500, 000 yuan.

相关知识
Relevant Knowledge

一、国际货运代理企业备案
Registration of International Freight Forwarding Corporation

国际货运代理企业备案程序如下。

The procedures for the registration of international freight forwarding corporation are as follows.

（一）领取《国际货运代理企业备案表》（以下简称《备案表》）

Collect the "International Freight Forwarders Registration Form"（hereinafter refered to as the "Registration Form"）

国际货代企业可以通过中华人民共和国商务部网站（http：//www. mofcom. gov. cn）下载，或者到所在地备案机关领取备案表。

Collect the International Freight Forwarders Registration Form（hereinafter referred to as the Registration Form）. International freight forwarding companies can download the documents through the website of the Ministry of Commerce of the People's Republic of China（http：// www. mofcom. gov. cn）or obtain a registration form from the local registration authority.

（二）填写《备案表》
Fill in the "Registration Form"

国际货代企业应按《备案表》要求认真填写所有事项的信息，并确保所填写内容完整、准确和真实；同时认真阅读《备案表》背面的条款，并由法定代表人签字、盖章。

Fill in the Registration Form. The legal representative of the international freight forwarding companies is supposed to fill in the information of all matters in accordance with the requirements of the Registration Form, ensuring that all the contents filled in are complete, accurate and truthful. At the same time, the legal representative is required to read carefully, then sign and seal the terms on the back of the Registration Form.

（三）向备案机关提交如下备案材料

Submit the Following Materials to the Registration Authority

（1）按本条第二款要求填写的《备案表》。

Completed Registration Form according to the above requirements.

（2）营业执照复印件。

Copy of business license.

（3）组织机构代码证书复印件。

Copy of organization code certificate.

备案机关应自收到国际货代企业提交的上述材料之日起5日内办理备案手续，在备案表上加盖备案印章。备案机关在完成备案手续的同时，应当完整、准确地记录和保存国际货代企业的备案信息材料，依法建立备案档案。国际货代企业应携带加盖备案印章的备案表在30日内到有关部门办理开展国际货代业务所需的有关手续。

The Registration Authority shall go through the registration procedures within 5 days from the date of receipt of the above-mentioned materials submitted by the International Freight Forwarding Company, and shall put a seal on the Registration Form. While completing the registration procedures, the Registration Authority should record as well as preserve the information materials of International Freight Forwarding Company for archival purposes completely and establish registration files in accordance with law accurately. International Freight Forwarding Company could go through relevant registration procedures for the international freight forwarding business on the basis of the registration form stamped and sealed within 30 days.

二、国际货运代理企业税务登记

Tax Registration of International Freight Forwarding Corporation

办理税务登记应当出示、提供以下证件资料（所提供资料原件用于税务机关审核，复印件留存税务机关，复印件一式两份，国税局、地税局各留存一份，纳税人须在复印件上逐页签字加盖公章，并签署“与原件相符”字样，同一证件资料如果页数较多，可仅在首页签署“与原件相符”字样并签字盖章，同时骑缝加盖公章。

For the tax registration, the following documents should be presented and provided.

The original documents provided shall be used for examination by the tax authorities, and the copy shall be retained by the tax authority. The copy shall be in duplicate, each of which needs to be kept for National Tax and Local Tax separately. The taxpayer must sign the copy page by page, stamp the official seal, and sign the words of "consistent with the original". For the same document containing a number of pages, the taxpayer can only sign the words of "consistent with the original" on the front page and meanwhile stamp the official paging seal.

（1）营业执照副本或其他核准执业证件原件及其复印件。

The original and copy of the business license or other approved practice documents.

（2）组织机构代码证书副本原件及其复印件。

The original and copy of organization code certificate.

（3）注册地址及生产、经营地址证明（产权证、租赁协议）原件及其复印件；如为自有房产，请提供产权证或买卖契约等合法的产权证明原件及其复印件；如为租赁的场所，请提供租赁协议原件及其复印件，出租人为自然人的请提供产权证明的复印件；如生产、经营地址与注册地址不一致，请分别提供相应证明。

The original and photocopies of the registration address and the proof of production and operation address (property right certificate and lease agreement). If it is a private property, please provide the original and photocopies of the legal property right certificate such as property right certificate or sales contract. If it is a leasing place, please provide the original and photocopies of the lease agreement. If the lessor is a natural person, please provide the copies of the certificate of property rights. If the production and business addresses are inconsistent with the registration addresses, please provide corresponding certificates separately.

（4）公司章程复印件。

Copy of the company's articles of association.

（5）有权力机关出具的验资报告或评估报告原件及其复印件。

The original and copy of the capital verification report or assessment report issued by the authority.

（6）法定代表人（负责人）居民身份证、护照或其他证明身份的合法证件原件及其复印件。

The original and copy of the legal representative's identity card, passport or other legal documents that certify his/her identity.

（7）纳税人跨省（市）设立的分支机构办理税务登记时，须提供总机构的税务登记证（国、地税）副本复印件。

When taxpayers conduct tax registration in branches established across provinces (cities), they must also provide copies of the tax registration certificates (national and local taxes) of the headquarters.

（8）改组改制企业须提供有关改组改制的批文原件及其复印件。

The reorganization and restructuring enterprises must provide the original and duplicate of the approval documents for reorganization and restructuring.

（9）外商投资企业须提供商务部门批复设立证书原件及复印件。

Foreign-invested enterprises also need to provide the original and duplicate of the certificate approved by the business department.

税务机关对对外贸易经营者报送的税务登记表应在受理之日起 30 日内审核完毕，符合规定的予以登记，发放税务登记证（或注册税务登记表）及其副本。

Tax authorities shall examine and verify the tax registration forms submitted by foreign trade operators within 30 days from the date of acceptance, register them in conformity with the regulations, and issue tax registration certificates (or registered tax registration forms) and copies thereof.

三、国际货运代理企业报检注册登记

Inspection & Quarantine of International Freight Forwarding Corporation

（一）国际货运代理企业报检注册登记许可条件

Conditions for Inspection and Registration of International Freight Forwarding Corporation

（1）取得工商行政管理部门颁发的《企业法人营业执照》。

Having the Business License for Enterprise Legal Person issued by the administrative department for industry and commerce.

（2）注册资金 150 万元以上。

Having the registered capital of more than 1.5 million yuan.

（3）有固定营业场所及符合办理检验检疫报检业务所需的设施。

Having a fixed business place and facilities that meet the requirements for quarantine inspection.

（4）有健全的有关代理报检的管理制度。

Having a sound management system for agent inspection.

（5）有不少于10名取得国家质量监督检验检疫总局（以下简称质检总局）颁发的《报检员资格证》人员。

There are not less than 10 persons who have obtained the Certificate of inspection issued by General Administration of Quality Supervision, Inspection and Quarantine of the People's Republic of China（AQSIQ）.

（二）许可程序

Licensing Procedures

（1）申请单位通过中国检验电子业务平台（www.eciq.cn）填写并提交申请，同时打印申请书（具体操作可查询"报检单位、报检员注册管理系统或企业用户操作说明"）。

The applicant fills in and submits the application through the China Inspection Electronic Business Platform（www.eciq.cn）, and prints the application form at the same time（for details, please refer to "the operation instructions of the inspection & registration management system enterprise user"）

（2）申请单位到受理地点向有关检验检疫局提交以下申请材料。

The applicant shall submit the following application materials to the relevant inspection and quarantine bureau at the place of acceptance.

①《代理出入境检验检疫报检注册登记申请书》。

Application for registration of entry and exit inspection and quarantine.

②《企业法人营业执照》或《营业执照》正本复印件（同时交验副本原件）。

A copy of the original Business License of Enterprise Legal Person or Business License（with the original copy submitted for examination）.

③《企业组织机构代码证》复印件（同时交验正本）。

A copy of the Enterprise Organization Code Certificate（with the original submitted for examination）.

④拟任报检员的《报检员资格证》复印件（同时交验正本）。

A copy of the "Inspector's Qualification Certificate" to be appointed as an inspector（with the original submitted for examination）.

⑤代理报检企业的印章印模。

A seal of the inspection and quarantine enterprises.

⑥企业声明。

Corporate statement.

⑦质检总局规定的其他材料。

Other materials as stipulated by AQSIQ.

（3）有关检验检疫局根据申请单位提交的材料是否齐全、是否符合法定形式作出受理或不予受理的决定，并按规定出具书面凭证。

The relevant Inspection and Quarantine Bureau shall make a decision of acceptance or inadmissibility on the basis of the completeness of the materials submitted by the applicant and the conformity with the legal form, and shall issue written certificates in accordance with the regulations.

（4）受理申请后，有关检验检疫局按规定对申请材料具体内容进行审查，对申请单位的营业场所和办公条件等进行现场核查，对其有关代理报检的管理制度进行评审。

After accepting the application, the relevant Inspection and Quarantine Bureau shall examine the specific contents of the application materials according to the regulations, conduct on-site verification of the business premises and office conditions of the applicant, and evaluate the management system of the inspection and quarantine.

（5）初步审查合格的，由有关检验检疫局将初审意见连同申请材料报送质检总局；初审不合格的，出具不予许可通知书并说明理由。

If the preliminary examination is qualified, the relevant Inspection and Quarantine Bureau shall submit the preliminary examination opinions together with the application materials to the AQSIQ. If the preliminary examination is unqualified, a notice of disapproval shall be issued and the reasons shall be explained.

（6）国家质检总局根据规定，对申请材料和初审意见进行审查，并提出具体审批意见。

According to the regulations, AQSIQ examines the application materials and the preliminary examination opinions, and proposes specific approval opinions.

（7）有关检验检疫局根据质检总局的审批意见做出准予许可或不予许可的决定。准予许可的，于10个工作日内颁发《出入境检验检疫代理报检注册登记证书》；不予许可的，书面说明理由。

The relevant Inspection and Quarantine Bureau shall decide whether to grant or not to grant permission in accordance with the approval opinions of the AQSIQ. If the license is granted, the "Registration Certificate of Entry-Exit Inspection and Quarantine" shall be issued within 10 working days. If the license is not granted, the reasons shall be stated in writing.

四、国际货运代理企业海关注册登记

Customs Registration of International Freight Forwarding Corporation

申请人申请报关企业注册登记，须附以下文件资料。

The applicant applies for the enterprise registration of customs declaration with the following documents.

（1）直属海关注册登记许可文件。

Registration and licensing documents.

（2）《企业法人营业执照》副本（分支机构提交营业执照）复印件。

A copy of the Business License of Enterprise Legal Person (the business license submitted by a branch).

（3）税务登记证书副本复印件。

A copy of the tax registration certificate.

（4）银行开户证明复印件。

A copy of bank account opening certificate.

（5）组织机构代码证书复印件。

A copy of organization code certificate.

（6）《报关单位情况登记表》（联系人填报关业务负责人）、《出资者情况登记表》《企业管理人员情况登记表》。

The Registration Form of Customs Declaration (the person in charge of customs declaration business filled out), the Registration Form of Investors and the Registration Form for Enterprise Management Personnel.

（7）报关企业与所聘报关员签订的用工劳动合同复印件。

A copy of the employment contract signed between the customs declaration enterprise and the customs declarant.

（8）法人身份证复印件。

A copy of ID card of legal representative.

（9）其他与报关注册登记有关的文件材料。

Other materials related to customs declaration and registration.

申请单位应当将以上资料的原件交给注册地海关验核，并在复印件上（A4 纸）加盖企业公章。注册地海关接受申请后 3 日内办妥注册登记，并对申请材料齐全、符合法定形式的申请人核发“中华人民共和国海关进出口货物收发货人报关注册登记证书”，有效期限为3年。

The applicant shall submit the original of the above materials to the Customs of the place of registration for verification, and affix the official seal of the enterprise on the copy (A4 paper). The Customs of the place of registration shall complete the registration within 3 days after accepting the application, and issue the "registration certificate of customs declaration for consignee and consignor's import and export goods in the People's Republic of China" to the applicants with complete materials and legal forms, valid for 3 years.

任务实施
Task Implementation

一、国际货运代理企业名称预先核准
Pre-approval of International Freight Forwarding Enterprise

新设立的企业，须依法经中华人民共和国国家市场监督管理总局核准名称，填写企业名称预先核准申请书（见表1-2）。

The newly established enterprise shall be subject to the name approved by the State Administration for Market Regulation (SAMR) in accordance with the law, and fill in the name of the enterprise. Application for pre-approval is shown in Table 1-2.

表1-2　　企业名称预先核准申请书

<table>
<tr><td colspan="4">□企业设立名称预先核准</td></tr>
<tr><td>申请企业名称</td><td colspan="3"></td></tr>
<tr><td rowspan="3">备选
企业字号</td><td colspan="3">1.</td></tr>
<tr><td colspan="3">2.</td></tr>
<tr><td colspan="3">3.</td></tr>
<tr><td>企业住所地</td><td colspan="3">__________省（市/自治区）__________市（地区/盟/自治州）
__________县（自治县/旗/自治旗/市/区）</td></tr>
<tr><td>注册资本
（金）</td><td>__________万元</td><td>企业类型</td><td></td></tr>
<tr><td>经营范围</td><td colspan="3"></td></tr>
</table>

续表

投资人	名称或姓名	证照号码
（指定代表或委托代理人、具体经办人身份证件复印件粘贴处）		
申请人 签字或盖章	年　　月　　日	

注：“企业类型”栏目应根据以下具体类型选择填写，有限责任公司、股份有限公司、分公司、非公司企业法人、营业单位、企业非法人分支机构、个人独资企业、合伙企业。

Table1-2　　Name Pre-approval of Application Form

Enterprise Name			
Alternatives	1.		
	2.		
	3.		
Enterprise Address	________province________city ________country		
Registered Capital	________yuan	Enterprise Type	
Business Scope			
Investors	Name	License Number	
Paste the copy of ID card of designated representative, entrusted agent or specific handler			
Signature or Seal by Applicant	Specific Date		

Remarks: The column “Types of Enterprises” should be filled in according to the following specific types, limited liability company, company limited by shares, branch company, non-corporate legal person, business company, non-corporate branch, sole proprietorship enterprise and partnership enterprise.

二、国际货运代理企业备案

Registration of International Freight Forwarding Enterprise

国际货运代理企业业务备案表（见表1-3）。

The registration form of international freight forwarding enterprise is shown in Table 1-3.

表1-3　　国际货运代理企业业务备案表

<table>
<tr><td>企业名称</td><td></td><td>经营代码</td><td></td></tr>
<tr><td>年末职工人数</td><td></td><td>取得国际货代资格证书人数</td><td></td></tr>
<tr><td>货运车辆（辆/吨）</td><td></td><td>集装箱卡车（标准箱）</td><td></td></tr>
<tr><td>自有仓库（平方米）</td><td></td><td>保税、监管库（平方米）</td><td></td></tr>
<tr><td>铁路专用线（条）</td><td></td><td>物流计算机信息管理系统（套）</td><td></td></tr>
<tr><td>海关注册登记证书号</td><td></td><td>商检报检单位登记号</td><td></td></tr>
<tr><td colspan="4">年度经营情况</td></tr>
<tr><td rowspan="2">运输方式</td><td colspan="3">全年出口</td></tr>
<tr><td>散货（吨）</td><td>集装箱货物（标准箱）</td><td>营业额（万元人民币）</td></tr>
<tr><td>海运</td><td></td><td></td><td></td></tr>
<tr><td>陆运</td><td></td><td></td><td></td></tr>
<tr><td>空运</td><td></td><td></td><td></td></tr>
<tr><td>快件</td><td colspan="2">件</td><td></td></tr>
<tr><td rowspan="2">运输方式</td><td colspan="3">全年进口</td></tr>
<tr><td>散货（吨）</td><td>集装箱货物（标准箱）</td><td>营业额（万元人民币）</td></tr>
<tr><td>海运</td><td></td><td></td><td></td></tr>
<tr><td>陆运</td><td></td><td></td><td></td></tr>
<tr><td>空运</td><td></td><td></td><td></td></tr>
<tr><td>快件</td><td colspan="2">件</td><td></td></tr>
<tr><td>仓储营业额</td><td>（　　万元人民币）</td><td>其他营业额</td><td>（　　万元人民币）</td></tr>
<tr><td>年营业总额</td><td colspan="3">其中美元（万元）：　　　　人民币（万元）：</td></tr>
<tr><td>年净利润总额
（万元人民币）</td><td></td><td>缴纳税金
（万元人民币）</td><td></td></tr>
<tr><td colspan="2">（企业公章）
年　月　日</td><td colspan="2">（法定代表人签名）</td></tr>
</table>

Table 1-3　The Registration Form of International Freight Forwarding Enterprise

Enterprise Name		Business Code	
Number of Employees at the End of the Year		Number of People who have Obtained International Freight Forwarding Qualification Certificate	
Freight Vehicle (vehicle/ton)		Container Truck (standard)	
Self-owned Warehouse (square meters)		Bonded and Supervised Warehouse (square meters)	
Special Railway (lines)		Logistics Computer Information Management System (sets)	
Customs Registration Certificate Number		Registration Number of Commodity Inspection	

Annual Operation			
Transport Modes	Annual Export		
	Bulk Cargo (tons)	Container Cargo (standard container)	Turnover (10, 000 yuan)
Ocean Shipping			
Road Transportation			
Air Freighting			
Express Delivery	Pieces		
Transport Modes	Annual Import		
	Bulk Cargo (tons)	Container Cargo (standard container)	Turnover (10, 000 yuan)
Ocean Shipping			
Road Transportation			
Air Freighting			
Express Delivery	Pieces		

Warehousing Turnover	(10, 000 yuan)	Other Turnover	(10, 000 yuan)
Annual Turnover	Including USD (10, 000):	RMB (10, 000):	
Total Annual Net Profit (10, 000 yuan)		Tax Payment (10, 000 yuan)	
(Corporate Seal) Specific Date		(Signature of Legal Representative)	

三、国际货运代理企业税务登记

Tax Registration of International Freight Forwarder Enterprise

国际货运代理企业税务登记，填写税务登记表（见表1-4）。

The tax registration of international freight forwarder enterprise, fill in the tax registration form（as shown in Table 1-4）.

表1-4　　税务登记表
（适用单位纳税人）

填表日期：

<table>
<tr><td>纳税人名称</td><td colspan="3"></td><td colspan="2">纳税人识别号</td><td colspan="2"></td></tr>
<tr><td>登记注册类型</td><td colspan="3"></td><td colspan="2">批准设立机关</td><td colspan="2"></td></tr>
<tr><td>组织机构代码</td><td colspan="3"></td><td colspan="2">批准设立证明或文件号</td><td colspan="2"></td></tr>
<tr><td>开业（设立）日期</td><td></td><td>生产经营期限</td><td></td><td>证照名称</td><td></td><td>证照号码</td><td></td></tr>
<tr><td>注册地址</td><td colspan="2"></td><td>邮政编码</td><td colspan="2"></td><td>联系电话</td><td></td></tr>
<tr><td>生产经营地址</td><td colspan="2"></td><td>邮政编码</td><td colspan="2"></td><td>联系电话</td><td></td></tr>
<tr><td>核算方式</td><td colspan="4">请选择对应项目打“√”　□独立核算
□非独立核算度</td><td>从业人数</td><td colspan="2">____（其中外籍人____）</td></tr>
<tr><td>单位性质</td><td colspan="7">请选择对应项目打“√”　□企业　□事业单位　□社会团体
□民办非企业单位　□其他</td></tr>
<tr><td>网站网址</td><td colspan="3"></td><td>国标行业</td><td colspan="3">□□□□□□□□□□</td></tr>
<tr><td>适用会计制度</td><td colspan="7">请选择对应项目打“√”
□企业会计制度　□小企业会计制度
□金融企业会计制度　□行政事业单位会计制度</td></tr>
<tr><td colspan="8">经营范围
主营：________________
____
兼营：________________
________________</td></tr>
</table>

续表

项目 内容 联系人	姓　名	身份证件		固定电话	移动电话	电子邮箱
		种类	号码			
法定代表人 （负责人）						
财务负责人						
办税人						

税务代理人名称	纳税人识别号	联系电话	电子邮箱

注册资本或投资总额	币种	金额	币种	金额	币种	金额

投资方名称	投资方 经济性质	投资比例	证件种类	证件号码	国籍 或地址	

自然人投资比例		外资投资比例		国有投资比例	

分支机构名称	注册地址	纳税人识别号

总机构名称		纳税人识别号	
注册地址		经营范围	

法定代表人姓名		联系电话		注册地址邮政编码	

代扣代缴 代收代缴 税款业务 情　　况	代扣代缴、代收代缴税款业务内容	代扣代缴、代收代缴税种

附报资料：	

经办人签章： 年　月　日	法定代表人（负责人）签章： 年　月　日	纳税人公章： 年　月　日

Table 1-4 **The Tax Registration Form**

(applicable to enterprise taxpayers)

Date of Filling

<table>
<tr><td>Taxpayer Name</td><td colspan="4"></td><td colspan="2">Taxpayer Identification Number</td><td colspan="2"></td></tr>
<tr><td>Registration Type</td><td colspan="3"></td><td colspan="3">Approval Authority</td><td colspan="2"></td></tr>
<tr><td>Organization Code</td><td colspan="3"></td><td colspan="3">Approval Certificateor Document Number</td><td colspan="2"></td></tr>
<tr><td>Establishment Date</td><td></td><td>Production and Operation Period</td><td></td><td>License Name</td><td colspan="2"></td><td>License Number</td><td></td></tr>
<tr><td>Registered Address</td><td colspan="3"></td><td>Postal Code</td><td></td><td>Contact Number</td><td colspan="2"></td></tr>
<tr><td>Production and Operation Address</td><td colspan="3"></td><td>Postal Code</td><td></td><td>Contact Number</td><td colspan="2"></td></tr>
<tr><td>Accounting Method</td><td colspan="4">Please tick "√" for the corresponding items
□Independent accounting
□Non-independent accounting</td><td colspan="2">Number of Employees</td><td colspan="2">________ Including
________ foreigners</td></tr>
<tr><td>Organization Type</td><td colspan="8">Please tick "√" for the corresponding items □Enterprise □Public institution
□Social organization □Private non-enterprise □Other</td></tr>
<tr><td>Website Address</td><td colspan="3"></td><td colspan="2">National Standard Industry</td><td colspan="3">□□□□□□□□</td></tr>
<tr><td>Applicable Accounting System</td><td colspan="8">Please tick "√" for the corresponding items
□Enterprise accounting system □Small business accounting system
□Financial enterprise accounting system □Administrative institution accounting system</td></tr>
<tr><td colspan="9">Business Scope
Main business: ________________________________
____
Secondary business: ________________________________
________________________________</td></tr>
</table>

Continued

Project / Content / Contact	Full Name	ID Card Type	ID Card Number	Fixed Telephone	Mobile Phone	E-mail Address
Legal Representative (person in charge)						
Financial Director						
Taxpayer						

Tax Agent	Taxpayer Identification Number	Contact Number	E-mail Address

Registered Capital or Total Investment	Currency	Amount	Currency	Amount	Currency	Amount

Investor Name	Economic Nature	Investment Proportion	Documents Types	Identification Number	Nationality or Address

Natural Investment Proportion		Foreign Investment Proportion		State-owned Investment Proportion	

Branch Name	Registered Address	Taxpayer Identification Number	

Headquarters Name		Taxpayer Identification Number			
Registered Address		Business Scope			
Legal Representative		Contact Number		Registered Address Zip Code	

Withholding, Collection and Payment of Taxes	Business Contents	Tax Category

Attached Information:		
Operator's Signature: Specific Date	Legal Representative's Signature: Specific Date	Taxpayer's Seal: Specific Date

四、国际货运代理企业报检注册登记

Inspection & Quarantine of International Freight Forwarder Enterprise

登录报检企业管理系统，进入报检企业管理页面。

Login inspection enterprise management system, enter the inspection management page.

国际货运代理企业报检注册登记，填写代理出入境检验检疫报检单位注册登记申请基本情况登记表，如表 1-5 所示。

The international freight forwarding enterprises shall register for inspection and fill in the form of registration application for Entry-Exit Inspection and Quarantine, as shown in Table 1-5.

表 1-5　　代理出入境检验检疫报检单位注册登记申请基本情况登记表

单位名称	中文						
	英文						
单位地址	注册地址					邮政编码	
	经营地址					邮政编码	
电话		传真		法人代表		电话	
工商营业执照号码		有效日期					
组织机构代码							
批准经营机构名称							
报检人员	姓名	报检员编号	联系电话	身份证号码	手签笔迹		

Table 1-5　The Form of Registration Application for Entry-Exit Inspection and Quarantine

<table>
<tr><td rowspan="2">Company Name</td><td>Chinese</td><td colspan="6"></td></tr>
<tr><td>English</td><td colspan="6"></td></tr>
<tr><td rowspan="2">Company Address</td><td>Registered Address</td><td colspan="4"></td><td>Postal Code</td><td></td></tr>
<tr><td>Business Address</td><td colspan="4"></td><td>Postal Code</td><td></td></tr>
<tr><td>Telephone Number</td><td></td><td>Fax Number</td><td></td><td>Legal Representative</td><td></td><td>Telephone Number</td><td></td></tr>
<tr><td>Business License Number</td><td></td><td>Effective Date</td><td colspan="5"></td></tr>
<tr><td>Organization Code</td><td colspan="7"></td></tr>
<tr><td>Approved Operation Agency</td><td colspan="7"></td></tr>
<tr><td rowspan="6">Inspection Personnel</td><td>Full Name</td><td colspan="2">Inspector Number</td><td>Contact Number</td><td colspan="2">Identification Number</td><td>Signature</td></tr>
<tr><td></td><td colspan="2"></td><td></td><td colspan="2"></td><td></td></tr>
<tr><td></td><td colspan="2"></td><td></td><td colspan="2"></td><td></td></tr>
<tr><td></td><td colspan="2"></td><td></td><td colspan="2"></td><td></td></tr>
<tr><td></td><td colspan="2"></td><td></td><td colspan="2"></td><td></td></tr>
<tr><td></td><td colspan="2"></td><td></td><td colspan="2"></td><td></td></tr>
</table>

2015 年 10 月 16 日，系统进行升级，升级后的系统报检企业备案登记表、报检人员备案登记表按照新格式进行双面打印。

On October 16, 2015, the system was upgraded. The upgraded registration forms for enterprises and personnel were printed on both sides in accordance with the new format.

五、国际货运代理企业报关注册登记

Customs Registration of International Freight Forwarding Enterprise

国际货运代理企业报关注册登记，填写报关单位情况登记表，如表 1-6 所示。

The international freight forwarder shall declare the registration and fill in the registration form of the customs declaration, as shown in Table 1-6.

表 1-6　　报关单位情况登记表

海关注册编码		预录入编号		注册海关	
组织机构代码		海关注册日期		海关首次注册日期	
中文名称					
英文名称					
工商注册地址				邮政编码	
英文地址					
其他经营地址				管理类别	
营业执照注册号		工商注册日期		工商注册有效期	
进出口经营权或报关权批准机关		批准文号		报关有效期	
开户银行		开户账号		注销标志	
注册资本（万元）		注册资本币制		注册资本（万元）	
投资总额（万元）		投资总额币制		投资总额（万美元）	
到位资金（万元）		到位资金币制		到位资金（万美元）	

续表

<table>
<tr><td>税务登记号</td><td></td><td>进出口代码</td><td></td><td>报关类别</td><td></td></tr>
<tr><td>行政区划</td><td></td><td>经济区划</td><td></td><td>经济类型</td><td></td></tr>
<tr><td>经营类别</td><td></td><td>组织机构类型</td><td></td><td>行业种类</td><td></td></tr>
<tr><td>企业传真</td><td></td><td>企业电子邮箱</td><td></td><td>企业网址</td><td></td></tr>
<tr><td>法定代表人（负责人）</td><td></td><td rowspan="2">法定代表人（负责人）电话</td><td></td><td rowspan="2">法定代表人（负责人）身份证件</td><td></td></tr>
<tr><td>法定代表人（负责人）电子邮箱</td><td></td><td></td><td></td></tr>
<tr><td rowspan="2">海关业务联系人</td><td rowspan="2"></td><td rowspan="2">海关业务联系人电话</td><td></td><td>海关业务联系人传真</td><td></td></tr>
<tr><td></td><td>海关业务联系人电子邮箱</td><td></td></tr>
<tr><td>员工人数</td><td></td><td>经营场所性质</td><td></td><td>经营总建筑面积</td><td></td></tr>
<tr><td>是否上市公司</td><td></td><td>是否实行会计电算化</td><td></td><td>财务管理软件名称</td><td></td></tr>
<tr><td>记账方式</td><td></td><td>委托代理记账单位名称</td><td></td><td></td><td></td></tr>
<tr><td>委托代理记账单位组织机构代码</td><td></td><td>委托代理记账单位地址</td><td></td><td></td><td></td></tr>
<tr><td>委托代理记账单位联系人</td><td></td><td>委托代理记账单位联系人电话</td><td></td><td></td><td></td></tr>
<tr><td>上级单位名称</td><td colspan="5"></td></tr>
<tr><td>上级单位组织机构代码</td><td></td><td>与上级单位关系</td><td></td><td>认证标准类型</td><td></td></tr>
</table>

续表

<table>
<tr><td>是否允许
异地报关</td><td></td><td>报关口岸</td><td colspan="2"></td></tr>
<tr><td>经营范围</td><td colspan="4"></td></tr>
<tr><td>备注</td><td colspan="4"></td></tr>
<tr><td>填表人
（签名）</td><td colspan="2"></td><td rowspan="2">单位公章</td><td rowspan="2"></td></tr>
<tr><td>填表日期</td><td colspan="2"></td></tr>
</table>

Table 1-6　　The Registration Form of the Customs Declaration

<table>
<tr><td>Customs Registration Code</td><td></td><td>Pre-entry Number</td><td></td><td>Registered Customs</td><td></td></tr>
<tr><td>Organization Code</td><td></td><td>Registration Date</td><td></td><td>First Date</td><td></td></tr>
<tr><td>Chinese Name</td><td colspan="5"></td></tr>
<tr><td>English Name</td><td colspan="5"></td></tr>
<tr><td>Business Registered Address</td><td colspan="3"></td><td>Postal Code</td><td></td></tr>
<tr><td>English Address</td><td colspan="5"></td></tr>
<tr><td>Other Business Address</td><td colspan="3"></td><td>Management Category</td><td></td></tr>
<tr><td>Business License Registration Number</td><td></td><td>Business Registration Date</td><td></td><td>Business Registration Validity</td><td></td></tr>
</table>

Continued

Approval Authority for Import / Export Operation or Declaration		Approval Number		Declaration Validity	
Deposit Bank		Opening Account		Cancellation Mark	
Registered Capital (10, 000 yuan)		Currency System		Registered Capital (10, 000 yuan)	
Total Investment (10, 000 yuan)		Currency System		Total Investment (USD 10, 000)	
Gained Capital (10, 000 yuan)		Currency System		Gained Capital (USD 10, 000)	
Tax Registration Number		Import and Export Code		Declaration Category	
Administration Division		Economy Division		Economy Type	
Business Category		Organization Type		Industry Category	
Corporate Fax		Enterprise E-mail		Enterprise Website	
Legal Representative (person in charge)		Telephone Number		Identification Number	
E-mail Address					
Customs Business Contact		Telephone Number		Fax Number	
				E-mail Address	

Continued

<table>
<tr><td>Number of Employees</td><td></td><td>Operation Nature</td><td></td><td>Total Area</td><td></td></tr>
<tr><td>Listed Company or not</td><td></td><td>Computerized Accounting or not</td><td></td><td>Accounting Software Name</td><td></td></tr>
<tr><td>Accounting Method</td><td></td><td>Company Name of Entrusted Accounting</td><td colspan="3"></td></tr>
<tr><td>Organization Code of Entrusted Accounting</td><td></td><td>Company Address of Entrusted Accounting</td><td colspan="3"></td></tr>
<tr><td>Contact of Entrusted Accounting</td><td></td><td>Telephone Number of Entrusted Accounting</td><td colspan="3"></td></tr>
<tr><td>Superior Company</td><td colspan="5"></td></tr>
<tr><td>Organization Code</td><td></td><td>Relationship with Superior Company</td><td></td><td>Certification Standard Type</td><td></td></tr>
<tr><td>Whether to Allow Customs Declaration in Different Places</td><td></td><td>Customs Port</td><td colspan="3"></td></tr>
<tr><td>Business Scope</td><td colspan="5"></td></tr>
<tr><td>Remarks</td><td colspan="5"></td></tr>
<tr><td>Completed by (signature)</td><td colspan="2"></td><td rowspan="2">Official Seal</td><td colspan="2" rowspan="2"></td></tr>
<tr><td>Date</td><td colspan="2"></td></tr>
</table>

持卡企业或无卡企业用户，在海关行政审批网上办理平台系统中，可以从报关企业注册登记菜单下报关企业许可事项的链接进入海关企业管理网上办事平台系统，进行报关企业行政许可的变更、延续及注销操作。

Users of cardholder enterprises or non-cardholder enterprises can enter the online management platform system of Customs enterprises from the links of the license items under the registration menu of customs declaration enterprises to change, extend and cancel the administrative license of customs declaration enterprises.

思考题

Questions

请根据国际货运代理企业设立的基本程序填表，如表 1-7 所示。

Please fill in the form according to the basic procedures established by the international freight forwarding enterprise, as shown in Table 1-7.

表 1-7　国际货运代理企业设立的基本程序表

设立环节	登记机构	提交的主要材料	主要申请表	获取证书

Table 1-7　The Form According to the Basic Procedures Established by the International Freight Forwarding Enterprise

Establishment Link	Registration Institution	Submitted Materials	Application Form	Obtained Certificates

任务二　海上货物运输
Task Two: Sea Freight Transportation

【知识目标】

Knowledge Goals

1. 能说明国际贸易的主要航线。

   To be able to explain the main routes of international trade.

2. 能说明海运出口业务的内容。

   To be able to illustrate the contents of the maritime export business.

3. 能说明提单的内容。

   To be able to list the contents of the bill of lading.

【技能目标】

Skill Goals

1. 能模拟货运代理公司的货代业务员，为客户报价。

   To be able to act as the freight forwarder and offer quotations for customers.

2. 能模拟货运代理公司的货代业务员，为客户订舱。

   To be able to act as the freight forwarder and book the space for customers.

3. 能模拟货运代理公司的货代业务员，为客户办理装箱送货事宜。

   To be able to act as the freight forwarder and handle packing and delivery for customers.

4. 能模拟货运代理公司的货代操作员，为客户整理货运单据。

   To be able to act as the freight forwarder and arrange shipping documents for customers.

5. 能模拟货运代理公司的货代操作员，协助办理报关事宜。

   To be able to act as the freight forwarder and assist in customs declaration.

6. 能模拟货运代理公司的货代操作员，办理海运提单确认事宜。

   To be able to act as the freight forwarder and fulfill confirmation of the bill of lading.

子任务之一　海运业务培训
Section One：Marine Business Training

任务引入
Task Introduction

小张刚入职某货运代理公司业务员岗位。今天，他接待了一位客户。该客户打算从天津新港运至苏丹港一批货物。请帮助小张为客户寻找该航线的相关信息。

Xiao Zhang has just joined in a freighting company and worked as a freight forwarder. Today, he received a client who intends to transport a batch of goods from New Port in Tianjin to Port Sudan. Please help Xiao Zhang find relevant information in terms of this route for the customer.

任务分析
Assignment Analysis

货运代理公司业务员，隶属于业务部，主要负责开发业务，并为货主选择最佳的承运人运输货物。货运代理业务员要了解多家承运人的价格、船期、服务等情况，为委托人选择最为满意的出运时间。因此，该岗位应熟悉国际贸易线路，应该熟悉主要的交通线路、港口的位置、转运地和内陆中心。

The freight forwarder, who belongs to the Business Department, is mainly responsible for developing the business and selecting the best carrier to transport the goods for the shipper. The freight forwarder needs to know about the different situations of various carriers, such as price, schedule, as well as service, and choose the most satisfactory delivery time for the client. Therefore, a freight forwarder ought to be familiar with international trade routes, together with significant traffic routes, location of ports, trans-shipment points and inland centers.

相关知识
Relevant Knowledge

一、港口基础知识

Basic Knowledges of Port

运输将全世界连成一片。世界上主要有三大航线：远东到北美航线；远东到欧洲、地中海航线；北美到欧洲、地中海航线。而港口是运输中的重要环节。世界上的发达国家一般都有自己的海岸线和功能较为完善的港口。

There is no doubt that transport connects the whole world. Up to now, there are three major routes in the world: Far East to North America; Far East to Europe and the Mediterranean; North America to Europe and the Mediterranean. To some degree, the port plays a huge role in transportation. The developed countries in the world generally come complete with their own coastline and functional ports.

表 2-1　　世界主要港口

地区	港口外文名称	港口中文名称	国家
美西	LOS ANGELES，CA	洛杉矶	美国
	LONG BEACH，CA	长滩	美国
	OAKLAND，CA	奥克兰	美国
	SEATTLE，WA	西雅图	美国
	TACOMA，WA	塔科马	美国
	PORTLAND，OR	波特兰	美国
美东	NEW YORK，NY	纽约	美国
	NORFOLK，VA	诺福克	美国
	CHARLESTON，SC	查尔斯顿	美国
	SAVANNAH，GA	萨凡纳	美国
	MIAMI，FL	迈阿密	美国
	HOUSTON，TX	休斯敦	美国
	JACKSONVILLE，FL	杰克逊维尔	美国
	NEW ORLEANS，LA	新奥尔良	美国
	PHILADELPHIA，PA	费城	美国
	BALTIMORE，MD	巴尔的摩	美国
	BOSTON，MA	波士顿	美国
加拿大（西）	VANCOUVER	温哥华	加拿大
加拿大（东）	MONTREAL	蒙特利尔	加拿大
	TORONTO	多伦多	加拿大
中美洲	PUERTO QUETZAL	夸特扎尔港	危地马拉
	ACAJUTLA	阿卡胡特拉	萨尔瓦多
	PUERTO CALDERA	卡尔德拉港	哥斯达黎加

续表

地区	港口外文名称	港口中文名称	国家
墨西哥	MANZANILLO	曼萨尼略	墨西哥
	LAZARO CARDENAS	拉萨罗卡德纳斯	墨西哥
南美西岸	BUENAVENTURA	布韦那文图拉	哥伦比亚
	GUAYAQUIL	瓜亚基尔	厄瓜多尔
	CALLAO	卡亚俄	秘鲁
	IQUIQUE	伊基克	智利
	ANTOFAGASTA	安托法加斯塔	智利
	SAN ANTONIO	圣安东尼奥	智利
	SAN VICENTE	圣文森特	智利
南美东岸	BUENOS AIRES	布宜诺斯艾利斯	阿根廷
	MONTEVIDEO	蒙得维的亚	乌拉圭
	RIO GRANDE	里奥格兰德	巴西
	RIO DE JANEIRO	里约热内卢	巴西
	ITAJAI	伊塔雅伊	巴西
	PARANAGU	巴拉那瓜	巴西
	SANTOS	桑托斯	巴西
加勒比海	COLON FREE ZONE	科隆自由贸易区	巴拿马
	KINSTON	金斯顿	牙买加
	CARTAGENA, CO	卡塔赫纳	哥伦比亚
	CAUCEDO	考赛多	多米尼加
	PORT OF SPAIN	西班牙港	特立尼达和多巴哥
	PUERTO CABELLO	卡贝略港	委内瑞拉
	LA GUAIRA	拉瓜伊拉	委内瑞拉
	HAVANA	哈瓦那	古巴
	PORT AU PRINCE	太子港	海地
欧基港	ANTWERP	安特卫普	比利时
	ROTTERDAM	鹿特丹	荷兰
	HAMBURG	汉堡	德国
	LE HAVRE	勒阿佛尔	法国
	FELIXSTOWE	弗利克斯托	英国
	SOUTHAMPTON	南安普顿	英国

续表

地区	港口外文名称	港口中文名称	国家
地中海西	FOS	福斯	法国
	GENOVA	热那亚	意大利
	LA SPEZIA	拉斯佩齐亚	意大利
	NAPOLI	那波利	意大利
	LEGHORN	里窝那	意大利
	ANCONA	安科纳	意大利
	VENICE	威尼斯	意大利
	TRIESTE	的里雅斯特	意大利
	BARCELONA	巴塞罗那	西班牙
	VALENCIA	瓦伦西亚	西班牙
	KOPER	科佩尔	斯洛文尼亚
地中海东	ISTANBUL	伊斯坦布尔	土耳其
	IZMIR	伊兹密尔	土耳其
	GEMLIK	盖姆利克	土耳其
	MERSIN	梅尔辛	土耳其
	LIMASSOL	利马索尔	塞浦路斯
	ALEXANDRIA	亚历山大	埃及
	PORT SAID	塞得港	埃及
	LATTAKIA	拉塔基亚	叙利亚
	BEIRUT	贝鲁特	黎巴嫩
	PIRAEUS	比雷埃夫斯	希腊
	THESSALONIKI	塞萨洛尼基	希腊
中东	JEBEL ALI	杰贝阿里	阿联酋
	ABU DHABI	阿布扎比	阿联酋
	SHARJAH	沙迦	阿联酋
	AJMAM	阿治曼	阿联酋
	KHOR FAKKAN	法坎	阿联酋
	DAMMAM	达曼	沙特阿拉伯
	RIYADH	利雅得	沙特阿拉伯
	BANDAR ABBAS	阿巴斯	伊朗

续表

地区	港口外文名称	港口中文名称	国家
中东	KUWAIT	科威特	科威特
	BAHRAIN	巴林	巴林
	DOHA	多哈	卡塔尔
	MUSCAT	马斯喀特	阿曼
	SOHAR	索哈	阿曼
	UMM QASAR	乌姆盖斯尔	伊拉克
印巴	NHAVA SHEVA	那瓦西瓦	印度
	MUMBAI	孟买	印度
	MUNDRA	蒙德拉	印度
	CHENNAI	钦奈	印度
	CALCUTTA	加尔各答	印度
	COLOMBO	科伦坡	斯里兰卡
	CHITTAGONG	吉大港	孟加拉国
	DHAKA	达卡	孟加拉国
	QASIM	卡西姆	巴基斯坦
	KARACHI	卡拉奇	巴基斯坦
红海	JEDDAH	吉达	沙特阿拉伯
	AQABA	亚喀巴	约旦
	SOKHNA	苏科纳	埃及
	PORT SUDAN	苏丹港	苏丹
东南亚	SINGAPORE	新加坡	新加坡
	JAKARTA	雅加达	印度尼西亚
	PORT KELANG（N）	巴生北港	马来西亚
	PORT KELANG（W）	巴生西港	马来西亚
	SURABAYA	泗水	印度尼西亚
	BANGKOK	曼谷	泰国
	LAEM CHABANG	林查班	泰国
	MANILA	马尼拉	菲律宾
	HOCHIMINH	胡志明市	越南
	HAIPHONG	海防	越南

续表

地区	港口外文名称	港口中文名称	国家
东南亚	PENANG	槟城	马来西亚
	SEMARANG	三宝垄	印度尼西亚
	SIHANOUKVILLE	西哈努克	柬埔寨
	PHNOM PENH	金边	柬埔寨
	YANGON	仰光	缅甸
西非	ABIDJAN	阿比让	科特迪瓦
	LOME	洛美	多哥
	COTONOU	科托努	贝宁
	LAGOS	拉各斯	尼日利亚
	APAPA	阿帕帕	尼日利亚
	TIN CAN	廷坎	尼日利亚
	TEMA	特马	加纳
	DUOALA	杜阿拉	喀麦隆
	LUANDA	罗安达	安格拉
	ONNE	奥纳	尼日利亚
东非	MOMBASA	蒙巴萨	肯尼亚
	DAR ES SALAAM	达累斯萨拉姆	坦桑尼亚
	PORT LOUIS	路易港	毛里求斯
	TAMATAVE	塔马塔夫	马达加斯加
南非	CAPE TOWN	开普敦	南非
	DURBAN	德班	南非
	JOHANNESBURG	约翰内斯堡	南非
	PRETORIA	比勒陀利亚	南非
澳新	BRISBANE	布里斯班	澳大利亚
	MELBOURNE	墨尔本	澳大利亚
	SYDNEY	悉尼	澳大利亚
	ADELAIDE	阿德莱德	澳大利亚
	FREMANTLE	弗里曼特尔	澳大利亚
	AUCKLAND	奥克兰	新西兰
	WELLINGTON	惠灵顿	新西兰

续表

地区	港口外文名称	港口中文名称	国家
关东	TOKYO	东京	日本
	NAGOYA	名古屋	日本
	YOKOHAMA	横滨	日本
关西	OSAKA	大阪	日本
	KOBE	神户	日本
	MOJI	门司	日本
日偏	HAKATA	博多	日本
	TOMAKOMAI	苫小牧	日本
	NIGATA	新潟	日本
	MIZUSHIMA	水岛	日本
韩国	BUSAN	釜山	韩国
	INCHON	仁川	韩国
	KWANGYANG	光阳	韩国
	PYEONGTAEK	平泽	韩国
	ULSAN	蔚山	韩国
中国台湾	KAOHSIUNG	高雄	中国
	KEELUNG	基隆	中国
	TAICHUNG	台中	中国
	TAIPEI	台北	中国

Table 2-1　　Main Ports

Regions	Ports	Chinese Translation	Countries
Western United States	LOS ANGELES, CA	洛杉矶	the United States
	LONG BEACH, CA	长滩	the United States
	OAKLAND, CA	奥克兰	the United States
Western United States	SEATTLE, WA	西雅图	the United States
	TACOMA, WA	塔科马	the United States
	PORTLAND, OR	波特兰	the United States
Eastern United States	NEW YORK, NY	纽约	the United States
	NORFOLK, VA	诺福克	the United States
	CHARLESTON, SC	查尔斯顿	the United States
	SAVANNAH, GA	萨凡那	the United States

Continued

Regions	Ports	Chinese Translation	Countries
Eastern United States	MIAMI, FL	迈阿密	the United States
	HOUSTON, TX	休斯敦	the United States
	JACKSONVILLE, FL	杰克逊维尔	the United States
	NEW ORLEANS, LA	新奥尔良	the United States
	PHILADELPHIA, PA	费城	the United States
	BALTIMORE, MD	巴尔的摩	the United States
	BOSTON, MA	波士顿	the United States
Canada (West)	VANCOUVER	温哥华	Canada
Canada (East)	MONTREAL	蒙特利尔	Canada
	TORONTO	多伦多	Canada
Central America	PUERTO QUETZAL	夸特扎尔港	Guatemala
	ACAJUTLA	阿卡胡特拉	El Salvador
	PUERTO CALDERA	卡尔德拉港	Costa Rica
Mexico	MANZANILLO	曼萨尼约	Mexico
	LAZARO CARDEDAS	拉萨罗卡德纳勒	Mexico
West coast of South America	BUENAVENTURA	布韦那文图拉	Columbia
	GUAYAQUIL	瓜亚基尔	Ecuador
	CALLAO	卡亚俄	Peru
	IQUIQUE	伊基克	Chile
	ANTOFAGASTA	安托法加斯塔	Chile
	SAN ANTONIO	圣安东尼奥	Chile
	SAN VICENTE	圣文森特	Chile
East coast of South America	BUENOS AIRES	布宜诺斯艾利斯	Argentina
	MONTEVIDEO	蒙得维的亚	Uruguay
	RIO GRANDE	里奥格兰德	Brazil
	RIO DE JANEIRO	里约热内卢	Brazil
	ITAJAI	伊塔亚伊	Brazil
	PARANAGU	帕拉那瓜	Brazil
	SANTOS	桑托斯	Brazil

Continued

Regions	Ports	Chinese Translation	Countries
Caribbean	COLON FFEE ZONE	科隆	Panama
	KINSTON	金斯顿	Jamaica
	CARTAGENA	卡塔赫纳	Colombia
	CAUCEDO	卡西多	Dominica
	PORT OF SPAIN	西班牙港	Trinidad and Tobago
	PUERTO CABELLO	卡贝略	Venezuela
	LA GUAIRA	拉瓜伊拉	Venezuela
	HAVANA	哈瓦那	Cuba
	PORT AU PRINCE	太子港	Haiti
Europe Basic Ports	ANTWERP	安特卫普	Belgium
	ROTTERDAM	鹿特丹	Netherlands
	HAMBURG	汉堡	Germany
	LE HAVRE	里哈弗	France
	FELIXSTOWE	菲利克斯托	Britain
	SOUTHAMPTON	南安普顿	Britain
Mediterranean West	FOS	福斯	France
	GENOA	热那亚	Italy
	LA SPEZIA	拉斯佩奇亚	Italy
	NAPOLI	那波利	Italy
	LIVORNO	里窝那	Italy
	ANCONA	安科纳	Italy
	VENICE	威尼斯	Italy
	TRIESTE	迪利亚斯特	Italy
	BARCELONA	巴塞罗那	Spain
	VALENCIA	巴伦西亚	Spain
	KOPER	科佩尔	Slovenia
Mediterranean East	ISTANBUL	伊斯坦布尔	Turkey
	IZMIR	伊兹密尔	Turkey
	GEMLIK	盖姆利克	Turkey
	MERSIN	梅尔辛	Turkey

Continued

Regions	Ports	Chinese Translation	Countries
Mediterranean East	LIMASSOL	利马索尔	Cyprus
	ALEXANDRA	亚历山大	Egypt
	PORT SAID	塞得港	Egypt
	LATTAKIA	拉塔基亚	Syria
	BEIRUT	贝鲁特	Lebanon
	PIRAEUS	比雷艾夫斯	Greece
	THESSALONIKI	塞萨洛尼基	Greece
Middle East	JEBEL ALI	吉拜阿里	the United Arab Emirates
	ABU DHABI	阿布扎比	the United Arab Emirates
	SHARJAH	沙迦	the United Arab Emirates
	AJMAN	阿治曼	the United Arab Emirates
	KHOR FAKKAN	豪尔法坎	the United Arab Emirates
	DAMMAN	达曼	Saudi Arabia
	RIYADH	利雅得	Saudi Arabia
	BANDAR ABBAS	（班达）阿巴斯	Iran
	KUWAIT	科威特	Kuwait
	BAHRAIN	巴林	Bahrain
	DOHA	多哈	Qatar
	MUSCAT	马斯喀特	Oman
	SOHAR	索哈	Oman
	UMM QASR	乌木卡萨	Iraq
India and Pakistan	NHAVA SHEVA	那瓦西瓦	India
	MUMBAI	孟买老	India
	MUNDRA	蒙德拉	India
	CHENNAI	青奈	India
	CALCUTTA	加尔各答	India
	COLOMBO	科伦坡	Sri Lanka
	CHITTAGONG	吉大港	Bangladesh
	DHAKA	达卡	Bangladesh
	PORT QASIM	卡西姆	Pakistan
	KARACHI	卡拉奇	Pakistan

Continued

Regions	Ports	Chinese Translation	Countries
Crimson Sea	JEDDAH	吉达	Saudi Arabia
	AQABA	阿卡巴	Jordan
	SOKHNA	索科纳	Egypt
	PORT SUDAN	苏丹港	Sudan
Southeast Asia	SINGAPORE	新加坡	Singapore
	JAKARTA	雅加达	Indonesia
	PORT KELANG	巴生	Malaysia
	SURABAYA	泗水	Indonesia
	BANGKOK	曼谷	Thailand
	LAEM CHABANG	林查邦	Thailand
	MANILA	马尼拉	Philippines
	HOCHIMINH	胡志明	Vietnam
	HAIPHONG	海防	Vietnam
	PENANG	槟城	Malaysia
	SEMARANG	三宝垄	Indonesia
	SIHANOUKVILLE	西哈努克	Cambodia
	PHNOM PENH	金边	Cambodia
	YANGON	仰光	Myanmar
West Africa	ABIDJAN	阿比让	Cote d'Ivoire
	LOME	洛美	Togo
	COTONOU	科托努	Benin
	LAGOS	拉各斯	Nigeria
	APAPA	阿帕帕	Nigeria
	TINCAN	挺坎	Nigeria
	TEMA	特马	Ghana
	DUOALA	杜阿拉	Cameroon
	LUANDA	卢安达	Angela
	ONNE	奥尼	Nigeria
East Africa	MOMBASA	蒙巴萨	Kenya
	DAR ES SALAAM	达累斯萨拉姆	Tanzania

Continued

Regions	Ports	Chinese Translation	Countries
East Africa	PORT LOUIS	路易港	Mauritius
	TAMATAVE	塔马塔夫	Madagascar
South Africa	CAPETOWN	开普敦	South Africa
	DURBAN	德班	South Africa
	JOHANNESBURG	约翰内斯堡	South Africa
	PRETORIA	比勒陀利亚	South Africa
Australia and New Zealand	BRISBANE	布里斯班	Australia
	MELBOURNE	墨尔本	Australia
	SYDNEY	悉尼	Australia
	ADELAIDE	阿得莱德	Australia
	FREMANTLE	弗里曼特尔	Australia
	AUCKLAND	奥克兰	New Zealand
	WELLINGTON	惠灵顿	New Zealand
Kansai	TOKYO	东京	Japan
	NOGOYA	名古屋	Japan
	YOKOHAMA	横滨	Japan
Kanto	OSAKA	大阪	Japan
	KOBE	神户	Japan
	MOJI	门斯	Japan
Japan Remote	HAKATA	博多	Japan
	TOMAKOMAI	占小牧	Japan
	NIIGATA	新潟	Japan
	MIZUSHIMA	水岛	Japan
South Korea	BUSAN	釜山	South Korea
	INCHON	仁川	South Korea
	KWANGYANG	光阳	South Korea
	PYONGTAEK	平泽	South Korea
	ULSAN	蔚山	South Korea
Taiwan, China	KAOHSIUNG	高雄	China
	KEELUNG	基隆	China
	TAICHUNG	台中	China
	TAIPEI	台北	China

二、术语分类

Classification of Terms

《2010年国际贸易术语解释通则》的11个术语分为两类。

The 11 terms of Incoterms 2010 could be divided into two distinct categories.

（一）适用于任一或多种运输方式的规则贸易术语条款

Terms for any Modes of Transport

1. 工厂交货（插入指定交货地点）

EXW, Ex Works (insert named place of delivery)

EXW意为卖方交货地点可以是卖方所在地，也可以是其他指定地点。

EXW means that the seller delivers the goods at the seller's location or other designated location.

2. 货交承运人（插入指定交货地点）

FCA, Free Carrier (insert named place of delivery)

FCA意为卖方在其所在地或其他指定地点将货物交给买方指定的承运人或其他人处置时，即完成交货。

FCA means that the seller delivers the goods to the carrier or another person nominated by the buyer at the seller's location or other designated location.

3. 运费付至（插入指定目的地）

CPT, Carriage Paid to (insert named place of destination)

CPT意为卖方将货物交给指定的承运人或其他人处置即完成交货，卖方必须按照合同支付将货物运到指定目的地所需要的运费。

CPT means that the seller delivers the goods to the carrier or another person nominated by the seller at an agreed place and that the seller must pay the freight required to transport the goods to the designated destination in accordance with the contract.

4. 运费和保险费付至（插入指定目的地）

CIP, Carriage and Insurance Paid to (insert named place of destination)

这是CPT和CIP仅有的不同。在CIP贸易术语下，卖方承担保险合同约定的对买方在运输货物期间货物损坏或丢失的风险。

Different from CPT, the seller assumes the risk of damage or loss to the buyer during the transportation of the goods as stipulated in the insurance contract, according to the terms of the CIP trade.

5. 运输终端交货（插入指定港口或目的地运输终端）

DAT, Delivered at Terminal（insert named terminal at port or place of destination）

DAT 意为卖方在指定港口或目的地的运输终端将货物从抵达的运输工具上卸下交给买方处置时即可完成交货。

DAT means that the seller unloads the goods from the vehicles and delivers the buyer for disposal at the terminal of the designated port or place of destination.

6. 目的地交货（插入指定目的地）

DAP, Delivered at Place（insert named place of destination）

DAP 意为卖方在指定目的地将货物放在已抵达的交通工具上交给买方处置时即可完成交货。

DAP means that the seller places the goods on the vehicles and delivers the buyer for disposal at the designated place of destination.

7. 完税后交货（插入指定目的地）

DDP, Delivered Duty Paid（insert named place of destination）

DDP 意为卖方在指定目的地将已完成进口清关且可供卸载的货物交给买方处置时即完成交货。

DDP means that the seller completes the import clearance and delivers the goods available for unloading to the buyer at the designated destination.

（二）水运贸易术语条款

Terms for Sea and Inland Waterway Transport

1. 船边交货（插入指定装运港）

FAS, Free Alongside Ship（insert named port of shipment）

FAS 意为卖方将货物在指定的装运港交到买方指定的船边、码头或者驳船。买方负担货物在指定装运港交到船边之后的一切丢失或破损风险和费用。

FAS means that the seller delivers when the goods are placed alongside the vessel（e. g. , on a quay or a barge）nominated by the buyer at the designated port of shipment and the buyer bears all costs caused by the risk of loss of or damage to the goods alongside the vessel.

2. 船上交货（插入指定装运港）

FOB，Free on Board（insert named port of shipment）

FOB 意为卖方将货物装到买方制动的船上或通过“取得”已交付至船上货物的方式交货。

FOB means that the seller delivers the goods on board the vessel nominated by the buyer at the designated port of shipment.

3. 成本加运费（插入指定目的地）

CFR，Cost and Freight（insert named port of destination）

不同于 FOB，在 CFR 术语下，卖方必须根据运输合同支付将货物运输至指定目的港所需要的运费。

Different from FOB, the seller must pay the freight required to transport the goods to the designated port of destination in accordance with the contract, according to the terms of the CFR trade.

4. 成本、保险费加运费（插入指定目的地）

CIF，Cost Insurance and Freight（insert named port of destination）

不同于 CFR，在 CIF 术语下，卖方承担买方运输期间货物丢失或破损的风险和费用。

Different from CFR, the seller assumes the risk of damage or loss to the buyer during the transportation of the goods as stipulated in the insurance contract, according to the terms of the CIF trade.

任务实施
Task Implementation

登录货运代理公司网站，查询天津新港到苏丹港的集装箱海运船期表。

Visit the website of the freight forwarding company and check the container shipping schedule between Tianjin Xingang and Port Sudan.

起运港：天津新港

Port of departure: Tianjin Xingang, China

中转港：宁波

Transit port: Ningbo, China

目的港：苏丹港

Port of Destination: Port Sudan, Sudan

船期：每周五

Shipping date: Every Friday

预计航程：35 天左右

Estimated range：about 35 days

思考题
Questions

1. 请为以下港口填写五字港口代码。

Please fill in the five-letter port code for the following ports.

表 2-2　　主要港口代码

地区	港口	中文港口	港口代码
美西	LOS ANGELES，CA	洛杉矶	
	LONG BEACH，CA	长滩	
	OAKLAND，CA	奥克兰	
	SEATTLE，WA	西雅图	
	TACOMA，WA	塔科马	
美东	NEW YORK，NY	纽约	
	NORFOLK，VA	诺福克	
	CHARLESTON，SC	查尔斯顿	
	HOUSTON，TX	休斯敦	
	NEW ORLEANS，LA	新奥尔良	
	BOSTON，MA	波士顿	
加拿大（西）	VANCOUVER	温哥华	
加拿大（东）	MONTREAL	蒙特利尔	
	TORONTO	多伦多	
欧基港	ANTWERP	安特卫普	
	ROTTERDAM	鹿特丹	
	HAMBURG	汉堡	
东南亚	SINGAPORE	新加坡	
	PORT KELANG	巴生	
关东	TOKYO	东京	
	NAGOYA	名古屋	
	YOKOHAMA	横滨	
关西	OSAKA	大阪	
	KOBE	神户	
韩国	BUSAN	釜山	
	INCHON	仁川	
中国台湾	KAOHSIUNG	高雄	
	KEELUNG	基隆	

Table 2-2　　　　Port Code

Regions	Ports	Chinese Translation	Port Code
Western United States	LOS ANGELES, CA	洛杉矶	
	LONG BEACH, CA	长滩	
	OAKLAND, CA	奥克兰	
	SEATTLE, WA	西雅图	
	TACOMA, WA	塔科马	
Eastern United States	NEW YORK, NY	纽约	
	NORFOLK, VA	诺福克	
	CHARLESTON, SC	查尔斯顿	
	HOUSTON, TX	休斯敦	
	NEW ORLEANS, LA	新奥尔良	
	BOSTON, MA	波士顿	
Canada (West)	VANCOUVER	温哥华	
Canada (East)	MONTREAL	蒙特利尔	
	TORONTO	多伦多	
Europe Basic Ports	ANTWERP	安特卫普	
	ROTTERDAM	鹿特丹	
	HAMBURG	汉堡	
Southeast Asia	SINGAPORE	新加坡	
	PORT KELANG	巴生	
Kansai	TOKYO	东京	
	NOGOYA	名古屋	
	YOKOHAMA	横滨	
Kanto	OSAKA	大阪	
	KOBE	神户	
Republic of Korea	BUSAN	釜山	
	INCHON	仁川	
Taiwan, China	KAOHSIUNG	高雄	
	KEELUNG	基隆	

2. 请填写《2010 通则》贸易术语比较表。

Please fill out the trade terms comparison table of "2010 general rules" .

表 2-3 《2010 通则》贸易术语比较表

国际代码	名称 中文	贸易术语/合同性质	交货地点	交货运输状态	风险转移	运输责任费用	保险责任费用	出口报关责任	进口报关责任	运输方式适用
EXW	工厂交货（插入指定交货地点）									
FAS	船边交货（插入指定装运港）									
FOB	船上交货（插入指定装运港）									
FCA	货交承运人（插入指定交货地点）									
CFR	成本加运费（插入指定目的港）									
CPT	运费付至（插入指定目的地）									
CIF	成本加保险费、运费（插入指定目的港）									
CIP	运费保险费付至（插入指定目的地）									
DAP	目的地交货（插入指定目的地）									
DAT	运输终端交货（插入指定港口或目的地的运输终端）									
DDP	完税后交货（插入指定目的地）									
备注	包装费：坚持合同优先原则。订立合同前卖方已知有关运输情况，卖方必须自费提供卖方在订立合同前已知的有关货物运输所要求的包装。 商检费：除 DDP 术语成交外，货物装运前检验费由买方承担：但是出口商检下，检验费由卖方承担（EXW 除外）。									

Table 2-3　Comparison of Trade Terms in 2010 General Principles

International Code	Names (English)	Trade Terms/Contract Nature	Place of Delivery	Transportation Conditions	Risk Transfer	Transportation Cost	Insurance Expenses	Export Declaration Responsibility	Import Declaration Responsibility	Transportation Modes
EXW	Ex Works (insert named place of delivery)									
FAS	Free Alongside Ship (insert named port of shipment)									
FOB	Free on Board (insert named port of shipment)									
FCA	Free Carrier (insert named place of delivery)									
CFR	Cost and Freight (insert named port of destination)									
CPT	Carriage Paid To (insert named place of destination)									
CIF	Cost Insurance and Freight (insert named port of destination)									
CIP	Carriage and Insurance Paid to (insert named place of destination)									

Continued

International Code	Names	Trade Terms/ Contract Nature	Place of Delivery	Transportation Conditions	Risk Transfer	Transportation Cost	Insurance Expenses	Export Declaration Responsibility	Import Declaration Responsibility	Transportation Modes
	English									
DAP	Delivered at Place（insert named place of destination）									
DAT	Delivered at Terminal（insert named terminal at port or place of destination）									
DDP	Delivered Duty Paid（insert named place of destination）									
Remarks	Packaging fee: adhere to the principle of contract priority. Prior to the conclusion of the contract, the seller has known the relevant transportation conditions, and the seller must, at its own expense, provide the packing required for the transportation of the relevant goods known to the seller prior to the conclusion of the contract. Commodity inspection fee: in addition to DDP terms, inspection fee before shipment shall be borne by the buyer; however, under export commodity inspection, inspection fee shall be borne by the seller（excluding EXW）.									

子任务之二　询价报价
Section Two：Inquiries and Offers

任务引入
Task Introduction

小张从事某货运代理公司业务员工作。今天，他接待了一位询价的客户。该批货物将从天津新港运至苏丹港。具体货物情况如下。

As a freight forwarder, Xiao Zhang received a customer who made an inquiry today. The goods will be shipped from Tianjin Xingang to Port Sudan. The details of the specific goods are as follows.

货名：彩涂卷

Goods description：PRE-PAINTED COLD ROLLED COILS

数量：278 卷

Quantity：278 COILS

总毛重：1300MT

Weight：1300MT

总体积：960 cbm

Volume：960 cbm

任务分析
Assignment Analysis

货代业务员需要为询价的客户报价，如海运费及相关的港杂费用，进而确定船期。

The freight forwarder needs to quote the customer for the inquiry, such as ocean freight and related port fees, so as to determine the shipping date.

相关知识
Relevant Knowledge

一、海运运费率的类型
Types of Ocean Freight Rate

海运运费费率可大致上分成不定期船运费率和班轮运费率。

Ocean freight rate may be broadly divided into tramp rate and liner freight rate.

（一）不定期船运费率
Tramp Rate

不定期船运费率随航运市场的供求关系而波动。在市场繁荣时期，不定期船运费率上升，在市场萧条时期，费率下降。

Tramp rates fluctuate with market conditions of supply and demand. In a boom period, the tramp rates rise. In a period of recession, the tramp rates decline.

（二）班轮运费率
Liner Freight Rate

班轮运费率由班轮公会和其他的班轮营运人确定；它们多与营运成本密切相关，在一定时期内保持相对稳定。

Liner freight rates are fixed by shipping conferences and other liner operators and related more to the costs of operation and remain comparatively steady over a period of time.

二、班轮运费费用的范围
Scope of Liner Freight Rate

货运代理主要涉及班轮运费率。

Freight forwarders are mainly concerned with liner freight rates.

尽管班轮公会或班轮经营人对班轮运费率的确定原则并不公开，但是很显然，提供班轮服务的运输成本应包括实际运输成本和利润额度。

Although the principles on which the liner freight rates are fixed have not been clarified by shipping conferences or operators, it is obvious that the shipping cost of providing liner services will cover actual costs and profit margins.

这些服务的全部费用由固定成本和可变成本两个部分组成。

The total costs of providing the services consist of fixed costs and variable costs.

（一）固定成本
Fixed Costs

1. 船员的工资
Crew Wages

2. 保险费

Insurance Costs

3. 维修和保养费

Repairs and Maintenance Costs

4. 物料费

Stores

5. 管理费用

Administrative Costs

6. 利息以及折旧

Interests and Depreciation

(二) 可变成本

Variable costs

1. 燃料费

Cost of Fuel

2. 装卸费

Loading and Unloading Expenses

3. 港口费

Port Costs

三、决定运费的因素

The Factor Determining the Freight

在确定运费率时，承运人还将考虑积载因数、航程以及一个很古老的原则，即“运输所能承受”的原则。

When determining the freight rate, the carrier will also consider stowage factor, distance and the age-old principle of “what the traffic can bear”.

实际上，“运输所能承受”原则是指高费率的商品可以补偿较低费率的商品。

In fact, the principle of “what the traffic can bear” in effect means that commodities which are highly rated subsidize those which are rated lower.

在过去，采用“运输所能承受”原则比“服务成本”原则更为普遍，这是由于实际单位成本计算时所涉及的问题。

This principle was more commonly adopted in the past than the “cost of service” principle because of the problems involved in the computation of the actual unit costs.

可是，计算集装箱运输的标准货物单位的服务成本要比不同种类的普通货物的服务成本容易得多。

However, containerization with standardized cargo units has made the calculation of the service cost per unit easier than heterogeneous break bulk cargoes.

特别考虑到竞争因素，因此如今承运人日益采用“服务成本”原则。

The carriers are therefore increasingly adopting the “service cost” principle nowadays, particularly with a view to fighting competition.

公开市场费率同样受到关注。当货物运输的数量大且易受到租船竞争的影响时，为了适合竞争环境，费率可能会公开，所以班轮运输在运费价格方面有了可供选择的权利。

The open market rates are also taken into account. When commodities move in large quantities and are susceptible to charter competition, the rates may be left “open” so that a liner has the option of charging whatever is considered appropriate in the competitive situation.

班轮运费率也受附加费和其他调节因素的影响而变化，这些费用可能会被不时征收，以使航运公司应付投入中的价格变化，比如货币贬值的影响、燃油价格变化的调整因素和港口拥挤附加费。

The liner rates are also subject to surcharges or adjustment factors which may be levied from time to time in order to enable the shipping lines to meet certain price variations in their inputs such as Currency Adjustment Factor (CAF), the Bunker Adjustment Factor (BAF) and port congestion surcharges.

任务实施
Task Implementation

登录某物流公司网站，查询天津新港到苏丹港的集装箱海运整箱运价表，如图 2-1 所示。

Visit the website of a logistics company and check the shipping tariff of container freight FCL from Tianjin Xingang to Port Sudan, as shown in Figure 2-1.

思考题
Questions

1. 海运运费率都有哪些类型？

What are the types of ocean freight rates?

2. 请通过网站查询，填写以下信息。

Please check the website and fill in the following form.

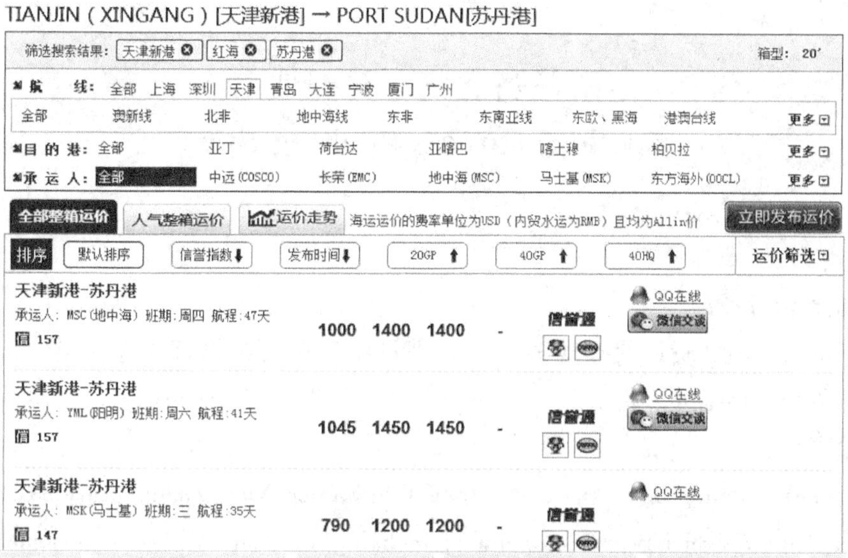

图 2-1　天津新港到苏丹港运价查询

表 2-4　　海运运费表

始发港	目的港	20 英尺小柜	40 英尺集装箱	40 英尺高柜	预计开航日	预计航程
天津新港	林查班，泰国					
	拉各斯，尼日利亚					
	拉合尔，巴基斯坦					
	拉尔维克，挪威					

Table 2-4　　Ocean Freight Price List

Port of Departure	Port of Destination	20GP	40GP	40HQ	Expected Sailing Date	Estimated Voyage
Tianjin Xingang	Laem Chabang, Thailand					
	Lagos, Nigeria					
	Lahore, Pakistan					
	Larvik, Norway					

子任务之三　订舱业务
Section Three: Booking Space

任务引入
Task Introduction

由于价格合适，货运代理业务员小张把订舱工作委托给货代操作员，包括收发货人信息、货物品名描述、件重尺、中文报关品名和报关 HS code。之后，货代业务员去安排订舱事宜。

Due to the appropriate price, the freight forwarder Xiao Zhang provided the booking delegation to the freight forwarding operator, including the consignee and consigner's information, the description of the goods' name, the weight of the goods, the name of the Chinese customs declaration, and the customs declaration HS code. Afterwards, the freight clerk went to arrange the booking.

货名：彩涂卷

Goods description: PRE-PAINTED COLD ROLLED COILS

数量：278 卷

Quantity: 278 COILS

总毛重：1300MT

Weight: 1300MT

总体积：960 cbm

Volume: 960 cbm

报关 HS code：7210701000

HS code: 7210701000

备注：申请目的港免用箱 21 天；显示目的港代理信息

Remarks: The port of destination will be exempted from the use of containers for 21 days. The destination port information will be displayed

任务分析
Assignment Analysis

货代操作员，隶属于操作部。负责与船公司、航空公司的操作制单人员联系，把信息传达给客户，起到中间传输的作用，并完成一些单证文件的制作。

The freight operator, who belongs to the Operation Department, is mainly responsible for liaising with the operators in shipping companies and airline companies, sending information to customers, acting as an intermediary, and completing the production of some documents.

客户在海运公司订舱出口货物时，应按订舱出口委托书内容进行填写，将填写好的托运单通过传真或邮件发至货运代理公司。有时货代操作也会根据客户提供的信息，协助客户填写托运单。

When a customer ships an export cargo at a shipping company, the customer should fill in the contents of the booking entrustment and fax or mail the completed booking note to the freight forwarding company. Sometimes the freight operator will also assist the customer in completing the booking note based on the information provided by the customer.

相关知识
Relevant Knowledge

一、托运单
Booking Note, B/N

托运单俗称下货纸，是托运人根据贸易合同和信用证条款内容填制的，向承运人或其代理办理货物托运的单证。承运人根据托运单内容，并结合船舶的航线、挂靠港、船期和舱位等条件考虑，认为合适后，即接受托运。托运单是运货人和托运人之间对托运货物的合约，其记载有关托运人与送货人相互间的权利和义务。运送人签收后，一份给托运人当收据，货物的责任从托运转至运送人，直到收货人收到货物为止。如发生托运人向运送人要求索赔时，托运单是托运单位必备的文件。运送人输入托运单上数据的正确与否，对后续程序影响甚大。

The booking note, commonly known as the "shipping paper", is the document that the shipper fills in based on the terms of the trade contract as well as the letter of credit and handles the consignment of the goods to the carrier or his agent. According to the contents of the booking note and the conditions of the shipping route, the port of call, the shipping date together with the shipping space, the carrier agrees to accept the consignment when deeming it appropriate. The consignment note is a contract between the shipper and the carrier on the consignment of the goods, which records the rights and obligations between the shipper and the carrier. As for the booking note signed by the shipper, one copy is given to the shipper as a receipt and the responsibility for the goods is transferred from the shipper to the carrier until the consignee receives the goods. In the event that the shipper requests a claim from the shipping company, the shipping company must have the necessary documents. The correctness of the data input on the booking note by the shipping company affects the followup operations.

二、海运出口托运单的填制

Filling in Booking Note of Ocean Transportation

海洋运输有两种方式：传统散货运输、现代集装箱运输。两种运输方式分别使用不同格式的托运单。

There are two ways of ocean transportation: traditional bulk transportation and modern container transportation, which are required to use different formats of booking notes separately.

（一）散货运输托运单

Booking Note for Bulk Cargo

散货运输托运单是在装货单和收货单（大副收据）基础上发展而成的一种多功能单据，其内容及填制方法如下。

The booking note for bulk cargo is a multifunctional document developed on the basis of loading list and goods receipt (major receipt), whose contents and filling methods are as follows.

（1）SHIPPER（托运人）。此处一般填写出口合同的卖方，信用证支付方式下应与信用证受益人的名称、地址一致。

SHIPPER. The seller of the export contract is generally filled here, who should be consistentwith the name and address of the beneficiary of the letter of credit.

（2）NO S/S（编号、船名）。此为托运单的顺序编号，船名可留给船方安排船只舱位后填写。

NO S/S (number, vessel name). This is the serial number of the booking note. The name of the vessel can be filled in after completing the arrangements of shipping space.

（3）FOR（目的港）。按合同或信用证规定填写目的港具体名称，遇世界重名港口时，应在港口名称后面加注国名。

FOR (destination port). According to the stipulations of the contract or letter of credit, the specific name of the destination port should be filled out. In the case of the same names, the name of the country should be added after the name of the port.

（4）MARKS & NOS（标记及号码）。本栏应按合同或信用证规定的内容和形式填写，如没有规定，可由出口商自己编制，没有唛头则填"N/M"。

MARKS & NOS (mark and number). This column should be completed according to the contents and forms stipulated in the contract or the letter of credit. If there is no provision, it can be worked out by the exporter himself. If there is no shipping mark, it will be filled with "N/M".

（5）QUANTITY（件数）。按最大包装实际件数填写，应与唛头中的件数一致。

QUANTITY (number of pieces). According to the maximum number of packages, the number of packages should be the same as those in the shipping marks.

（6）DESCRIPTION OF GOODS（货名）。本栏填写货物大类名称或统称，与发票（信用证）中的货名一致。运费到付（FREIGHT TO COLLECT）或运费预付（FREIGHT PREPAID）也可借用此栏加以注明。

DESCRIPTION OF GOODS (goods name). This column will be filled in the general name of major category of the goods, which is in conformity with the name of the goods in the invoice (L / C). FREIGHT TO COLLECT or FREIGHT PREPAID may also be noted in this column.

（7）WEIGHT（重量）。本栏内容是计算船只受载吨位和运费的基础资料，以千克为单位，须分别填写整批货物的毛重和净重。

WEIGHT. The contents of this column are the basic data for calculating the tonnage and freight charges of the vessel. The gross and net weight of the entire cargo must be filled separatelyin the unit of kilograms.

（8）MEASUREMENT（尺码）。本栏填写整批货物的体积实数，以立方米为单位，是计算运费的主要依据之一，计算应务求准确。

MEASUREMENT (size). This column is filled with the actual volume of the entire shipment in the unit of cubic meters, which should be accurate functioning as one of the main basis for the calculation of freight.

（9）PARTIAL SHIPMENT, TRANSSHIPMENT（分批转船）。本栏应严格按合同或信用证填写"允许"或"不允许"。

PARTIAL SHIPMENT, TRANSSHIPMENT. This column should be filled with "permitted" or "not allowed" in accordance with the contract or letter of credit.

（10）DATE OF SHIPMENT, DATE OF EXPIRY（装运期、有效期）。本栏根据信用证规定的最迟装运期和议付有效期分别填写。

DATE OF SHIPMENT, DATE OF EXPIRY (shipment period, expiration date). This column is filled out according to the latest shipment period and the negotiation validity period stipulated in the L/C.

（11）CONSIGNEE（收货人）。本栏一般根据信用证要求填写"TO ORDER/TO ORDER OF SHIPPER"。

CONSIGNEE. This column is generally filled in "TO ORDER/TO ORDER OF SHIPPER" according to the letter of credit.

（12）NOTIFY（通知人）。本栏填写接受船方发出货到通知的人的名称与地址。

NOTIFY. This column is filled with the name and address of the person who accepts the ship's delivery notice.

（13）备注。本栏填写信用证中有关运输方面的特殊要求。

Remarks. This column contains the special requirements for transportation in the letter of credit.

（二）集装箱货物托运单

Booking Note for Container Cargo

集装箱货物托运单（见表2-5）与海运散货出口托运单基本相同，发货人在办理集装箱货物托运时，除应填写与海运散货出口托运单相似栏目内容外，还应标明托运货物的交接方式，如CY—CY、CFS—CFS等，以及集装箱货物的种类，如普通、冷藏、液体等。

The booking note for container cargo (as shown in Table 2-5) is basically the same as the one just mentioned above. When the consignor is handling consignment of container cargo, he ought to indicate the delivery methods (CY-CY, CFS-CFS) and cargo types (Common, Refrigerated, Liquid), in addition to the similar contents of the booking note for bulk cargo.

表 2-5　　**集装箱货物托运单**

<table>
<tr><td colspan="6">发货人
TIANJIN TIFERT TEXTILES IMPORT & EXPORT CORP. 86，ZHUJIANG ROAD，HEXT DISTRICT，TIANJIN，CHINA</td><td colspan="2" rowspan="5">D/R NO（编号）104975

集装箱货物托运单

货主留底</td></tr>
<tr><td colspan="6">收货人
TO ORDER OF SHIPPER</td></tr>
<tr><td colspan="6">通知人
OVERSEAS TRADING CO. LTD.，
100 JULAA SULTAN#01-20　SULTAN PLAZASINGAPORE</td></tr>
<tr><td colspan="3">前程运输</td><td colspan="3">收货地点</td></tr>
<tr><td colspan="2">船名
VICTORY</td><td colspan="2">航次
VH-07861</td><td colspan="2">装货港
TIANJIN，CHINA</td></tr>
<tr><td colspan="3">卸货港
SINGAPORE</td><td colspan="3">交货地点
SINGAPORE</td><td colspan="2">目的地</td></tr>
<tr><td>集装箱号</td><td>封志号
标记与号码
O. T. C SC300762
NO1-8</td><td>箱数或件数
8</td><td colspan="2">包装种类与货名
BALES
(6, 300. 00YARDS)
OF BLEACHED
SHIRTING
“FREIGHT PREPAID”</td><td>毛重/千克
568. 00KGS</td><td colspan="2">尺码/
立方米
34. 462FEET3
($0.975M^3$)</td></tr>
<tr><td colspan="2">集装箱数或件数合计（大写）</td><td colspan="6">EIGHT BALES ONLY</td></tr>
<tr><td colspan="2">运费与附加费</td><td>运费吨</td><td>运费率</td><td>每</td><td colspan="2">运费预付</td><td>到付</td></tr>
<tr><td>兑换率</td><td colspan="2">预付地点 TIANJIN，CHINA</td><td colspan="2">到付地点</td><td colspan="3">签发地点 TIANJIN，CHINA</td></tr>
<tr><td></td><td colspan="2">预付总额</td><td colspan="2">正本提单份数 B (S) /L THREE</td><td colspan="3"></td></tr>
<tr><td rowspan="2">种类</td><td colspan="4">□ 普通　□ 冷藏　□危险品　□裸装车辆</td><td rowspan="2">危险品</td><td colspan="2" rowspan="2">等级：
性质：
《国际海运危险货物规则》所在页码：
UN 编号</td></tr>
<tr><td colspan="4">□ 液体　□ 活动物　□散货</td></tr>
<tr><td colspan="2">可否转船　NOT</td><td colspan="3">可否分批　ALLOWED</td><td colspan="3" rowspan="4"></td></tr>
<tr><td colspan="2">装期　NOV 20, 20××</td><td colspan="3">有效期　DEC 15，20××</td></tr>
<tr><td colspan="2">金额　USD 9, 139. 20</td><td colspan="3"></td></tr>
<tr><td colspan="2">制单日期　20××-11-06</td><td colspan="3"></td></tr>
</table>

Table 2-5　　Booking Note for Container Cargo

<table>
<tr><td colspan="4">Shipper
TIANJIN TIFERT TEXTILES IMPORT & EXPORT CORP.
86, ZHUJIANG ROAD, HEXT DISTRICT, TIANJIN, CHINA</td><td colspan="2" rowspan="5">D/R NO 104975

Booking Note for
Container Cargo

Reserved by Owners</td></tr>
<tr><td colspan="4">Consignee
TO ORDER OF SHIPPER</td></tr>
<tr><td colspan="4">Notify Party
OVERSEAS TRADING CO. LTD.,
100 JULAH SULTAN# 01-20 SULTAN PLAZASINGAPORE</td></tr>
<tr><td colspan="2">Pre-carriaged by</td><td colspan="2">Place of Receipt</td></tr>
<tr><td>Ocean Vessel
VICTORY</td><td colspan="2">Voy No
VH-07861</td><td>Port of Loading
TIANJIN, CHINA</td></tr>
<tr><td colspan="2">Port of Discharge
SINGAPORE</td><td colspan="2">Place of Delivery
SINGAPORE</td><td colspan="2">Final Destination</td></tr>
<tr><td>Container No.</td><td>Seal No Marks & Nos.
O. T. C
SC300762
SINGAPORE
NO1-8</td><td>No. of Containers or Pkgs.
8</td><td>Kind of Packages and Description of Goods
BALES
(6,300.00YARDS)
OF BLEACHED SHIR-
TING
"FREIGHT PREPAID"</td><td>Gross Weight
568.00KGS</td><td>Measurement
34.462FEET3
(0.975M^3)</td></tr>
<tr><td colspan="2">Total Number of Containers or Packages (in words)</td><td colspan="4">EIGHT BALES ONLY</td></tr>
<tr><td>Freight & Charges</td><td>Revenue Tons</td><td>Rate</td><td>Per</td><td>Prepaid</td><td>Collect</td></tr>
<tr><td>Ex Rate</td><td colspan="2">Prepaid at
TIANJIN, CHINA</td><td colspan="2">Payable at</td><td>Place of Issue
TIANJIN, CHINA</td></tr>
<tr><td></td><td colspan="2">Total Prepaid</td><td colspan="2">No. of Original
B (S) /L THREE</td><td></td></tr>
</table>

Continued

<table>
<tr><td rowspan="2">Type of Goods</td><td colspan="2">□Ordinary, □Reefer, □Dangerous, □Auto.</td><td rowspan="2">Dangerous</td><td rowspan="2">Class:
Property:
IMDG Code Page:
UN No. (UN)</td></tr>
<tr><td colspan="2">□Liquid, □Live animal, □Bulk</td></tr>
<tr><td colspan="2">Transshipment
NOT</td><td>Partial
ALLOWED</td><td colspan="2" rowspan="4"></td></tr>
<tr><td colspan="2">Date of Shipment
NOV 20, 20××</td><td>Expiry Date
DEC 15, 20××</td></tr>
<tr><td colspan="2">Amount of Money
USD 9, 139. 20</td><td></td></tr>
<tr><td colspan="2">Date of Filling
20××-11-06</td><td></td></tr>
</table>

任务实施
Task Implementation

托运单上必须注明下列事项：托运人；收货人；通知方；起运港；目的港；箱型、箱量；件数、毛重、体积；运费条款（预付、到付、第三地付款）；货名（如系危险品请标明危险等级和有关的注意事项、冷冻箱请注明冷冻温度）；船公司或无船承运人（若指定）；其他要求。

The following items must be noted on the booking note: shipper, consignee, notify party, port of departure, port of destination, container type, container volume, number of pieces, gross weight, volume, freight terms (prepayment, payment, third payment), cargo name (As for the dangerous goods, please indicate the hazard level and related precautions; As for the freezer, please indicate the freezing temperature), shipping company or NVOCC (if you specify), other requirements.

托运单要根据客人的要求进行填写，如：客人要求在目的港需要申请免堆期，就需要及时在托运单上体现，如图 2-2 所示。

The booking note must be filled in according to the requirements of the customers. For example, if the customer requests to apply for an exemption period at the port of destination, it is necessary to reflect it on the booking note in time, as shown in Figure 2-2.

SHIPPER	BL NO.	
XXX CO.,LTD ADD:XXX		

CONSIGNEE		
XXX CO.,LYD ADDRESS:XXXX SUDAN	订舱协议号:	
	舱位公司:	
	付款方式:	预付
NOTIFY	提单类型:	正本
SAME AS CONSINGEE	运输条款:	CY/CY
	订舱人:	

箱型	数量
20GP	48
20RF	
40GP	
40HC	
40OT	
40FR	
40RH	

VESSEL	VOY	PLACE OF RECEIPT	PORT OF LOADING
			TIANJIN, CHINA
ETD		PORT OF DISCHARGE	PLACE OF DELIVERY
		SUDAN PORT	

MARK	DESCRIPTION	QUANTITY	PACKAGE	WEIGHT(KG)	VOLUME(CBM)
N/M	PRE-PAINTED COLD ROLLED COILS	278 COILS		1300MT	960
				单位：KG	单位：CBM
			冷柜温度:		℃
			危险品UN NO.:		

提单备注	订舱备注
	申请目的港免用箱21天 彩涂卷 HS 7210701000 显示目的港代理信息

图 2-2 托运单

货代业务员接到托运单后，根据和客户谈好的情况向船公司订舱，船代出口舱单表格模板，如表 2-6 所示。船公司确认后，具体订舱信息如图 2-3 所示。

After receiving the booking note, the freight forwarder will make a booking with the shipping company according to the customer's requirements and work out the export manifest template, as shown in Table 2-6. After confirmation of the shipping company, the specific booking information is shown in Figure 2-3.

表 2-6

船代出口舱单表格模板

<table>
<tr><td colspan="9">箱型尺寸：参考“箱型尺寸”页，输入“KEY_VALUE”列的值
包装种类：参考“包装种类”页，输入“KEY_NME”列的值</td></tr>
<tr><td>订舱号</td><td>发货人</td><td>发货人地址</td><td>收货人</td><td>收货人地址</td><td>通知方</td><td>通知方地址</td><td>到付/预付</td><td></td></tr>
<tr><td>575021××5</td><td>××× CO. , LTD.</td><td>ROOM 1×××, NO. × BUILDING NO. ××× ROAD, ××, ××. P. R. C</td><td>××</td><td>×× FREE ZONE, ×× ROAD, ×× LOCAL GOVERNMENT AREA, ××</td><td>×××</td><td>×× FREE ZONE, ×× ROAD, ×× LOCAL GOVERNMENT AREA, ××</td><td>PREPAYMENT</td><td></td></tr>
<tr><td>总单号</td><td>分单号</td><td>箱号</td><td>铅封号</td><td>箱型尺寸</td><td>件数</td><td>货重</td><td>体积</td><td>货物详细描述</td></tr>
<tr><td></td><td></td><td>TCLU 1411909</td><td>CN 7379394</td><td>20GP</td><td>1</td><td>30232KGS</td><td></td><td>PRE-PAINTED COLD ROLLED COILS</td></tr>
</table>

Table 2-6 **Export Manifest Template**

Container Size: refer to the page of "container size" and enter the value in the "KEY_ VALUE" column
Package Type: refer to the page of "package type" and enter the value in the "KEY_ NME" column

Booking Number	Consignor	Consignor Address	Consignee	Consignee Address	Notifier	Notifier Address	Payment on Arrival/ Prepayment	
575021××5	××× CO., LTD	ROOM 1×××, NO. × BUILDING NO. ××× ROAD, ××, ××. P. R. C	××	×× FREE ZONE, ×× ROAD, ×× LOCAL GOVERNMENT AREA, ××	×××	×× FREE ZONE, ×× ROAD, ×× LOCAL GOVERNMENT AREA, ××	PREPAYMENT	
General Order Number	**Sub-order Number**	**Container Number**	**Seal Number**	**Container Size**	**Number of Pieces**	**Cargo Weight**	**Volume**	**Full Description of Goods**
		TCLU 1411909	CN 7379394	20GP	1	30232KGS		PRE-PAINTED COLD ROLLED COILS

MAERSK LINE

BOOKING AMENDMENT

Booking No.: **575021 5**　　　　打印时间:　2018-01-30 04:16 UTC

订舱人:	SINOTRANS SHANDONG CO LTD	交接方式:	CY/CY
联系人:	LIW LI N	收货地:	Xingang,Tianjin,China
订舱人参考号:		交货地:	Port Sudan,Sudan
合约号:	202 5	客人提供货物描述:	mma PREPAINTED STEEL COILS
合约客户:	CHEMPLUS INDUSTRY COMPANY LIMITED	受理订舱分公司:	Maersk China Shipping (Qingdao)
参考号:		Shipper Ref. No:	

您的马士基客服电话:86-532-80951000 邮箱：CN.NORTH.EXPORT@maersk.com

MMA的货物（具体品名为金属卷/金属条/金属管类）；请于开港前(CY Open)24小时（工作日）务必提供装箱照片(可联系装箱公司/或者客户自行提供装箱照片，邮件正文中请注明:提单号，箱号，货物单件重量，总重，件数，货物生产商名称，目的港，起运港,柜底支撑木条规格:长/宽/高)于我司，待鉴定合格之后，方可入港。如果照片不合格或者未经允许提前入港产生的费用及损失由客户自行承担。另外，北美内陆不接受金属卷。

尊敬的客人，您申请的场站信息更改已处理完毕，请参照以下场站信息

提箱场地:
操　作:　　刘 9　　E-MAIL:h n_liu@ .com
8　　E-MAIL: @tj com
箱　管:　　分 022-25
*请严格按照箱体标示的有效载荷安排装箱，超出箱体载重量的集装箱，整票将不予装载
*自2012年起，除了某些特殊情况，熏蒸货物将被算作危险品，请务必按照相关规定申报。

船名/航次(Vessel):　　BALLENITA(巴伦尼塔)/180
船舶劳氏编码:　　9603609
航线(Trade code):　　PH1
挂靠码头:　　联盟国际(Tianjin Port Alliance Terminal)
开港时间(CY open):　　2018-02-06 00:00（集装箱开始入港时间）
截港时间(CY cut off)/MSK VGM 截止时间：　2018-02-07 00:00（请在此时间前完成集装箱入港）
加载申请截止时间:　　2018-02-07 12:00
样单截止时间(SI cut off):　　2018-02-06 09:00
(1.需要申报欧盟舱单的货物，请严格按照此时间提交提单样本，及完整信息包括所有品名的6位HS商品编码，托运人和收货人（或通知方）公司名称，街道地址，城市等。2.
如有在釜山或者光阳中转的货物，请严格按照此时间提交提单样本，否则发货人将承担由此产生的罚金及后果。)
舱单(入港清单)截止时间: 2018-02-05 17:00(超尺货物请提供超尺数据，冻柜请提供温度设置）

船代 VGM 截止时间:2018-02-05 17:00
舱单(入港清单)联系人:
邮箱:　　x @pen tj.com
电话:　　022-833 47;13820163

开船后，更改海关清洁舱单联系人:
邮箱:　　@p tj.com
电话:　　022-8332 1

集装箱信息

数量	尺寸/箱型/高度 (英尺.)是否可折叠	替代箱型	货物总重量	包装数量/种类	货物体积
10	20 DRY 8 6		150000.000 KGS		

预期运输计划

This document is subject to following:
- This booking and carriage are subject to the Maersk Line Terms and Conditions of Carriage which are available upon request from the carrier or his representatives and are furthermore accessible on the Maersk Line website "<http://www.maerskline.com>" under "Services" / "General Business Terms".
- The shipment is subject to tariff rates unless a correct and applicable service contract number is available
- The carrier's right to substitute the named and/or performing vessel(s) with another vessel or vessels at any time.
- Arrival, berthing, departure and transit times are estimated and given without guarantee and subject to change without prior notice
- All dates/times are given as reasonable estimates only and subject to change without prior notice.

Shipments destined for or carried/transhipped via the USA:
- This document is given subject to the customer providing the correct cargo description in accordance with U.S. law, including U.S. Customs requirements as described in Customs Rules and Regulations, 19 CFR Parts 4, 113 and 178 of October 31, 2002

图 2-3　订舱信息

思考题
Questions

1. 请通过调研，收集某一货代公司的托运单。

Please collect the booking note of a freight forwarding company through investigation.

2. 请模拟一订舱过程，填写下列出口托运单。

Please simulate a booking process and fill out the following export booking note.

表 2-7 **托运单**

年　月　日

<table>
<tr><td>托运人</td><td colspan="3"></td><td>发票号
提单号</td></tr>
<tr><td>收货人</td><td colspan="3"></td><td></td></tr>
<tr><td>通知方</td><td colspan="3"></td><td></td></tr>
<tr><td colspan="5">船名、航次</td></tr>
<tr><td colspan="2">装货港</td><td colspan="3">卸货港</td></tr>
<tr><td colspan="2">正本提单数量</td><td colspan="3">副本提单数量</td></tr>
<tr><td>唛头</td><td>包装数量</td><td>货物描述</td><td>毛重
（千克）</td><td>体积
（立方米）</td></tr>
<tr><td colspan="5">×××××××（总计）</td></tr>
<tr><td colspan="5">特殊条款：
1）
2）
3）</td></tr>
</table>

Table 2-7　　　　　　　　**Booking Note**

Specific Date

<table>
<tr><td>Shipper</td><td colspan="3"></td><td>INV No.
B/L No.</td></tr>
<tr><td>Consignee</td><td colspan="3"></td><td></td></tr>
<tr><td>Notify Party</td><td colspan="3"></td><td></td></tr>
<tr><td colspan="5">Vessel & Voy.</td></tr>
<tr><td colspan="2">Port of Loading:</td><td colspan="3">Port of Discharge:</td></tr>
<tr><td colspan="2">No of Original B/L:</td><td colspan="3">Copy of B/L:</td></tr>
<tr><td>Shipping Marks</td><td>No. of Packages</td><td>Description of Goods</td><td>G. W. KGS</td><td>MEAS. CBM</td></tr>
<tr><td colspan="5">Total　×××××××　only.</td></tr>
<tr><td colspan="5">Special provisions:
1)
2)
3)</td></tr>
</table>

子任务之四　装箱送货
Section Four: Packing and Delivery

任务引入
Task Introduction

订舱完毕后，货代业务员需要安排后续装箱送货事宜。由于该批货物需要到工厂进行装箱，请帮助货代业务员办理装箱送货事宜。

After the booking is completed, the freight forwarder has to arrange for subsequent packing and delivery. As the goods need to be packed at the factory, please help the freight forwarder to handle the packing and delivery.

任务分析
Assignment Analysis

装箱一般分两种，一种是提箱去工厂产装，需要联系车队拿空箱提交单去船公司指定堆场提箱，在船公司要求报数据时间截止前到工厂装箱，一般工厂是要装完箱之后有具体的数据。另一种是工厂安排送货到船公司指定堆场进行装箱，要求堆场按照客户分箱明细装箱，装完箱之后提供分箱明细对应的箱封号，以便于客户填写数据和做之后的相关单据。

Generally speaking, packing can be divided into two kinds: one is that the factory contacts the vehicle team, fetches the container at the designated yard with Equipment Dispatch Order, and does packing at the factory before the deadline when the shipping company claims to report the data. Therefore, the factory is to have concrete data after packing the container. The other is that the factory arranges delivery to the shipping company's designated yard for packing, which is required to pack goods in accordance with the customer's detailed packing list. After the packing, the container number corresponding to the details of the list will be provided, so that the customer can fill in the data and make the related documents.

相关知识
Relevant Knowledge

一、空箱提交单
Equipment Dispatch Order

空箱提交单又称集装箱发放通知单，俗称提箱单，是船公司或其代理人指示集装箱堆场将空集装箱及其他设备提交给本单持有人的书面凭证。

Equipment Dispatch Order, also known as Container Release Order, is commonly referred to as the "container order". It is the written document that the shipping company or its agent instructs the container yard to submit empty containers and other equipment to the holder.

在集装箱运输中，发货人如使用船公司的集装箱，并为了要把预定的货物装在箱内，就要向集装箱堆场或空箱储存场租借空箱，通常是由船公司提供空集装箱，借给发货人或集装箱货运站。在这种情况下，船公司或其代理人要对集装箱堆场或空箱储存场发出交箱指示，但是由于空集装箱是一个售价较高的设备，因此不能只靠简单的口头指示，还要向发货人或其代理人提交空箱提交单，集装箱堆场或空箱储存场只对持有本单证的人提交空集装箱，以确保交接安全。

During the transit of containers, if the consignor wants to use the container of the shipping company in order to store the scheduled goods, he has to rent the empty container from the container yard or empty container storage yard. Usually, the shipping company provides empty containers and lends them to the consignor or container freight station. In this case, the shipping company or its agent must issue a delivery instruction to the container yard or empty storage yard. However, since the empty container is a high-priced equipment, it is dependent on the submission of equipment dispatch order to the consignor or its agent, rather than through simple oral instructions. In short, the empty container should be only submitted to the person holding equipment dispatch order to ensure the safety of handover.

集装箱的空箱提交单一式 3 份，发货人或其代理人凭订舱委托书，接受订舱委托后，由船公司或其代理人签发，除自留一联备查外，发货人或其代理人和存箱的集装箱堆场或空箱储存场各执一联。

Equipment dispatch order should be provided in three copies, which are held by the shipping company or its agent, the consignor or its agent, and the container yard or empty container storage yard respectively.

二、装箱单

Container Loading Plan (CLP)

CLP 是指 Container Loading Plan，集装箱装箱单，如表 2-8 所示。在出口时工厂、货主、码头、船公司、货代用以核对装箱数据的单证。

CLP refers to the Container Loading Plan, as shown in Table 2-8, which is the document used by factories, shippers, wharfs, shipping companies and freight forwarders to check the packing data.

P/L 是指 Packing List，作为报关资料的装箱单。

P/L refers to the Packing List, as a packing list for customs declaration data.

从装货明细这个角度来看，两者本质上一样——都是列名货物的详细信息——包括包装方式、件数、毛重、净重，每件的尺寸、体积等。

From the perspective of loading, the two are essentially the same—both of which are detailed information for single shipment, including the packaging method, number of pieces, gross weight, net weight, size and volume of each item.

从用途上来看，两者有所不同。CLP 是货物出口时，货主、码头、承运人、货运代理人等用于核对装箱数据的单证，主要说明整个集装箱所装载货物的详细情况。P/L 一般用作报检或报关资料的装箱单。

From the perspective of usage, the two are different. CLP is a document used by shippers, docks, carriers, freight forwarders, etc. to verify packing data when the goods are exported, so as to mainly illustrate the details of the goods loaded in the entire container. P/L is generally used as a packing list for inspection or customs declaration.

三、装箱注意事项

Cautions for Packing

（一）混装注意事项

Cautions for Container Mixing

一般企业出口时，在装柜过程中主要担心的是货物数据错误、货物损坏和数据与报关数据不符合，从而导致海关不会放行。因此，在装柜前，发货人、仓库、货代必须协调周到，以避免这种情况的发生。

When a company exports, the main concern during the loading process is incorrect cargo data, damaged goods, and in-conformity between the information and the customs declaration data, which will result in the customs not releasing. Therefore, before loading the container, the consignor, the warehouse and the freight forwarder must be well coordinated to avoid this situation.

（1）不同形状、不同包装的货物尽可能不要装在一起。

The goods with different shapes and different packages should not be packed together as much as possible.

（2）从包装中会渗出灰尘、液体、潮气、臭气等的货物，尽可能不要与其他货物放在一起。不得已的情况下，就要用帆布、塑料薄膜或其他材料隔开。

The goods with dust, liquid, moisture, odor, etc. should not be put together with others as far as possible. In case of necessity, it should be separated by canvas, plastic film or other materials.

（3）重量轻的货物放在重量相对较重的货物上面。

Light weight goods are placed on the goods with relatively heavy weight.

（4）包装强度弱的货物要放在包装强度强的货物上面。

The goods with weak packaging strength should be placed on the goods with strong packaging strength.

（5）液体类货物和清洁类货物要尽量放在其他货物下面。

Liquid goods and clean goods should be placed under other goods as far as possible.

（6）带有尖角或有突出部分的货物，需将其遮盖，以避免将其他货物损坏。

Goods with sharp corners or protruding parts need to be covered to avoid damage to other goods.

（二）集装箱装货技巧

Container Loading Skills

（1）任何情况下货物装柜时，箱内所装货物重量不能超过集装箱的最大装载量，即集装箱总量减去集装箱的自重所得。一般情况下，总重和自重都会标在集装箱的箱门上。

In any cases, when the goods are loaded, the weight of the goods cannot exceed the maximumload of the container, that is, the total amount of the container minus the weight of the container. Under normal circumstances, the total weight and the weight of the container will be marked on the container door.

（2）每个集装箱的单位容重是一定的，因此在箱内装载同种货物时，只要知道货物密度，就可以断定出是重货还是轻货。如果货物密度大于箱的单位容重就是重货，反之则为轻货。及时并明确区分这两种不同的情况，对提高装箱效率很重要。

The unit weight of each container is certain, so when the same kind of cargo is loaded in the box, it can be determined whether it is heavy or light cargo as long as the density of the cargo is known. If the cargo density is greater than the unit weight of the container, it is heavy cargo, and vice versa, it is light cargo. Timely and clearly distinguish between these two different situations is fairly crucial to improve the packing efficiency.

（3）装载时要使箱底上的负荷平衡，特别要严格禁止负荷重心偏在一端的情况。

The load on the bottom of the container should be balanced when loading, especially the load center of gravity at one end is strictly prohibited.

（4）避免产生集中载荷。如在装载机械设备等重货时，箱底应铺上木板等衬垫材料，尽量分散其负荷。

Avoid concentrated loads. When loading heavy equipment such as machinery and equipment, the bottom of the container should be covered with wood and other cushioning materialsto disperse the load as much as possible.

（5）使用人力装货时要注意包装上有无“不可倒置”“平放”“竖放”等装卸指示标志。务必正确使用装货工具，捆包货禁止使用手钩。箱内所装的货物要装载整齐、紧密堆装。容易散捆和包装脆弱的货物，要使用衬垫或在货物间插入胶合板，防止货物在箱内移动。

When using human loading, pay attention to whether there are loading and unloading instruction signs such as "no inversion", "flat position" and "vertical placement" on the packaging. Make sure the correct use of loading tools and avoid the hooks for bundled goods. The goods in the container must be loaded neatly and packed closely. For the loose and fragile goods, we had better use padded or insert plywood to prevent the goods from moving inside the container.

（6）装载货板时，要确切掌握集装箱内部尺寸和货物包装的外部尺寸，以便计算装载件数，以达到尽量减少弃位、多装货物的目的。

When loading the pallet, it is necessary to accurately grasp the internal dimensions of the container and the external dimensions of the goods packaging in order to calculate the number of loads so as to achieve the purpose of minimizing abandonment and multi-packaging.

（7）用叉式装卸车装箱时，将受到机械的自由提升高度和门架高度的限制。

When using the forklift truck to pack, it will be restricted by the height of the machine's free lifting and the height of the gantry.

（8）货物最好不要裸装，最起码要有包装，不要一味地为节省空间而导致货物受损。

It's best not to put the goods naked. At the very least, there must be packaging. Do not blindly save the space and cause damage to the goods.

任务实施
Task Implementation

考虑到该批货物需要到工厂进行装箱，因此工厂需要联系车队拿空箱提交单去船公司指定堆场提箱，在船公司要求报数据时间截止前到工厂装箱。工厂应按照客户分箱明细装箱，填写装箱单，如表 2-8 所示。装完箱之后提供分箱明细对应的箱封号，575021165 彩涂卷的分箱情况，如表 2-9 所示。

Because the goods need to be packed in the factory, the factory has to contact the vehicle team, fetch the container at the designated yard with Equipment Dispatch Order, and do packing at the factory before the deadline when the shipping company claims to report the data. The factoryshall pack the container according to the details of the customer's requirements, fill in the container loading plan, as is shown in Table 2-8. After the packing, the container number of 575021165 corresponding to the details of the list will be provided, as is shown in Table 2-9.

表 2-8　　装箱单

<table>
<tr><td colspan="5">装　　箱　　单</td><td colspan="2">集装箱号</td><td>集装箱规格
20　40</td></tr>
<tr><td colspan="5"></td><td colspan="2">铅封号</td><td>冷藏温度　℉　℃</td></tr>
<tr><td colspan="2">船名　　航次</td><td colspan="2">收货地点</td><td>装货港</td><td>卸货港</td><td colspan="2">交货地点</td></tr>
<tr><td>箱主</td><td>提单号码</td><td>1. 发货人
2. 收货人
3. 通知人</td><td>标志与和号码</td><td>件数及包装种类</td><td>货名</td><td>重量（公斤）</td><td>尺码（立方米）</td></tr>
<tr><td rowspan="2"></td><td rowspan="2"></td><td rowspan="2">底
门</td><td rowspan="2"></td><td rowspan="2"></td><td></td><td></td><td></td></tr>
<tr><td>总件数
重量及尺码总计</td><td></td><td></td></tr>
</table>

续表

<table>
<tr><td rowspan="3">危险品要注意危险品标志及闪点</td><td colspan="2"></td><td>开封原因</td><td>封箱日期........................
封箱地点........................
（地点及国名）</td><td></td><td>皮重</td></tr>
<tr><td>出口</td><td>驾驶员签收</td><td>堆场签收</td><td rowspan="2">封箱人
发货人　货运站

....
（签署）</td><td></td><td>总毛重</td></tr>
<tr><td>进口</td><td>驾驶员签收</td><td>货运站签收</td><td colspan="2">发货人或货运站留存
一式十份 此栏每份不同</td></tr>
</table>

Table 2-8 **Container Loading Plan**

<table>
<tr><td colspan="5" rowspan="2">Container Loading Plan</td><td>Container No.</td><td colspan="2">Type of Container
20　40</td></tr>
<tr><td>Seal No.</td><td colspan="2">℉　℃
Reefer Temp Required</td></tr>
<tr><td colspan="2">Ocean Vessel　Voy. No.</td><td colspan="2">Place of Receipt</td><td>Port of loading</td><td>Port of Discharge</td><td colspan="2">Place of Delivery</td></tr>
<tr><td>Owner</td><td>B/L　No.</td><td>1. Shipper
2. Consignee
3. Notify</td><td>Marks & Number</td><td>No. &Kind of Pkgs</td><td>Description of Goods</td><td>Weight (kgs)</td><td>Measurement (Cubic meter)</td></tr>
<tr><td rowspan="2"></td><td rowspan="2"></td><td rowspan="2">Fron
Door</td><td rowspan="2"></td><td rowspan="2"></td><td></td><td></td><td></td></tr>
<tr><td>Total Number of Packages
Total Weight & Measurement</td><td></td><td></td></tr>
</table>

Continued

<table>
<tr><td rowspan="3">In case of dangerous goods pales enter the label classifi – cation and flash point of the goods</td><td colspan="2">New Seal No.</td><td>Reason for Breaking Seal</td><td>Date of Vanning ------------------
at ------------------
（Place & Country）</td><td></td><td>Tare Weight</td></tr>
<tr><td>Export</td><td>Received by Driver</td><td>Received by CY</td><td rowspan="2">Packed by
（shipper/CFS） ------------------
Signed</td><td></td><td>Gross Weight</td></tr>
<tr><td>Import</td><td>Received by Driver</td><td>Received by CFS</td><td colspan="2">1. SHIPPER/CFS</td></tr>
</table>

表 2-9　　彩涂卷的分箱情况汇总

575021165　10 * 20GP（GP：通用集装箱）													
规格	颜色	卷号	吨位	柜号	件数	毛重	箱号	封号	箱门重	加固材料	VGM	体积	VGM
0. 22 * 1200	9016	180120A18	4. 612										
0. 22 * 1200	9016	180120A19	4. 516										
0. 48 * 1200	9016	180120A20	4. 332										
0. 48 * 1200	9016	180120A21	4. 804										
0. 33 * 1200	9016	180120A22	4. 088										
0. 33 * 1200	9016	180120A29	5. 48										
			27. 832	1	6	27832KGS	TCLU 1411909	CN 7379394	2300KGS	100	30232KGS	20	30232KGS
0. 33 * 1200	9016	180120A24	4. 512										
0. 48 * 1200	9016	180120A25	5. 344										
0. 33 * 1200	9016	180120A26	4. 652										
0. 33 * 1200	9016	180120A27	4. 802										
0. 33 * 1200	9016	180120A28	4. 502										
0. 33 * 1200	9016	180120A23	4. 128										
			27. 94	2	6	27940KGS	MRKU 6929352	CN 7379396	2170KGS	100	30210KGS	20	30210KGS

续表

575021165　10 * 20GP（GP：通用集装箱）													
规格	颜色	卷号	吨位	柜号	件数	毛重	箱号	封号	箱门重	加固材料	VGM	体积	VGM
0. 33 * 1200	9016	180120A31	5. 352										
0. 33 * 1200	9016	180120A32	4. 53										
0. 33 * 1200	9016	180120A33	5. 388										
0. 26 * 1200	9016	180120A34	4. 22										
0. 26 * 1200	9016	180120A35	4. 232										
0. 26 * 1200	9016	180120A36	3. 868										
			27. 59	3	6	27590KGS	MSKU 7782247	CN 7379399	2170KGS	100	29860KGS	20	29860KGS
0. 33 * 1200	9016	180120A30	4. 524										
0. 26 * 1200	9016	180120A37	4. 554										
0. 26 * 1200	9016	180120A38	4. 542										
0. 26 * 1200	9016	180120A39	4. 426										
0. 26 * 1200	9016	180120A40	4. 404										
0. 26 * 1200	9016	180120A41	4. 546										
			26. 996	4	6	26996KGS	MRKU 7005585	CN 7379400	2170KGS	100	29266KGS	20	29266KGS

续表

575021165　10 * 20GP（GP：通用集装箱）													
规格	颜色	卷号	吨位	柜号	件数	毛重	箱号	封号	箱门重	加固材料	VGM	体积	VGM
0. 26 * 1200	9016	180120A43	4. 528										
0. 26 * 1200	9016	180120A44	4. 486										
0. 26 * 1200	9016	180120A45	4. 488										
0. 26 * 1200	9016	180120A46	4. 424										
0. 26 * 1200	9016	180120A47	4. 304										
0. 26 * 1200	9016	180120A56	4. 814										
			27. 044	5	6	27044KGS	TEMU 0697591	CN 7379391	2180KGS	100	29324KGS	20	29324KGS
0. 26 * 1200	9016	180120A42	4. 432										
0. 26 * 1200	9016	180120A48	4. 41										
0. 26 * 1200	9016	180120A49	4. 552										
0. 26 * 1200	9016	180120A50	4. 488										
0. 26 * 1200	9016	180120A51	4. 386										
0. 26 * 1200	9016	180120A52	4. 458										
			26. 726	6	6	26726KGS	MRKU 9071101	CN 7379393	2170KGS	100	28996KGS	20	28996KGS

续表

575021165　10＊20GP（GP：通用集装箱）													
规格	颜色	卷号	吨位	柜号	件数	毛重	箱号	封号	箱门重	加固材料	VGM	体积	VGM
0. 26＊1200	9016	180120A53	4. 428										
0. 26＊1200	9016	180120A54	4. 454										
0. 26＊1200	9016	180120A55	4. 434										
0. 26＊1200	9016	180120A59	4. 476										
0. 26＊1200	9016	180120A60	4. 476										
0. 26＊1200	9016	180120A61	4. 67										
			26. 938	7	6	26938KGS	PONU 0198150	CN 7379398	2300KGS	100	29338KGS	20	29338KGS
0. 26＊1200	9016	180120A63	4. 49										
0. 26＊1200	9016	180120A64	4. 116										
0. 26＊1200	9016	180120A65	4. 402										
0. 26＊1200	9016	180120A66	4. 406										
0. 26＊1200	9016	180121B01	4. 47										
0. 26＊1200	9016	180121B11	4. 91										
			26. 794	8	6	26794KGS	MRKU 7756816	CN 7379397	2150KGS	100	29044KGS	20	29044KGS

续表

575021165　10 * 20GP（GP：通用集装箱）													
规格	颜色	卷号	吨位	柜号	件数	毛重	箱号	封号	箱门重	加固材料	VGM	体积	VGM
0. 26 * 1200	9016	180121B02	4. 094										
0. 26 * 1200	9016	180121B03	4. 364										
0. 26 * 1200	9016	180121B04	4. 346										
0. 26 * 1200	9016	180121B05	4. 926										
0. 26 * 1200	9016	180121B06	4. 484										
0. 26 * 1200	9016	180121B07	4. 482										
			26. 696	9	6	26696KGS	PONU 0198150	CN 7379395	2300KGS	100	29096KGS	20	29096KGS
0. 16 * 1200	9016	180123A03	4. 342										
0. 16 * 1200	9016	180123A04	4. 34										
0. 2 * 1200	9016	180123A11	5. 11										
0. 2 * 1200	9016	180123A12	4. 528										
0. 2 * 1200	9016	180123A13	4. 624										
0. 2 * 1200	9016	180123A14	4. 87										
			27. 814	29	6	27814KGS	TCLU 6122431	CN 7379389	2380KGS	100	30294KGS	20	30294KGS
					60	272370KGS							

Table 2-9 **Summary of Loading for PRE-PAINTED COLD ROLLED COILS**

575021165 10 * 20GP													
Specification	Colour	Volume Number	Tonnage	Cabinet Number	Number of Pieces	Gross Weight	Container Number	Seal Number	Container Door Weight	Reinfor-cement Material	VGM	Volume	VGM
0. 22 * 1200	9016	180120A18	4. 612										
0. 22 * 1200	9016	180120A19	4. 516										
0. 48 * 1200	9016	180120A20	4. 332										
0. 48 * 1200	9016	180120A21	4. 804										
0. 33 * 1200	9016	180120A22	4. 088										
0. 33 * 1200	9016	180120A29	5. 48										
			27. 832	1	6	27832KGS	TCLU 1411909	CN 7379394	2300KGS	100	30232KGS	20	30232KGS
0. 33 * 1200	9016	180120A24	4. 512										
0. 48 * 1200	9016	180120A25	5. 344										
0. 33 * 1200	9016	180120A26	4. 652										
0. 33 * 1200	9016	180120A27	4. 802										
0. 33 * 1200	9016	180120A28	4. 502										
0. 33 * 1200	9016	180120A23	4. 128										
			27. 94	2	6	27940KGS	MRKU 6929352	CN 7379396	2170KGS	100	30210KGS	20	30210KGS

Continued

575021165　10 * 20GP													
Specification	Colour	Volume Number	Tonnage	Cabinet Number	Number of Pieces	Gross Weight	Container Number	Seal Number	Container Door Weight	Reinfor-cement Material	VGM	Volume	VGM
0. 33 * 1200	9016	180120A31	5. 352										
0. 33 * 1200	9016	180120A32	4. 53										
0. 33 * 1200	9016	180120A33	5. 388										
0. 26 * 1200	9016	180120A34	4. 22										
0. 26 * 1200	9016	180120A35	4. 232										
0. 26 * 1200	9016	180120A36	3. 868										
			27. 59	3	6	27590KGS	MSKU 7782247	CN 7379399	2170KGS	100	29860KGS	20	29860KGS
0. 33 * 1200	9016	180120A30	4. 524										
0. 26 * 1200	9016	180120A37	4. 554										
0. 26 * 1200	9016	180120A38	4. 542										
0. 26 * 1200	9016	180120A39	4. 426										
0. 26 * 1200	9016	180120A40	4. 404										
0. 26 * 1200	9016	180120A41	4. 546										
			26. 996	4	6	26996KGS	MRKU 7005585	CN 7379400	2170KGS	100	29266KGS	20	29266KGS

Continued

575021165 10 * 20GP													
Specification	Colour	Volume Number	Tonnage	Cabinet Number	Number of Pieces	Gross Weight	Container Number	Seal Number	Container Door Weight	Reinfor-cement Material	VGM	Volume	VGM
0. 26 * 1200	9016	180120A43	4. 528										
0. 26 * 1200	9016	180120A44	4. 486										
0. 26 * 1200	9016	180120A45	4. 488										
0. 26 * 1200	9016	180120A46	4. 424										
0. 26 * 1200	9016	180120A47	4. 304										
0. 26 * 1200	9016	180120A56	4. 814										
			27. 044	5	6	27044KGS	TEMU 0697591	CN 7379391	2180KGS	100	29324KGS	20	29324KGS
0. 26 * 1200	9016	180120A42	4. 432										
0. 26 * 1200	9016	180120A48	4. 41										
0. 26 * 1200	9016	180120A49	4. 552										
0. 26 * 1200	9016	180120A50	4. 488										
0. 26 * 1200	9016	180120A51	4. 386										
0. 26 * 1200	9016	180120A52	4. 458										
			26. 726	6	6	26726KGS	MRKU 9071101	CN 7379393	2170KGS	100	28996KGS	20	28996KGS

Continued

575021165　10 * 20GP													
Specification	Colour	Volume Number	Tonnage	Cabinet Number	Number of Pieces	Gross Weight	Container Number	Seal Number	Container Door Weight	Reinfor-cement Material	VGM	Volume	VGM
0. 26 * 1200	9016	180120A53	4. 428										
0. 26 * 1200	9016	180120A54	4. 454										
0. 26 * 1200	9016	180120A55	4. 434										
0. 26 * 1200	9016	180120A59	4. 476										
0. 26 * 1200	9016	180120A60	4. 476										
0. 26 * 1200	9016	180120A61	4. 67										
			26. 938	7	6	26938KGS	PONU 0198150	CN 7379398	2300KGS	100	29338KGS	20	29338KGS
0. 26 * 1200	9016	180120A63	4. 49										
0. 26 * 1200	9016	180120A64	4. 116										
0. 26 * 1200	9016	180120A65	4. 402										
0. 26 * 1200	9016	180120A66	4. 406										
0. 26 * 1200	9016	180121B01	4. 47										
0. 26 * 1200	9016	180121B11	4. 91										
			26. 794	8	6	26794KGS	MRKU 7756816	CN 7379397	2150KGS	100	29044KGS	20	29044KGS

Continued

575021165 10 * 20GP													
Specification	Colour	Volume Number	Tonnage	Cabinet Number	Number of Pieces	Gross Weight	Container Number	Seal Number	Container Door Weight	Reinfor-cement Material	VGM	Volume	VGM
0. 26 * 1200	9016	180121B02	4. 094										
0. 26 * 1200	9016	180121B03	4. 364										
0. 26 * 1200	9016	180121B04	4. 346										
0. 26 * 1200	9016	180121B05	4. 926										
0. 26 * 1200	9016	180121B06	4. 484										
0. 26 * 1200	9016	180121B07	4. 482										
			26. 696	9	6	26696KGS	PONU 0198150	CN 7379395	2300KGS	100	29096KGS	20	29096KGS
0. 16 * 1200	9016	180123A03	4. 342										
0. 16 * 1200	9016	180123A04	4. 34										
0. 2 * 1200	9016	180123A11	5. 11										
0. 2 * 1200	9016	180123A12	4. 528										
0. 2 * 1200	9016	180123A13	4. 624										
0. 2 * 1200	9016	180123A14	4. 87										
			27. 814	29	6	27814KGS	TCLU 6122431	CN 7379389	2380KGS	100	30294KGS	20	30294KGS
					60	272370KGS							

思考题
Questions

1. CLP 与 P/L 的区别是什么？

What is the difference between CLP and P/L?

2. 请说明集装箱混装的注意事项。

Please specify the cautions for container mixing.

子任务之五　整理单据
Section Five：Documents Collection

任务引入
Task Introduction

在工厂装完箱，确定好箱封号之后，货运代理操作员需要根据船公司报数据格式填写提单样本、VGM EXCLE 表格和声明，将所有表格填写完毕统一发给船代。

After packing the container in the factory and determining the seal number, the freight operator needs to fill in the bill of lading, VGM EXCLE form and declaration according to the data provided by the shipping company, and send all the forms to the shipping agent.

任务分析
Assignment Analysis

作为货运代理操作员，应该做的就是关注船的动态集港开始的时间到集港结束截关的时间，这些都是需要特别清楚的，一定要在截关时间之前安排货物放行。

The freight operator, should to pay attention to the time from the start of the harboring to the end of the berthing and make arrangements for the cargo before the cut-off time.

相关知识
Relevant Knowledge

一、核实的集装箱总重（VGM）
Verified Gross Mass Statement（VGM）

2014 年 5 月，国际海事组织海上安全委员会批准修改《海上生命安全公约》（SO-

LAS）中对托运人强制验证集装箱重量的要求。

In May 2014, the IMO'S Maritime Safety Committee approved changes to the Safety of Life at Sea (SOLAS) convention regarding a mandatory container weight verification requirement on shippers.

DSC 的报告被海上安全委员会于 2014 年 5 月批准并在 2014 年 11 月进行了修订。

The DSC report was approved by the Maritime Safety Committee in May 2014 and adopted by the committee in November 2014.

把集装箱重量检验作为船舶装载的条件这一要求自 2016 年 7 月 1 日开始具备法律约束效力。

The requirement making container weight verification a condition for vessel loading has become legally binding on 1st July, 2016.

SOLAS 公约修订案明确了责任的分配，归纳如下。

The SOLAS amendments are clear in assigning responsibilities, summarized below.

托运人有责任提供精确的经核实的载货集装箱毛重。

The shipper is responsible for providing an accurate "verified gross mass".

在没有获取经核实的载货集装箱毛重时，船长（船东）和码头经营人有权拒绝将该集装箱装载到船舶上。

The vessel operator and the terminal operator must not load a container aboard a vessel without a VGM.

VGM 托运人声明，如表 2-10 所示。

The Declaration of VGM Consignor as shown in Table 2-10.

表 2-10　　VGM 托运人声明

<table>
<tr><td colspan="2">订舱编号或提单号</td><td colspan="3"></td></tr>
<tr><td colspan="2">船舶名称</td><td></td><td>航次编号</td><td></td></tr>
<tr><td colspan="2">托运人</td><td colspan="3">名称　　地址　　电话</td></tr>
<tr><td>序号</td><td>集装箱编号</td><td colspan="3">验证后的载货集装箱的重量（公斤）及称重点信息</td></tr>
<tr><td>1</td><td></td><td colspan="3"></td></tr>
<tr><td>2</td><td></td><td colspan="3"></td></tr>
<tr><td>3</td><td></td><td colspan="3"></td></tr>
<tr><td>4</td><td></td><td colspan="3"></td></tr>
<tr><td>5</td><td></td><td colspan="3"></td></tr>
<tr><td>6</td><td></td><td colspan="3"></td></tr>
<tr><td>7</td><td></td><td colspan="3"></td></tr>
<tr><td>8</td><td></td><td colspan="3"></td></tr>
<tr><td>9</td><td></td><td colspan="3"></td></tr>
<tr><td>10</td><td></td><td colspan="3"></td></tr>
</table>

□　本托运人声明：该文件资料所含载货集装箱重量信息系按照《1974 年国际海上人命安全公约》第 VI/2. 4. 1 条所述方法（方法一整体称重法）获得，称重点的称重设备已取得计量监督部门颁发的计量检定证书，且获得重量的日期在证书的有效期范围内。

□　本托运人声明：该文件资料所含载货集装箱重量信息系按照《1974 年国际海上人命安全公约》第 VI/2. 4. 2 条所述方法（方法二累加计算法）获得，该方法符合主管机关制定并公布的《载货集装箱累加计算法重量验证指南》的要求。

（请根据实际使用的称重方法，在□中加上√。）

本声明由____________________________________（托运人公司）授权________________（声明人姓名）负责提交。

声明人签名（请手签）：________________

托运人公司（请盖章）________________

日期：________________

本声明书只适用中国地区使用，其他国家、地区应以当地主管机构公布的声明书为准。如需要使用本声明书，请根据当地主管机构的要求做相应调整。

VGM 声明上传网址：http：//111. 160. 55. 66：6666/cdfiles/

上传文件名格式为提单号，不带字母前缀，如 7020837240. doc 或 7020837240. pdf 等。

Table 2-10　　The Declaration of VGM Consignor

<table>
<tr><td colspan="2">Booking Number or Bill of Lading Number</td><td colspan="4"></td></tr>
<tr><td colspan="2">Vessel Name</td><td colspan="2"></td><td>Voyage Number</td><td></td></tr>
<tr><td colspan="2">Consignor</td><td colspan="4">Name　　Address　　Telephone Number</td></tr>
<tr><td>Serial Number</td><td colspan="2">Container Number</td><td colspan="3">Weight (kg) and key information of verified cargo container</td></tr>
<tr><td>1</td><td colspan="2"></td><td colspan="3"></td></tr>
<tr><td>2</td><td colspan="2"></td><td colspan="3"></td></tr>
<tr><td>3</td><td colspan="2"></td><td colspan="3"></td></tr>
</table>

Continued

Serial Number	Container Number	Weight (kg) and key information of verified cargo container
4		
5		
6		
7		
8		
9		
10		

The consignor declares that the weight information of the cargo container contained in the document is obtained in accordance with the method (Method I Overall Weighing Method) described in Article VI / 2. 4. 1 of the 1974 International Convention for the safety of life at sea, and that the key weighing equipment has obtained the measurement & inspection certificate issued by the measurement supervision department, and the date of obtaining the weight is within the validity period of the certificate.

The consignor declares that the weight information of the cargo container contained in the document is obtained in accordance with the method (Method II Cumulative Calculation Method) described in Article VI / 2. 4. 2 of the 1974 International Convention for the safety of life at sea, which conforms to the requirements of the weight verification guide for the cumulative calculation method of cargo containers formulated and published by the competent authority.

Please add √ to□according to the actual weighing method.

This declaration is authorized by (shipping company) and submitted by (declarant).

Signature of declarant (please sign by hand):

Shipping company (please seal):

Date:

This declaration is only applicable in China, and other countries and regions shall be subject to the declaration issued by the local competent authority. If you need to use this declaration, please make corresponding adjustment according to the requirements of the local competent authority.

upload URL: http: //111. 160. 55. 66: 6666/cdfiles/

The format of the uploaded file name is B/L number without letter prefix, such as 7020837240. doc or 7020837240. pdf, etc.

二、获取载货集装箱经核实毛重的方法

Method for Obtaining Verified Gross Weight of Cargo Container

托运人有两种方法获取载货集装箱经核实毛重的方法。

For shippers to establish an accurate verified gross mass, two methods are available.

（1）在完成集装箱装箱和上封后，托运人可自行或安排第三方对载货集装箱进行称重。

After packing and sealing the containers, the shipper may carry out the weighing of the loaded containers by himself or by a third party.

（2）托运人可自行或安排第三方对所有的货物包装和组件进行称重，包括集装箱内的衬盘、衬垫和其他包装及系固材料，然后将这些重量和集装箱的皮重相加。

The shipper (or by arrangement of the shipper, a third party) may weigh all packages and cargo items and add the tare mass of the container to the sum of the single masses of the container's contents.

任务实施

Task Implementation

货运代理操作员制提单（如图 2-4 所示）、VGM 表格（如表 2-11 所示）和载货集装箱重量验证声明，如表 2-12 所示。

The freight forwarder develops the bill of lading (as shown in Figure 2-4), the VGM form (as shown in Table 2-11), and the weight verification statement for the loaded container, as shown in Table 2-12.

船代在收到货代操作员递交的所有表格之后，安排制作舱单，如表 2-13 所示。

After receiving all the forms submitted by the freight operator, the shipping agent sets about the manifest, as shown in Table 2-13.

提单号：575021165
出单方式：正本

SHIPPER:
T TD
ADD:
TEL:

CNEE:
Y
ADD: N
TEL: +3

NOTIFY:

ADD: K
TEL: +3

船名航次：BALLENITA / 1804

起运港:XINGANG CHINA 目的港:PORT SUDAN 最终卸货港:PORT SUDAN

唛头	总件数以及单位	货描	总重	总体积
N/M	278COILS	PRE-PAINTED COLD ROLLED COILS	1315220KGS	960M3

FREIGHT PREPAID
++++以下为提供但不显示内容
H.S. CODE: 7210701000

箱封号 件 重 尺 箱型 超尺寸数据

箱号	封号	件数	毛重	体积	箱型
TCLU1411909	CN7379394	6	27832	20	20GP
MRKU6929352	CN7379396	6	27940	20	20GP
MSKU7782247	CN7379399	6	27590	20	20GP
MRKU7005585	CN7379400	6	26996	20	20GP
TEMU0697591	CN7379391	6	27044	20	20GP
MRKU9071101	CN7379393	6	26726	20	20GP
PONU0939930	CN7379398	6	26938	20	20GP
MRKU7756816	CN7379397	6	26794	20	20GP
PONU0198150	CN7379395	6	26696	20	20GP
TCLU6122431	CN7379389	6	27814	20	20GP
MSKU7137562	CN7378326	6	27692	20	20GP
TGHU2390517	CN7378340	6	26988	20	20GP
PONU0934604	CN7378331	6	27902	20	20GP
PONU2038504	CN7378332	6	27556	20	20GP
PONU0502370	CN7378330	6	27694	20	20GP

图 2-4 提单样本

表 2-11　　VGM 模板

船名航次	BALLENITA		1804	订舱代理	TJWY06	提单承运人	MAE				
VGM 信息说明	此表须全英文填写		称重方式：（M1：整体称重；M2：累加计算）								
箱号（必填）	提单号（必填）	箱形尺寸（必填）	VGM 总称重（千克）（必填）	称重方式（必填）	称重日期（必填）	托运人名称（必填）	托运人联系人（必填）	托运人联系电话（必填）	托运人签名（必填）	VGM 称重公司（必填）	VGM 证书编号
TCLU1411909	575021165	20GP	30232	M2	201802051100	SHIPPER	SUN	0315-3232266	SUN	SHIPPER	
MRKU6929352	575021165	20GP	30210	M2	201802051100	SHIPPER	SUN	0315-3232266	SUN	SHIPPER	
MSKU7782247	575021165	20GP	29860	M2	201802051100	SHIPPER	SUN	0315-3232266	SUN	SHIPPER	
MRKU7005585	575021165	20GP	29266	M2	201802051100	SHIPPER	SUN	0315-3232266	SUN	SHIPPER	
TEMU0697591	575021165	20GP	29324	M2	201802051100	SHIPPER	SUN	0315-3232266	SUN	SHIPPER	
MRKU9071101	575021165	20GP	28996	M2	201802051100	SHIPPER	SUN	0315-3232266	SUN	SHIPPER	
PONU0939930	575021165	20GP	29338	M2	201802051100	SHIPPER	SUN	0315-3232266	SUN	SHIPPER	
MRKU7756816	575021165	20GP	29044	M2	201802051100	SHIPPER	SUN	0315-3232266	SUN	SHIPPER	
PONU0198150	575021165	20GP	29096	M2	201802051100	SHIPPER	SUN	0315-3232266	SUN	SHIPPER	
TCLU6122431	575021165	20GP	30294	M2	201802051100	SHIPPER	SUN	0315-3232266	SUN	SHIPPER	

Table 2-11 **The Template of VGM**

Vessel Name Voyage Number	BALLENITA		1804	Booking Agent	TJWY06	Bill of Lading Carrier	MAE				
VGM message description	This form must be completed in English!		Weighing method:（M1: overall weighing; M2: cumulative calculation）								
Container Number（required）	Bill of Lading Number（required）	Container Size（required）	VGM Total Weighing KGS（required）	Weighing Method（required）	Weighing Date（required）	Shipper Name（required）	Shipper Contact（required）	Shipper's Contact Number（required）	Shipper's Signature（required）	VGM Weighing Company（required）	VGM Certificate Number
TCLU1411909	575021165	20GP	30232	M2	201802051100	SHIPPER	SUN	0315-3232266	SUN	SHIPPER	
MRKU6929352	575021165	20GP	30210	M2	201802051100	SHIPPER	SUN	0315-3232266	SUN	SHIPPER	
MSKU7782247	575021165	20GP	29860	M2	201802051100	SHIPPER	SUN	0315-3232266	SUN	SHIPPER	
MRKU7005585	575021165	20GP	29266	M2	201802051100	SHIPPER	SUN	0315-3232266	SUN	SHIPPER	
TEMU0697591	575021165	20GP	29324	M2	201802051100	SHIPPER	SUN	0315-3232266	SUN	SHIPPER	
MRKU9071101	575021165	20GP	28996	M2	201802051100	SHIPPER	SUN	0315-3232266	SUN	SHIPPER	
PONU0939930	575021165	20GP	29338	M2	201802051100	SHIPPER	SUN	0315-3232266	SUN	SHIPPER	
MRKU7756816	575021165	20GP	29044	M2	201802051100	SHIPPER	SUN	0315-3232266	SUN	SHIPPER	
PONU0198150	575021165	20GP	29096	M2	201802051100	SHIPPER	SUN	0315-3232266	SUN	SHIPPER	
TCLU6122431	575021165	20GP	30294	M2	201802051100	SHIPPER	SUN	0315-3232266	SUN	SHIPPER	

表 2-12　　载货集装箱重量验证声明

船名航次：BALLENITA 1804
中文报关品名：

订舱号（必填）	箱号（必填）	是否自有箱（选填）	箱皮重（选填）	验证重量（必填）	计量单位（必填 KGM）
575021165	TCLU1411909			30232	KGM
575021165	MRKU6929352			30210	KGM
575021165	MSKU7782247			29860	KGM
575021165	MRKU7005585			29266	KGM
575021165	TEMU0697591			29324	KGM
575021165	MRKU9071101			28996	KGM
575021165	PONU0939930			29338	KGM
575021165	MRKU7756816			29044	KGM
575021165	PONU0198150			29096	KGM
575021165	TCLU6122431			30294	KGM

本托运人声明：该文件资料所含载货集装箱重量信息系按照《1974 年国际海上人命安全公约》第 VI/2. 4. 2 条所述方法获得，该方法符合主管机关制定并公布的《载货集装箱累加计算法重量验证指南》的要求。

本托运人确认，本声明的电子版本与其原件具有相同的法律效力。

托运人公司名称：

职位：OP

签字：

日期：2018. 2. 5

盖公章

Table 2-12 Verified Gross Mass Statement

Vessel & Voy: BOALLENITA 1804

Chinese Name:

Booking Reference (required)	Container Number (required)	SOC (Y if Yes) (optional)	Tare Weight (optional)	VGM (required)	UOM (KGM required)
575021165	TCLU1411909			30232	KGM
575021165	MRKU6929352			30210	KGM
575021165	MSKU7782247			29860	KGM
575021165	MRKU7005585			29266	KGM
575021165	TEMU0697591			29324	KGM
575021165	MRKU9071101			28996	KGM
575021165	PONU0939930			29338	KGM
575021165	MRKU7756816			29044	KGM
575021165	PONU0198150			29096	KGM
575021165	TCLU6122431			30294	KGM

The consignor declares that the weight information of the cargo container contained in the document is obtained in accordance with the method described in Article VI / 2.4.2 of the 1974 International Convention for the safety of life at sea, which conforms to the requirements of the weight verification guide for the cumulative calculation method of cargo containers formulated and published by the competent authority.

This shipper confirms that the electronic version of this declaration has the same legal effect as the original.

Shipping company name:

Position: OP

Sign:

Date: February 5, 2018

Official seal

表 2-13　　**舱单**

船名航次：BALLENITA 1804

提单号：575021165

箱号	封号	箱门重	件数	毛重	加固材料	VGM	体积	VGM
TCLU1411909	CN7379394	2300	6	27832	100	30232	20	30232
MRKU6929352	CN7379396	2170	6	27940	100	30210	20	30210
MSKU7782247	CN7379399	2170	6	27590	100	29860	20	29860
MRKU7005585	CN7379400	2170	6	26996	100	29266	20	29266
TEMU0697591	CN7379391	2180	6	27044	100	29324	20	29324
MRKU9071101	CN7379393	2170	6	26726	100	28996	20	28996
PONU0939930	CN7379398	2300	6	26938	100	29338	20	29338
MRKU7756816	CN7379397	2150	6	26794	100	29044	20	29044
PONU0198150	CN7379395	2300	6	26696	100	29096	20	29096
TCLU6122431	CN7379389	2380	6	27814	100	30294	20	30294
合计			60	272370				

Table 2-13 **The Manifest**

Vessel Name & Voyage Number：BALLENITA 1804

B/L Number：575021165

Container Number	Seal Number	Container Door Weight	Quantity	Gross Weight	Reinforcing Material	VGM	Volume	VGM
TCLU1411909	CN7379394	2300	6	27832	100	30232	20	30232
MRKU6929352	CN7379396	2170	6	27940	100	30210	20	30210
MSKU7782247	CN7379399	2170	6	27590	100	29860	20	29860
MRKU7005585	CN7379400	2170	6	26996	100	29266	20	29266
TEMU0697591	CN7379391	2180	6	27044	100	29324	20	29324
MRKU9071101	CN7379393	2170	6	26726	100	28996	20	28996
PONU0939930	CN7379398	2300	6	26938	100	29338	20	29338
MRKU7756816	CN7379397	2150	6	26794	100	29044	20	29044
PONU0198150	CN7379395	2300	6	26696	100	29096	20	29096
TCLU6122431	CN7379389	2380	6	27814	100	30294	20	30294
Total			60	272370				

思考题
Questions

1. 请结合自己的理解，介绍一下 VGM。

Please introduce VGM with your own understanding.

2. 请谈谈获得载货集装箱经核实毛重的方法。

Please talk about how to obtain the verified gross weight of the container.

子任务之六　协助报关
Section Six：Assisting Customs Declaration

任务引入
Task Introduction

舱单确认之后，由堆场货车队将集装箱运至堆场，即可安排报关。货运代理业务员需要协助办理报关事宜。作为货代业务员，该如何完成该项工作呢？

After the confirmation of the manifest, the container will be transported to the yard by the truck team. Freight forwarder should assist to deal with customs declaration. What should freight forwarder do?

任务分析
Assignment Analysis

如涉及查验，货运代理业务员须联系报关行和堆场车队安排此票货物不集港，并告知集装箱的所在位置，进而安排提箱验货。如货物通关放行，整个出口流程已进行大半，要根据船的动态查是否集港，能否上船。

If the inspection is involved, the freight forwarder should contact the customs broker as well as the vehicle team, inform the location of the container, and then arrange the inspection of the goods. If the goods are cleared and released, the entire export process has already been carried out for the most part. According to the ship's dynamics, it is necessary to check whether the port is ready for shipment.

相关知识
Relevant Knowledge

一、报关
Customs Clearance

（一）海关放行的主要措施
Customs Clearance Measures

海关放行的主要措施包括声明、文件检查、完税、货物检查和货物放行。

Customs clearance measures mainly include declaration, document－checking, duty－paying, cargo-examination and cargo－release.

1. 声明

Declaration

报关单和相关论文给海关检查。

Bill of Entry and relevant papers to the Customs for checking.

通常包含一些详细的情况，例如价格、货物描述、船名、装运港和其他一些细节作为规定通过主管机。

It usually contains particulars such as value, description of goods, name of the ship, port of shipment, and such other particulars as may be prescribed by the customs authorities.

根据《中华人民共和国海关法》，声明进口货物必须在收货人向海关申报的 14 天内运输到达；声明出口货物必须在发货人装货 24 小时之前到达海关的监视区，除非有特殊批准的海关证明。

According to Customs Law of the People's Republic of China, declaration of import goods shall be made to the Customs by the consignee within 14 days from the date of the declaration of the arrival of the means of transport, and declaration of export goods shall be made by the consignor upon the arrival of the goods at the customs surveillance zone and 24hours prior to loading, unless otherwise specially approved by the Customs.

2. 检查文件

Document－checking

3. 货物查验

Cargo－examination

4. 完税

Duty-paying

进口货物的收货人、出口货物的发货人和进出境物品的所有人是关税的纳税义务人。

The consignee for import goods, the consignor for export goods and the owner of inward and outward articles shall be the persons obligated to pay customs duties.

5. 货物放行

Cargo-release

（二）进出口货代报关流程

Procedures Involved in Customs Declaration

（1）客户提供到货通知书、正本提单或电放保函及换单费、THC 费等交给货代企业，由货代企业代客户到所属船公司换取进口提货单。

The customer provides the arrival notice, the original bill of lading or the telex guarantee letter and replacement fee, THC fee, etc. to the freight forwarding company. The freight forwarding company exchanges the import bill of lading on behalf of the customer to the shipping company.

（2）准备进口报关所需单证。

Documents Needed for Customs Declaration.

①必备单证：清单、发票、合同一式一份、报关、报检委托书各一份。

Essential documents: one copy for list, invoice, contract, customs declaration, and inspection commission.

②从欧盟、美国、韩国、日本进口货物，如是木制包装箱的，需提供热处理证书或植物检疫证书；如是非木制的，提供无木制包包装。

Import goods from the and Japan. As for wooden package, heat treatment certificates or phytosanitary certificates must be provided. As for non-wooden package, there should be no wood packaging.

③税则所规定的各项证件（如进口许可证、机电证、重要工业品证书）

Various documents stipulated by the tax (such as import licenses, mechanical and electrical certificates, certificates of major industrial products).

④有减免税手册的提供减免税证明手册。

There is a tax deduction certificate manual available from the Tax Reduction and Exemption Manual.

（3）进口申报后如海关审价需要，客户须提供相关价格证明。如信用证、保单、原厂发票、招标书等海关所要求的文件。

After the import declaration, if the customs needs to review the price, the customer must provide the relevant price certificate, such as letters of credit, insurance policies, original invoices, tenders and other documents required by the customs.

（4）海关打印税单后，客户须在 7 个工作日缴纳税费。如超过期限，海关按日计征滞纳金。

After the customs has printed the tax bill, the customer must pay the tax within 7 working days. If it exceeds the deadline, the customs shall collect the overdue payment on a daily basis.

（5）报关查验放行后，客户须及时到货代企业缴纳报关、报检代垫代办费。

After the customs inspection is released, the customer shall promptly arrive at the freight forwarding agency to pay the Customs declaration and inspection service fee.

（三）注意事项

Precautions Involved in Customs Declaration

货物到港后 14 日内必须向海关申报。如超过期限海关按日计征滞报金（按货物价值万分之五）超过 3 个月，海关将作无主货物进行变卖。

The goods must be declared to the customs within 14 days after arrival. Otherwise, the customs shall collect the overdue payment on a daily basis (according to the value of the goods, five-tenths of a million). If the time limit exceeds three months, the customs will make the sale of the goods.

二、报检

Inspection and Quarantine

2000 年 1 月 1 日海关报关机构建立了一个新的通关系统项目，中国接受在通关单之前进行检验检疫的实践。入境货物通关单和出境货物通关单已经被实施在货物进出境检验检疫项目检验合格后用特殊的印章盖章。

China adopted the practice of "quarantine inspection before customs declaration" in customs clearance following the establishment of a new clearance system for goods subject to inspection and quarantine on 1st January 2000. Import Goods Clearance Slips and Export

Goods Clearance Slips stamped with the special seal of inspection and quarantine authorities are issued to goods subject to entry-exit inspection and quarantine upon satisfactory inspection.

任务实施
Task Implementation

本任务涉及的报关要素有以下内容。

The customs declaration elements involved in this task include below.

商品编码：7210701000

Product Code: 7210701000

商品名称：彩涂卷

Product Name: Pre-painted cold rolled coils

请提供申报要素：

Please provide the elements of declaration:

（1）品牌类型：0

Brand Type: 0

（2）出口享惠情况：0

Export Enjoyment: 0

（3）形状：卷

Shape: Coil

（4）材质：非合金钢

Material: non-alloy steel

（5）加工方法：经涂层

Processing Method: coated

（6）成分含量：非合金元素的含量（C：0.06%；Si：0.12%；Mn：0.17%；P：0.017%；S：0.013%）

Composition Content: the content of non-alloy elements (C: 0.06%; Si: 0.12%; Mn: 0.17%; P: 0.017%; S: 0.013%)

（7）规格：0.16mm×1200mm；0.20mm×1200mm；0.22mm×1200mm；0.26mm×1200mm；0.33mm×1200mm；0.48mm×1200mm

Specifications: 0.16mm×1200mm; 0.20mm×1200mm; 0.22mm×1200mm; 0.26mm×1200mm; 0.33mm×1200mm; 0.48mm×1200mm

（8）涂层种类：涂漆

Coating Type: Painting

（9）钢号：q195

Steel Number：q195

（10）境内货源地：山东

Source of Goods：Shandong

根据申报要素、箱单（见图 2-5）、合同（见图 2-6）、发票（见图 2-7）的数据制作报关单草单，由报关行生成报关单预录入单（见图 2-8），进而生成报关单（见图 2-9）向海关申报。

According to the declaration elements, the packing list (as shown in Figure 2-5), the contract (as shown in Figure 2-6) and the invoice (as shown in Figure 2-7), a Customs Declaration Form (shown in Figure 2-8) is finally generated for customs declaration.

PACKING LIST

Contract No.: TL171227 **Date: 01 Feb. 2018**

The SELLER: T[illegible] D

The BUYER: [illegible] Y

Article 1. COMMODITY, SPECIFICATION, QUANTITY, PRICE & AMOUNT

1. The Commodity: PRE-PAINTED COLD ROLLED COILS

ITEM	THICKNESS(MM)	WIDTH(MM)	QUANTITY(MT)	NO. OF COILS
1	0.16	1200	8.682	2
2	0.20	1200	19.132	4
3	0.22	1200	9.128	2
4	0.26	1200	168.99	38
5	0.33	1200	51.958	11
6	0.48	1200	14.48	3
TOTAL	272.37 MT AND 60 COILS			

- Loading port and discharging port: From Xingang to Port Sudan by sea.

- Total net weight: 272.37mts.

- Total coils: 60coils

图 2-5 报关箱单

CONTRACT

Contract No.: TL171227　　　　Date: 27 Dec. 2017

The SELLER: [redacted]

The BUYER: [redacted]

THE BUYER AGREES TO BUY AND THE SELLER AGREES TO SELL PREPAITED STEEL COIL WITH TERMS AND CONDITIONS SET OUT HEREINAFTER AS FOLLOWS:

Article 1. COMMODITY, SPECIFICATION, QUANTITY, PRICE & AMOUNT

1. The Commodity: PRE-PAINTED COLD ROLLED COILS

ITEM	THICKNESS(MM)	WIDTH(MM)	QUANTITY(MT)	UNIT PRICE(USD)
1	0.16	1200	8.682	860
2	0.20	1200	19.132	825
3	0.22	1200	9.128	810
4	0.26	1200	168.99	790
5	0.33	1200	51.958	755
6	0.48	1200	14.48	745
TOTAL	214162.09USD			

THICKNESS TOLERANCE: +/-0.02MM.
COLOR: WHITE.
PAINTING: TOP: Not less than 17 μm; BACK: Not less than 5 μm.

- Total weight: 272.37 mts..

- Price term: FOB TIANJIN, CHINA (Incoterms 2010)

- Total amount : USD214162.09

-Tolerance on Quantity: +/-10% of Quantity of each size and in total.

2. Marking and Packing: As mill's seaworthy packing

3. Origin: China

4. Loading port and discharging port: From Tianjin port to Sudan port by sea.

5. Shipment date: Before 28th Feb 2018.

Article 2. TERMS OF PAYMENT
The buyer shall paid 30% T/T in advance as down payment to seller within 5 days after contract signed, and balance paid within 5 days by T/T against P/L, CI, before shipment.

Signed for and on behalf of BUYER　　　　**Signed for and on behalf of SELLER**

图 2-6　合同

INVOICE

Contract No.: TL171227　　　　Date: 01 Feb. 2018

The SELLER:

The BUYER:

Article 1. COMMODITY, SPECIFICATION, QUANTITY, PRICE & AMOUNT

1. The Commodity: PRE-PAINTED COLD ROLLED COILS

ITEM	THICKNESS(MM)	WIDTH(MM)	QUANTITY(MT)	UNIT PRICE(USD)
1	0.16	1200	8.682	860
2	0.20	1200	19.132	825
3	0.22	1200	9.128	810
4	0.26	1200	168.99	790
5	0.33	1200	51.958	755
6	0.48	1200	14.48	745
TOTAL	214162.09USD			

- Loading port and discharging port: From Xingang to Port Sudan by sea.

- Total net weight: 272.37 mts.

- Price term: FOB TIANJIN, CHINA (Incoterms 2010)

- Total: USD214162.09

图 2-7　发票

对于货运代理业务员来说，及时拿到预录单可以和发给船代的舱单进行核对，防止更改舱单。因为更改舱单比较难操作，如果修改不成功，就无法退还核销单给客户，给客户带来损失。

As for the freight forwarder, the timely receipt of the pre-entry form can be checked with the shipping manifest sent to the shipping agent to prevent the change of the manifest. Because it is more difficult to change the manifest, if the modification is unsuccessful, it will not be possible to refund the write-off order to the customer, causing losses to the customer.

2018-02-05 16:30 bannan

系统编号：Z11000001304858736

中华人民共和国海关出口货物预录入报关单

预录入编号：　　　　申报现场：新港海关(0202)　　海关编号：

收发货人 [illegible] 司	出口口岸 新港海关(0202)	出口日期	申报日期
生产销售单位 (1[illegible])() [illegible]]	运输方式 水路运输	运输工具名称 BALLENITA/1804	提运单号 575021165
申报单位 (1207480018)() 天津中远国际航空货运代理有限公司	监管方式(0110) 一般贸易	征免性质(101) 一般征税	备案号
贸易国(地区) (246) 苏丹	运抵国(地区) (246) 苏丹	指运港 (1761) 苏丹港	境内货源地 (37909) 山东其他
许可证号	成交方式 FOB　运费	保费	杂费
合同协议号 [illegible]	件数 60　包装种类 其它	毛重（公斤） 272370	净重（公斤） 272370
集装箱号 TEMU0697591 * 10(10)	随附单证		

集装箱号: TCLU6122431 TCLU1411909 PONU0939930 PONU0198150 MSKU7782247 MRKU9071101 MRKU7756816 MRKU7005585 MRKU6929352

随附单证号:

备注: 港集金狮

标记唛码及备注:

特殊关系确认：否　　价格影响确认：否　　与货物有关的特许权使用费支付确认：否

成交数量共：272.37吨 法定数量共：272370千克 第二数量共：　所有货物总价：214162.09美元

项号	商品编号	商品名称、规格型号	数量	单位	最终目的国(地区)	单价	总价	币制	征免
1	7210701000	彩涂卷 0|0|卷|非合金钢|经涂层|C:0.06% Si:0.12% Mn:0.17% P:0.017% S:0.013%|0.16mm×1200mm|涂漆|q195	8682 8.682	千克 吨	苏丹(246) 原产国:中国	860.0000	7466.52	美元	照章征税
2	7210701000	彩涂卷 0|0|卷|非合金钢|经涂层|C:0.06% Si:0.12% Mn:0.17% P:0.017% S:0.013%|0.20mm×1200mm|涂漆|q195	19132 19.132	千克 吨	苏丹(246) 原产国:中国	825.0000	15783.90	美元	照章征税
3	7210701000	彩涂卷 0|0|卷|非合金钢|经涂层|C:0.06% Si:0.12% Mn:0.17% P:0.017% S:0.013%|0.22mm×1200mm|涂漆|q195	9128 9.128	千克 吨	苏丹(246) 原产国:中国	810.0000	7393.68	美元	照章征税
4	7210701000	彩涂卷 0|0|卷|非合金钢|经涂层|C:0.06% Si:0.12% Mn:0.17% P:0.017% S:0.013%|0.26mm×1200mm|涂漆|q195	168990 168.99	千克 吨	苏丹(246) 原产国:中国	790.0000	133502.10	美元	照章征税
5	7210701000	彩涂卷 0|0|卷|非合金钢|经涂层|C:0.06% Si:0.12% Mn:0.17% P:0.017% S:0.013%|0.33mm×1200mm|涂漆|q195	51958 51.958	千克 吨	苏丹(246) 原产国:中国	755.0000	39228.29	美元	照章征税
6	7210701000	彩涂卷 0|0|卷|非合金钢|经涂层|C:0.06% Si:0.12% Mn:0.17% P:0.017% S:0.013%|0.48mm×1200mm|涂漆|q195	14480 14.48	千克 吨	苏丹(246) 原产国:中国	745.0000	10787.60	美元	照章征税

图 2-8　预录入报关单

中华人民共和国海关出口货物报关单

预录入编号：　　　　　　　　　　　　　　海关编号：

<table>
<tr><td colspan="2">收发货人　18 位统一社会代码</td><td colspan="2">出口口岸
天津新港</td><td>出口日期</td><td>申报日期</td></tr>
<tr><td colspan="2">生产销售单位　18 位统一社会代码</td><td>运输方式
水路运输</td><td colspan="2">运输工具名称
BALLENITA 1804</td><td>提运单号
575021165</td></tr>
<tr><td colspan="2">申报单位</td><td colspan="2">监管方式
一般贸易</td><td>征免性质
一般征税</td><td>备案号</td></tr>
<tr><td>贸易国（地区）
苏丹</td><td colspan="3">运抵国（地区）
苏丹</td><td>指运港
苏丹</td><td>境内货源地
山东</td></tr>
<tr><td>许可证号</td><td>成交方式
FOB</td><td colspan="2">运费</td><td>保费</td><td>杂费</td></tr>
<tr><td>合同协议号
TL171227</td><td>件数
60</td><td colspan="2">包装种类
卷</td><td>毛重（公斤）
272370KGS</td><td>净重（公斤）
272370KGS</td></tr>
<tr><td>集装箱号
TCLU1411909*10(20GP)</td><td colspan="5">随附单证
MRKU6929352　MSKU7782247　MRKU7005585　TEMU0697591　MRKU9071101　PONU0939930
MRKU7756816　PONU0198150　TCLU6122431</td></tr>
<tr><td colspan="6">标记唛码及备注：
N/M</td></tr>
</table>

项目	商品编号	商品名称、规格型号	数量及单位	最终目的国（地区）	单价	总价	币制	征免
01	72107010	彩涂卷 1.规格：0.16mm×1200mm 2.形状：卷 3.材质：非合金钢 4.加工方式：经涂层 5.成分含量：非合金元素的含量（C:0.06%　Si:0.12%　Mn:0.17%　P:0.017%　S:0.013%） 6.涂层种类：镀锌 7.钢号：q195 8.品牌：0 9.出口享惠：0	8.682TONS 8682 千克	苏丹	860	7466.52	USD	照章征免
02	72107010	彩涂卷 1.规格：0.20mm×1200mm 2.形状：卷 3.材质：非合金钢 4.加工方式：经涂层 5.成分含量：非合金元素的含量（C:0.06%　Si:0.12%　Mn:0.17%　P:0.017%　S:0.013%） 6.涂层种类：镀锌 7.钢号：q195 8.品牌：0 9.出口享惠：0	19.132TONS 19132 千克	苏丹	825	15783.9	USD	照章征免
03	72107010	彩涂卷 1.规格：0.22mm×1200mm 2.形状：卷 3.材质：非合金钢 4.加工方式：经涂层	9.128TONS 9128 千克	苏丹	810	7393.68	USD	照章征免

图 2–9　报关单

思考题
Questions

1. 简述进出口货运代理报关流程。

Briefly describe the declaration procedures carried out by the freight forwarder.

2. 请说明报关的注意事项。

Please explain the precautions of customs declaration.

子任务之七 提单确认
Section Seven: Bill Confirmation

任务引入
Task Introduction

货运代理业务员需要为即将从天津新港出发运至苏丹港的货物确认海运提单内容。

The freight forwarder needs to confirm the contents of the bill of lading for the goods to be shipped from Tianjin Xingang to Port Sudan.

具体货物情况如下：

The details of the specific goods are as follows:

货名：彩涂卷

Goods description: PRE-PAINTED COLD ROLLED COILS

数量：278 卷

Quantity: 278 COILS

总毛重：1300MT

Weight: 1300MT

总体积：960 cbm

Volume: 960 cbm

任务分析
Assignment Analysis

一般船公司要求的提单样本须一次性准确，并在提供之后让客户核对格式单，确认提单内容以及确认出单的方式。之后有任何更改均会产生改单费。

The sample of the bill of lading required by the shipping company must be accurate and exact, which needs to be checked by the customer so as to confirm the contents and the method. Any subsequent changes will result in a change of fees.

相关知识
Relevant Knowledge

一、海运提单的概念
General Concept of Marine Bills of Lading

海运提单主要用于国际货物销售的海上运输中。

Marine Bills of Lading are used primarily in international sales of goods where the carriage of goods is by sea.

每个国家对于提单的定义各有不同。总体而言，提单是货物装船的收据；它由达成货物运输协议的承运人签字，上有货物送到船上及被船方接收的条款。

Definitions of the Bill of Lading vary from country to country. Broadly, the bill of lading has been defined as receipt for goods shipped on board a ship, signed by the person (or his agent) contracts to carry them, and stating the terms on which the goods were delivered to and received by the ship.

提单不是实际的合同，却是构成据以履行合同条款极好的保证。

It is not the actual contract, but forms excellent evidence of the terms of the contract.

提单样单标准模板，如表 2-14 所示。

The standard template of Bill of lading, as shown in Table 2-14.

二、海运提单的作用
Functions of the Marine Bills of Lading

1. 货物装船的收据
Receipt for the Goods Shipped

提单是由承运人签发的有关承运人已接管提单所明确记载的货物或将货物装船的证明。

A bill of lading is a receipt issued by a carrier that an identifiable consignment of goods has been received by him for shipment, or actually loaded on board his ship.

表 2-14　　提单样单标准模板

发货人		
HOU YOU (HONG KONG)LIMITED ADD: RM D, 10/F, TOWER A, BILLION CTR, 1 WANG KWONG RD, KLN BAY, KLN HONG KONG	提单号	COUS6177648370
	出单方式 付款方式 HS CODE	正本 预付 68114010　48181000
收货人	注意：HS CODE 必须提供，但可以不显示。（√）	
KUNDA MANUFACTURING LIMITED ADD: NSAWAM ROAD, OPP RADIANCE FILLING STATION NSAWASM	显示HS COOE 显示目的港代理 显示运费 异地放单	是（　）　否（　） 是（√）　否（　） 是（　）　否（　） 是（　）　否（　）
	注意：无上述特殊要求可以填写	
	其他特殊要求请标注下栏（不要直接写在货描处或其他地方）	
通知人	申请目的港的免用箱21天	
KUNDA MANUFACTURING LIMMITED ADD:NSAWAM ROAD, OPP RADIANCE FILLING STATION NSAWASM		
船名　航次	装货港	
CSCL LONG BEACH 024E	TEMA PORT, GHANA	
卸货港	最终目的地	

唛头	总件数	货描	总重	体积
N/M	5861 PACKAGES	ROOFING SLATE TISSUE PAPER	168300KGS	$60M^3$

以下为对应需要填写的分箱信息，请根据实际情况填写清楚

集装箱号	铅封号	种类	件数	重量	尺码
TGHU1237268	G489904	20GP	945	28050KGS	10
FCIU5242331	G489903	20GP	964	28000KGS	10
FCIU5019647	G489906	20GP	960	28100KGS	10
UETU2242406	G489905	20GP	974	28050KGS	10
FCIU6133994	G489908	20GP	1034	28000KGS	10
BEAU2041449	F489843	20GP		28100KGS	10

Table 2-14　　The Bill of Lading

Shipper		
HOU YOU (HONG KONG)LIMITED ADD: RM D, 10/F, TOWER A, BILLION CTR, 1 WANG KWONG RD, KLN BAY, KLN HONG KONG	B/L No.	COUS6177648370
	Issuing Metbod Payment Method HS CODE:	Original Prepaid 68114010　48181000
Consignee	Note: HS CODE must be provided, but may not be displayed. (√)	
KUNDA MANUFACTURING LIMITED ADD: NSAWAM ROAD, OPP RADIANCE FILLING STATION NSAWASM	Display HS CODE Display Destination Code Display Freight Remote Billing	YES (　)　NO (　) YES (√)　NO (　) YES (　)　NO (　) YES (　)　NO (　)
	Dote: Thereis no need to fillin without the above special require ments.	
	Please mark the following column for other special requirements (do not write directlhy on the container or other places)	

Continued

<table>
<tr><td colspan="3">Notify Pary</td><td colspan="3" rowspan="2">Apply for free container at the port of destination for 21days</td></tr>
<tr><td colspan="3">KUNDA MANUFACTURING LIMITED
ADD: NSAWAM ROAD, OPP RADIANCE FILLING STATION NSAWASM</td></tr>
<tr><td colspan="2">Ocean Vessel</td><td>Voy.No.</td><td colspan="3">Port of Loading</td></tr>
<tr><td colspan="3">CSCL LONG BEACH 024E</td><td colspan="3">TEMA PORT,GHANA</td></tr>
<tr><td colspan="2">Port of Discharge</td><td></td><td colspan="3">Final Destination</td></tr>
<tr><td colspan="2"></td><td colspan="4"></td></tr>
<tr><td>Marks</td><td>No of PKGS</td><td colspan="2">Description of Goods</td><td>Gross Weight</td><td>Measurement</td></tr>
<tr><td>N/M</td><td>5861
PACKAGES</td><td colspan="2">ROOFING SLATE
TISSUE PAPER</td><td>168300KGS</td><td>$60M^3$</td></tr>
<tr><td colspan="6"></td></tr>
<tr><td>Container No</td><td>Seal No</td><td>Type</td><td>No of PKGS</td><td>Gross Weight</td><td>Measurement</td></tr>
<tr><td>TGHU1237268</td><td>G489904</td><td>20GP</td><td>945</td><td>28050KGS</td><td>10</td></tr>
<tr><td>FCIU5242331</td><td>G489903</td><td>20GP</td><td>964</td><td>28000KGS</td><td>10</td></tr>
<tr><td>FCIU5019647</td><td>G489906</td><td>20GP</td><td>960</td><td>28100KGS</td><td>10</td></tr>
<tr><td>UETU2242406</td><td>G489905</td><td>20GP</td><td>974</td><td>28050KGS</td><td>10</td></tr>
<tr><td>FCIU6133994</td><td>G489908</td><td>20GP</td><td>1034</td><td>28000KGS</td><td>10</td></tr>
<tr><td>BEAU2041449</td><td>F489843</td><td>20GP</td><td></td><td>28100KGS</td><td>10</td></tr>
</table>

提单作为收据将会列明所装载货物的数量和情况、船舶的名称、装运港、目的地，以及详细的日期等。

The bill of lading as a receipt will show the quantity and condition of the cargo loaded, ship's name, port of loading, the destination, details of date and so on.

2. 货物的物权凭证

Document of Title to the Goods

提单是货物的物权凭证，持有提单在法律上等同于持有货物。

A bill of lading is a document of title to the goods. The possession of a bill of lading is equivalent in law to possession of the goods.

提单的持有者可以在目的港提取货物并且在货物的运输期间可以仅仅通过背书提单将货物卖掉。

The holder of the bill of lading is able to obtain delivery of the goods at the port of destination and during transit the goods can be sold merely by endorsing the bill of lading.

3. 合同的证明

Evidence of Contract

另外，提单的条款也为承运人与托运人之间运输合同提供了证明。提单的条款包含了合同中的条款。

Additionally, the terms of the bill of lading provide evidence of the contract of carriage between the carrier and the shipper. The terms of the bill of lading contain the terms of the contract.

三、海运提单的类型

Types of Marine Bills of Lading

1. 指示提单

Order Bills of Lading

指示提单是由承运人签发给指定的托运人或者收货人。

Order bills are issued by carriers to the order of shipper or consignee.

承运人、船东、租船人或者船长将在目的港交货，不用单独交付给指定的收货人，可交付给任何其指定的人。

The carrier, ship owner, charterer or master will deliver the goods at the port of destination not solely to the named consignee, but to any person designated by him.

一份指示提单是一份可转让单据。

An order bill of lading is a negotiable document.

提单载明收货人或“由某人指示”的指示提单可通过收货人或指示人背书进行转让。

Order bills made out to consignee “or order” can be transferred by them by endorsement.

2. 记名提单

Straight Bills of Lading

与指示提单相比，记名提单载明指定的收货人而没有附加“由某人指示”的措辞。

In contrast with the order bills of lading, straight bills are those made out to named consignees without the addition of the words “or order” .

记名提单是不可转让的，不能转让给第三方。

Straight bills of lading is not negotiable and cannot be transferred to third parties.

只能由指定的收货人提取货物。

Delivery of goods can only be taken by the named consignee.

3. 已装船提单

Shipped Bills of Lading

已装船提单明确表明货物已装船，确定货物已实际装上船舶。

Shipped bills state definitely that the goods have been loaded, it confirms that the goods are actually on board the vessel.

大部分提单格式都会被打印成已装船提单格式并且标注“已装船外表状况明显良好”的措辞。

Most bills of lading forms are printed as shipped bills and commence with wording “Shipped in apparent good order and condition”.

4. 收货待运提单

Received for Shipment Bills of Lading

收货待运提单表明货物已经收货待运，但是不显示实际的装载日期。

Received for shipment bills state that the goods have been received for shipment, and do not indicate the actual date of loading.

收货待运提单因班轮运输业务的发展而成长起来，并逐渐成为惯例，船东在实际装载期之前几个小时甚至几天收到货物。

The received for shipment bill of lading grew up because with the development of the liner services it became the custom for the shipowner to receive the cargo some hours or even days before it was actually loaded.

5. 直达提单

Direct Bills of Lading

直达提单是货物从装运港直接运至目的港卸货的提单。

Direct bills of lading are those covering shipments between direct ports of loading or discharge.

6. 联运提单

Through Bills of Lading

联运提单是由两个或者两个以上的海运或铁路运输公司负责货物两个至多个港口间的运输。

Through bills of lading cover shipment from or to ports involving transport by two or more shipping or railways companies.

海运公司将承担额外的运费保证货物到达目的地。

The shipping company, for additional freight, undertakes to make all arrangements to get the goods to their destination.

7. 清洁提单

Clean Bill of Lading

清洁提单载明货物收货时无损坏、无异常或无短装现象，通常提单上会注明“货物外表状态良好”“清洁已装船”或类似的字样。

The clean bill of lading bears an indication that the goods were received without damages, irregularities or short shipment, usually the words "apparent good order and condition", "clean on board" or the like are indicated on the B/L.

8. 不清洁提单

Unclean Bills of Lading

不清洁提单是与清洁提单相对立的提单。提单上载明货物收货时有损坏、有异常或短装，通常会标注“不清洁已装船”或类似的字样，比如“包装不良”“缺少安全封条”或“一箱短装”等字样。

The unclean bill of lading, dirty bill of lading or claused bill of lading is the opposite of the clean bill of lading. It bears an indication that the goods were received with damages, irregularities or short shipment, usually the words "unclean on board" or the like are indicated on the B/L, for example, "insufficient packing", "missing safety seal" and "one carton short".

四、其他货运单证

Shipping Documents

海上货物运输常用的单证包括提单、海运单、舱单、托运单、提货单和大副收据。

The documents commonly used in carriage of goods by sea are bills of lading, sea waybills, manifests, shipping notes, delivery orders and mate's receipts.

1. 海运单

Sea Waybill

海运单替代了传统的海洋提单。

A sea waybill is the replacement of the traditional ocean bill of lading.

海运单是一种不可流通的单证，且填写了经承认的指定收货人，在提供了货物身份证明后，无须出示提单即可提货。

The waybill is a non-negotiable document and made out to a named consignee who is allowed, upon production of proper identification, to claim the goods without presenting the waybill.

2. 货物舱单

Cargo Manifest

货物舱单提供已装船货物的信息。

A cargo manifest provides information regarding cargo on board.

货物舱单提供了运费、附加费、折扣等信息

A freight manifest gives information regarding freight rates, surcharges, rebates, etc.

货物舱单是由承运人代理准备的，但是货运代理人必须持有海关和港务局开具的货物舱单（办理货物进出口）。

The manifest is prepared by the carrier's agent but the freight forwarder has to handle it while dealing with the customs and port authorities.

3. 托运单

Shipping Note

托运单是托运人签发给承运人要求分配舱位的单证。

A shipping note is issued by the shipper to the carrier requesting allocation of shipping space.

托运单是托运人委托运输货物，是准备提单的基础。

It is a commitment on the part of the shipper to ship the goods and serves as the basis for the preparation of the bill of lading.

4. 提货单

Delivery Order

提货单是由承运人或其代理签发给收货人或其代理，使后者能够从船上提货。

A delivery order is issued by the carrier or his agent to enable the consignee or his forwarding agent to take delivery of the cargo (import cargo) from the vessel.

5. 大副收据

Mate's Receipts

大副收据是由承运人签发，是对货物装船的确认，以后可用大副收据换取提单。

A mate's receipt is the receipt issued by the carrier in the acknowledgement of the goods received on board (export cargo) which is subsequently exchange for the bill of lading.

任务实施

Task Implementation

货运代理业务员需要确认提单样本（如图 2-10 所示）的准确性，并在提供之后让客户核对格式单，确认提单内容以及确认出单的方式，即是正本还是电放。

The freight forwarder needs to confirm the accuracy of the bill of lading (as shown in Figure 2-10) and provide the client with a check on the format, ensuring the contents of the bill of lading and the method of delivery order, that is, the original or the telex.

Please find payterm and payer details on end of every page and revert if any changes required before container get load.

MAERSK LINE

BILL OF LADING FOR OCEAN TRANSPORT OR MULTIMODAL TRANSPORT

SCAC MAEU
B/L No. 575021165

Shipper
T[illegible]G CO.,LTD
ADD: [illegible]E ZONE
[illegible]

Booking No.
575021165,596607474,596607476

Export references

Svc Contract
2022125

Onward inland routing (Not part of Carriage as defined in clause 1. For account and risk of Merchant)

Consignee (negotiable only if consigned "to order", "to order of" a named Person or "to order of bearer")
[illegible]
ADD: [illegible]N
[illegible]

Notify Party (see clause 22)
[illegible]
ADD: [illegible] SUDAN
[illegible]

Vessel (see clause 1 + 19)	Voyage No.	Place of Receipt. Applicable only when document used as Multimodal Transport B/L. (see clause 1)
BALLENITA	1804	
Port of Loading	**Port of Discharge**	**Place of Delivery. Applicable only when document used as Multimodal Transport B/L. (see clause 1)**
XINGANG CHINA	PORT SUDAN	

PARTICULARS FURNISHED BY SHIPPER

Kind of Packages; Description of goods; Marks and Numbers; Container No./Seal No. | Weight: 1315220.000 KGS | Measurement: 960.0000 CBM

48 containers said to contain 278 COILS

PRE-PAINTED COLD ROLLED COILS

N/M

Container No.	Seal No.	Type	Packages	Weight	Measurement
TGHU0604646	ML-CN7378339	20 DRY 8'6	6 COILS	27626.000 KGS	20.0000 CBM
TGHU2390517	ML-CN7378340	20 DRY 8'6	6 COILS	26988.000 KGS	20.0000 CBM
MSKU7137562	ML-CN7378326	20 DRY 8'6	6 COILS	27692.000 KGS	20.0000 CBM
MSKU3879938	ML-CN7378325	20 DRY 8'6	5 COILS	27062.000 KGS	20.0000 CBM
GATU1297037	ML-CN7378321	20 DRY 8'6	5 COILS	26668.000 KGS	20.0000 CBM
MRKU7787530	ML-CN7379367	20 DRY 8'6	6 COILS	27980.000 KGS	20.0000 CBM
MRKU6618345	ML-CN7379362	20 DRY 8'6	6 COILS	27922.000 KGS	20.0000 CBM
PONU0934604	ML-CN7378331	20 DRY 8'6	6 COILS	27902.000 KGS	20.0000 CBM
MSKU2469498	ML-CN7378323	20 DRY 8'6	6 COILS	27540.000 KGS	20.0000 CBM
MSKU3604484	ML-CN7378324	20 DRY 8'6	5 COILS	26760.000 KGS	20.0000 CBM
PONU0939930	ML-CN7379398	20 DRY 8'6	6 COILS	26938.000 KGS	20.0000 CBM
TCLU6122431	ML-CN7379389	20 DRY 8'6	6 COILS	27814.000 KGS	20.0000 CBM
MSKU7549343	ML-CN7379375	20 DRY 8'6	6 COILS	27832.000 KGS	20.0000 CBM
MRKU7368214	ML-CN7379365	20 DRY 8'6	5 COILS	27430.000 KGS	20.0000 CBM
MRKU7093420	ML-CN7379364	20 DRY 8'6	6 COILS	27112.000 KGS	20.0000 CBM
PONU2038504	ML-CN7378332	20 DRY 8'6	6 COILS	27556.000 KGS	20.0000 CBM
PONU0354988	ML-CN7378329	20 DRY 8'6	6 COILS	27550.000 KGS	20.0000 CBM
MSKU7510927	ML-CN7378327	20 DRY 8'6	6 COILS	27234.000 KGS	20.0000 CBM

Below freight details will not be part of Original Bill of Lading unless requested by customer
Above particulars as declared by Shipper, but without responsibility of or representation by Carrier (see clause 14)

Freight & Charges	Rate	Unit	Currency	Prepaid	Collect

Charges Name	Terms	Invoice Party
Basic Ocean Freight	P	SINOTRANS SHANDONG CO LTD
Terminal Handling Service - Destination	C	EDWARD STEEL FACTORY
Export Service	P	SINOTRANS SHANDONG CO LTD

Carrier's Receipt (see clause 1 and 14). Total number of containers or packages received by Carrier.	Place of Issue of B/L
48 containers	Qingdao
Number & Sequence of Original B(s)/L	**Date of Issue of B/L**
THREE/3	
Declared Value (see clause 7.3)	**Shipped on Board Date (Local Time)**
	2018-02-08

SHIPPED, as far as ascertained by reasonable means of checking, in apparent good order and condition unless otherwise stated herein, the total number or quantity of Containers or other packages or units indicated in the box entitled "Carrier's Receipt" for carriage from the Port of Loading (or the Place of Receipt, if mentioned above) to the Port of Discharge (or the Place of Delivery, if mentioned above), such carriage being always subject to the terms, rights, defences, provisions, conditions, exceptions, limitations, and liberties hereof (INCLUDING ALL THOSE TERMS AND CONDITIONS ON THE REVERSE HEREOF NUMBERED 1-26 AND THOSE TERMS AND CONDITIONS CONTAINED IN THE CARRIER'S APPLICABLE TARIFF) and the Merchant's attention is drawn in particular to the Carrier's liberties in respect of on deck stowage (see clause 18) and the carrying vessel (see clause 19). Where the bill of lading is non-negotiable the Carrier may give delivery of the Goods to the named consignee upon reasonable proof of identity and without requiring surrender of an original bill of lading. Where the bill of lading is negotiable, the Merchant is obliged to surrender one original, duly endorsed, in exchange for the Goods. The Carrier accepts a duty of reasonable care to check that any such document which the Merchant surrenders as a bill of lading is genuine and original. If the Carrier complies with this duty, it will be entitled to deliver the Goods against what it reasonably believes to be a genuine and original bill of lading, such delivery discharging the Carrier's delivery obligations. In accepting this bill of lading, any local customs or privileges to the contrary notwithstanding, the Merchant agrees to be bound by all Terms and Conditions stated herein whether written, printed, stamped or incorporated on the face or reverse side hereof, as fully as if they were all signed by the Merchant.
IN WITNESS WHEREOF the number of original Bills of Lading stated on this side have been signed and wherever one original Bill of Lading has been surrendered any others shall be void.

Signed for the Carrier Maersk Line A/S

As Agent(s)

This transport document has one or more numbered pages

图 2-10 提单样本

B/L: 575021165 Page : 2

PONU0303928 ML-CN7379376 20 DRY 8'6 5 COILS 27166.000 KGS 20.0000 CBM
MSKU2077389 ML-CN7379372 20 DRY 8'6 6 COILS 27466.000 KGS 20.0000 CBM
MSKU3864394 ML-CN7379374 20 DRY 8'6 6 COILS 27006.000 KGS 20.0000 CBM
PONU0502370 ML-CN7378330 20 DRY 8'6 6 COILS 27694.000 KGS 20.0000 CBM
MRKU7005585 ML-CN7379400 20 DRY 8'6 6 COILS 26996.000 KGS 20.0000 CBM
PONU0198150 ML-CN7379395 20 DRY 8'6 6 COILS 26696.000 KGS 20.0000 CBM
MRKU8548822 ML-CN7379369 20 DRY 8'6 5 COILS 27150.000 KGS 20.0000 CBM
MRKU7555848 ML-CN7379366 20 DRY 8'6 6 COILS 27372.000 KGS 20.0000 CBM
PONU0656817 ML-CN7379377 20 DRY 8'6 6 COILS 27748.000 KGS 20.0000 CBM
MRKU9802145 ML-CN7379371 20 DRY 8'6 6 COILS 27702.000 KGS 20.0000 CBM
MSKU7782247 ML-CN7379399 20 DRY 8'6 6 COILS 27590.000 KGS 20.0000 CBM
PONU2077373 ML-CN7378333 20 DRY 8'6 6 COILS 27800.000 KGS 20.0000 CBM
TEMU3896365 ML-CN7378337 20 DRY 8'6 6 COILS 27926.000 KGS 20.0000 CBM
TCLU6181619 ML-CN7378336 20 DRY 8'6 6 COILS 27242.000 KGS 20.0000 CBM
TEMU0697591 ML-CN7379391 20 DRY 8'6 6 COILS 27044.000 KGS 20.0000 CBM
MRKU6929352 ML-CN7379396 20 DRY 8'6 6 COILS 27940.000 KGS 20.0000 CBM
MRKU9071101 ML-CN7379393 20 DRY 8'6 6 COILS 26726.000 KGS 20.0000 CBM
MRKU6855711 ML-CN7379363 20 DRY 8'6 5 COILS 27898.000 KGS 20.0000 CBM
TCLU0693454 ML-CN7379378 20 DRY 8'6 6 COILS 27422.000 KGS 20.0000 CBM
MRKU8441140 ML-CN7379368 20 DRY 8'6 6 COILS 27856.000 KGS 20.0000 CBM
PONU0009889 ML-CN7378328 20 DRY 8'6 5 COILS 26792.000 KGS 20.0000 CBM
MRKU7756816 ML-CN7379397 20 DRY 8'6 6 COILS 26794.000 KGS 20.0000 CBM
TCLU1411909 ML-CN7379394 20 DRY 8'6 6 COILS 27832.000 KGS 20.0000 CBM
MSKU3095319 ML-CN7379373 20 DRY 8'6 6 COILS 26318.000 KGS 20.0000 CBM
MRKU8833964 ML-CN7379370 20 DRY 8'6 6 COILS 27842.000 KGS 20.0000 CBM
TCLU6122215 ML-CN7378335 20 DRY 8'6 6 COILS 27620.000 KGS 20.0000 CBM
TEXU2251431 ML-CN7378338 20 DRY 8'6 6 COILS 27822.000 KGS 20.0000 CBM
TCLU2207361 ML-CN7378334 20 DRY 8'6 6 COILS 27772.000 KGS 20.0000 CBM
MSKU2381560 ML-CN7378322 20 DRY 8'6 5 COILS 27220.000 KGS 20.0000 CBM
IPXU3401429 ML-CN7379361 20 DRY 8'6 5 COILS 27162.000 KGS 20.0000 CBM
DTHC collect in Sudan

SHIPPER'S LOAD, STOW, WEIGHT AND COUNT

FREIGHT PREPAID

Freight & Charges	Rate	Unit	Currency	Prepaid	Collect

Charges Name	Terms	Invoice Party
Free Out Service	C	EDWARD STEEL FACTORY
Import Service	C	EDWARD STEEL FACTORY
Terminal Handling Service - Origin	P	SINOTRANS SHANDONG CO LTD
Documentation fee - Destination	C	EDWARD STEEL FACTORY
Documentation Fee - Origin	P	SINOTRANS SHANDONG CO LTD
Switch Transport Document Service	P	SINOTRANS SHANDONG CO LTD

图 2-10 提单样本（序）

B/L: 575021165　　Page：3

CY/CY

Freight & Charges	Rate	Unit	Currency	Prepaid	Collect

Charges Name	Terms	Invoice Party

图 2-10　提单样本（序）

船开之后要等船公司的报号，所谓报号就是船公司所报的箱号已经上船，顺利出运。最后一个阶段是一般船开三到四个工作日，船公司正式出具提单正本或者等消息安排提单电放。接下来就是定期查询船动态，查询预计到达目的港的时间。

After the ship departs, it is necessary to wait for the shipping company's report number, which means the container having been shipped smoothly. During the three to four working days after the departure, the shipping company will formally issue an original bill of lading or wait for news to arrange the bill of lading. The next step is to check the vessel schedule regularly and estimate the time to reach the destination port.

思考题
Questions

1. 海运提单的类型有哪些？

What are the types of bills of lading?

2. 请说明海上货物运输常用的单证，包括提单、海运单、舱单、托运单、提货单和大副收据各自的特点。

Please explain the characteristics of the documents commonly used in the delivery of goods by sea, including bill of lading, sea waybill, cargo manifest, shipping note, delivery order and mate's receipt.

任务三　航空货物运输
Task Three：Air Freight Transportation

【知识目标】

Knowledge Goals

1. 能说明航空运费的计费方法。

   To be able to explain the billing method of air freight.

2. 能说明航空出口业务的内容。

   To be able to illustrate the contents of aviation export business.

3. 能说明航空货物运单的内容。

   To be able to list the contents of the air cargo waybill.

【技能目标】

Skill Goals

1. 能模拟货运代理公司的货代业务员，为客户报价。

   To be able to act as the freight forwarder and offer quotations for customers.

2. 能模拟货运代理公司的货代业务员，接受客户的委托运输。

   To be able to act as the freight forwarder and accept clients' entrusted transportation.

3. 能模拟货运代理公司的货代业务员，协助办理报关事宜。

   To be able to act as the freight forwarder and assist in customs declaration.

4. 能模拟货运代理公司的货代业务员，完成航空运单缮制。

   To be able to act as the freight forwarder and complete the air waybill.

5. 能模拟货运代理公司的货代业务员，为客户办理货物跟踪查询事宜。

   To be able to act as the freight forwarder and offer tracking and inquiry for customers.

子任务之一　空运业务培训
Section One：Air Freight Training

任务引入
Task Introduction

小张刚入职某货运代理公司业务员岗位。今天，他即将接受的培训内容为航空货物运价的计算。

Xiao Zhang, who has just joined in a freighting company and worked as a freight forwarder, is about to receive the training for the calculation of air cargo freight rates today.

任务分析
Assignment Analysis

为了更好地为客户服务，航空货运代理人必须非常熟悉国际货物运输的业务内容，能够及时地掌握航空运输的全过程，保证货物运输顺畅并及时运送到收货人的手中。

In order to provide high-quality service for customers, the air freight forwarder must be very familiar with the business contents of international cargo transport and the entire process of air transportation to make sure of smooth transportation and timely delivery.

具体操作时，货代业务员须及时向客户介绍本公司的业务范围、服务项目、各项收费标准，特别是向客户介绍本公司的优惠运价和服务优势等。

During the specific operation, the freight forwarder needs to introduce the company's business scope, the service items, the charging standards, especially the company's preferential freight rates and service advantages to the customer in a timely manner.

相关知识
Relevant Knowledge

一、航空公司舱位业务员的原则
Principles of Airline Clerk

（1）保证有固定舱位配额的货物。

Guarantee the goods with fixed space quotas.

（2）保证邮件、快件舱位。

Guarantee the mail and the express.

(3) 优先预定运价较高的货物舱位。

Give priority to the cargo with higher freight rates.

(4) 保留一定的零散货物舱位。

Keep a certain space for scattered goods.

(5) 未订舱的货物按交运时间的先后顺序安排舱位。

Arrange the unbooked cargoes according to the order of delivery time.

二、普通货物运价（GCR）的计算步骤

Calculation Procedure of General Cargo Rate（GCR）

（一）术语

Terms

体积（Volume）、体积重量（Volume Weight）、计费重量（Chargeable Weight）、适用运价（Applicable Rate）、航空运费（Weight Charge）。

（二）计算步骤

Calculation Procedures

第一步：计算出航空货物的体积及体积重量。

Step 1：Calculate the Volume and Volume Weight of air cargo.

体积重量的折算，换算标准为每 6000 立方厘米折合 1 千克。即：

The conversion of Volume Weight is equivalent to 1 kilograms per 6000 cubic centimeters. That is：

体积重量（千克）= 货物体积/6000（cm^3/KG）

Volume Weight（KG）= Cargo Volume /6000（cm^3/KG）

第二步：计算货物的总重量。

Step 2：Calculate the Gross Weight of the goods.

总重量=单个商品重量×商品总数

Total Weight = the weight of a single good × the total number of goods

第三步：比较体积重量与总重量，取大者为计费重量。

Step 3：Compare the Volume Weight and the total weight，and take the bigger weight as the Chargeable Weight.

根据国际航协规定，国际货物的计费重量以 0.5 千克为最小单位，重量尾数不足 0.5 千克的，按 0.5 千克计算；0.5 千克以上不足 1 千克的，按 1 千克计算。

According to the provisions of the International Aviation Association, the Chargeable Weight of international goods is 0.5 KG as the minimum unit. If the weight mantissa is less than 0.5 KG, it shall be calculated as 0.5 KG; if it is more than 0.5 KG but less than 1 KG, it should be 1 KG.

第四步：根据公布运价，找出适合计费重量的适用运价。

Step 4: Based on the published freight rates, find out the Applicable Rate applicable to the Chargeable Weight.

（1）计费重量小于45千克时，适用运价为GCR N的运价（GCR为普通货物运价，N表示重量在45千克以下的运价）。

When the Chargeable Weight is less than 45 KG, the Applicable Rate is GCR N (GCR is the general freight rate, and the N represents the freight rate below 45 KG).

（2）计费重量大于45千克时，适用运价为GCR Q45、GCR Ql00、GCR Q300等与不同重量等级分界点相对应的运价（航空货运对于45千克以上的不同重量分界点的普通货物运价均用“Q”表示）。

When the Chargeable Weight is more than 45 KG, the Applicable Rates are the ones corresponding to the demarcation points of different weight grades such as GCR Q45, GCR Ql00, GCR Q300, etc. (Air freight for ordinary goods of more than 45 kilograms at different weight points are expressed in “Q”).

第五步：计算航空运费。

Step 5: Calculate the Weight Charge.

航空运费=计费重量×适用运价

Weight Charge = Chargeable Weight ×Applicable Rate

第六步：若采用较高重量分界点的较低运价计算出的运费比第五步计算出的航空运费低时，取低者。

Step 6: If the freight rate calculated by the lower freight rate of the higher weight dividing point is lower than that calculated in Step 5, take the lower one.

第七步：比较第六步计算出的航空运费与最低运费M，取高者。

Step 7: Compare the air freight and the minimum freight M calculated in Step 6 and take the higher one.

（三）航空货运单运费计算栏的填制

Filling of Air Freight Bill Calculation Column

（1）No. of Pieces RCP：填写货物的数量。

No. of Pieces RCP: fill in the quantity of the goods.

(2) Gross Weight：货物的总重量。

Gross Weight: fill in the total weight of the goods.

(3) KG Lb：以千克为单位用代号“K”，以磅为单位用代号“L”。

KG lb: use the code name “K” in kilograms, and use the code “L” in pounds.

(4) Rate Class：若计费重量小于 45 千克，填写 N；若计费重量大于 45 千克，填写 Q；若航空运费为最低运费，则填写 M。

Rate Class: if the Chargeable Weight is less than 45KG, fill in N; if the Chargeable Weight is greater than 45KG, fill in Q; if the air freight is the lowest one, fill in the M.

(5) Commodity Item No.：普通货物此栏不填。

Commodity Item No.: This column is not filled with ordinary goods.

(6) Chargeable Weight：填写计费重量。

Chargeable Weight: fill in the Chargeable Weight.

(7) Rate/Charge：填写适用运价。

Rate/Charge: fill in the Applicable Rate.

(8) Total：填写航空运费。

Total: fill in air freight.

(9) Nature and Quantity of Goods (Incl dimension or volume)：填写商品品名及商品的尺寸。

Nature and Quantity of Goods (Incl dimension or volume): fill in the commodity name and the commodity size.

任务实施
Task Implementation

例 1. Routing：BEIJING，CHINA (BJS) to AMSTERDAM，HOLLAND (AMS)；Commodity：PARTS；Gross Weight：38.6KGS；Dimensions：101CM×58CM×32CM。计算其航空运费。公布运价（CNY）如下：M 320.00；N 50.22；45 41.53；300 37.52。

Example 1: Routing: BEIJING, CHINA (BJS) to AMSTERDAM, HOLLAND (AMS); Commodity: PARTS; Gross Weight: 38.6KGS; Dimensions: 101CM×58CM×32CM. Calculate its air freight. The published freight rates (CNY) are as follows: M 320.00; N 50.22; 45 41.53; 300 37.52.

解：(1) 按实际重量计算，Volume：$101\times58\times32=187456\text{cm}^3$

Volume Weight：187456/6000 = 31.24KG ≈ 31.5KG

Gross Weight：38.6KG　　Chargeable Weight：39.0KG

体积重量小于总重量，所以按总重量来计算。

Applicable Rate：GCR N 50. 22CNY/KG

Weight charge：39. 0×50. 22＝CNY1958. 58

Solution：(1) Calculated by actual weight，Volume：101×58×32＝187456cm^3

Volume Weight：187456/6000＝31. 24KG≈31. 5KG

Gross Weight：38. 6KG　　Chargeable Weight：39. 0KG

The volume weight is less than the total weight，so the total weight is calculated.

Applicable Rate：GCR N 50. 22CNY/KG

Weight charge：39. 0×50. 22＝CNY1958. 58

（2）采用较高重量分界点的较低运价计算：

Chargeable Weight：45. 0KG

Applicable Rate：GCR Q 41. 53CNY/KG

Weight charge：41. 53×45＝CNY1868. 85

Calculate the lower freight rate using the higher weight dividing point：

Chargeable Weight：45. 0KG

Applicable Rate：GCR Q 41. 53CNY/KG

Weight charge：41. 53×45＝CNY1868. 85

（1）与（2）比较，取运费较低者。

Take the lower freight by comparing (1) with (2).

例2. 从北京运往新加坡一箱水龙头接管，毛重40. 2千克，根据公布运价，如表3-1所示，请计算其航空运费，并按计算结果填制航空运单运费计算栏，如表3-2所示。

Example 2：A case of faucet with a gross weight of 40. 2 kilograms will be shipped from Beijing to Singapore. You are required to calculate the air freight charge on the basis of the published freight rates as shown in the Table 3-1 and fill in the air freight charge calculation column according to the calculation results as shown in Table 3-2.

表3-1　　公布运价

北京人民币	中国CNY（人民币代码）		BJS（北京城市码）KGS
新加坡	新加坡	M N 4 5	200. 00 0 30. 50 22. 49

Table 3-1　　Published Freight Rate

BEIJING Y. RENMINBI	CN CNY		BJS KGS
SINGAPORE	SN	M N 4 5	200. 00 0 30. 50 22. 49

表 3-2　　　　　　　　　　　　　　**航空运单运费计算栏**

货物件数	毛重	重量单位		费率等级	计费重量	费率/费用	总计	货物描述（包括数量及尺码）
				商品编号				

Table 3-2　　　　　　　　　　**Air Waybill Freight Calculation Column**

No. of Pieces RCP	Gross Weight	Kg Lb		Rate Class	Chargeable Weight	Rate/ Charge	Total	Nature and Quantity of Goods (incl dimensions or volume)
				Commodity Item No.				

答案：

Solution:

（1）按实际重量计算：40.2×30.5=CNY1226.1。

Calculated by actual weight, Volume: 40.2×30.5=CNY1226.1cm³.

（2）采用较高重量分界点的较低运价计算：45×22.49=CNY1012.05。

Calculate the lower freight rate using the higher weight dividing point: 45 × 22.49 = CNY1012.05cm³.

（1）与（2）比较，取运费较低者。所以填表，如表 3-3 所示：

Take the lower freight by comparing (1) with (2) and fill in the air freight calculation column as shown in Table 3-3.

表 3-3　　　　　　　　　　　　　　**航空运单运费计算栏**

货物件数	毛重	重量单位		费率等级	计费重量	费率/费用	总计	货物描述（包括数量及尺码）
				商品编号				
1	40.2				45	22.49	1012.05	

Table 3-3　　　　　Air Waybill Freight Calculation Columm

No. of Pieces RCP	Gross Weight	KG Lb		Rate Class / Commodity Item No.	Chargeable Weight	Rate/ Charge	Total	Nature and Quantity of Goods (incl dimensions volume)
1	40.2				45	22.49	1012.05	PIPE FILLING

思考题
Questions

1. 某货代公司接受 A、B 两个货主的航空货运委托，配载同一个航班。货物 A：500KG 1.5m^3；货物 B：300KG 3m^3。计算：

A freight forwarding company accepts the air freight entrustment from two shippers and stows the same flight. (Cargo A: 500KG 1.5m^3; Cargo B: 300KG 3m^3.) Calculate:

（1）A、B 货物计费重量分别是多少？

What are the chargeable weights of A and B respectively?

（2）两货混载后计费重量是多少？

What is the billable weight after the two goods are mixed?

（3）如与泡货货主按吃泡部分 3/7 分成，货代得到多少重量的操作利润？

How much operating profit does the freight forwarder get from the 3/7 share of the foam part with the foam owner?

（4）泡货货主按多少重量支付运费？

How much weight does the cargo owner pay for the freight?

2. 航空货运单运费计算栏的填制内容有哪些？

What are the contents of the calculation column of air waybill freight?

子任务之二　市场销售
Section Two: Market Sales

任务引入
Task Introduction

小张刚入职某货运代理公司业务员。今天，他接待了一位客户。该客户打算从中国天津到德国克内瑟贝克（Knesebeck）通过航空运输一批货物（不锈钢连接件）。请帮助小张为客户进行报价。

Xiao Zhang, who has just joined in a freighting company and worked as a freight forwarder. Today, he received a client, who intends to transport a shipment (Stainless Steel Flexible Couplings) from Tianjin, China to Knesebeck, Germany. Please help Xiao Zhang to offer a quotation for the customer.

任务分析
Assignment Analysis

承揽货物处于整个航空货物出口运输代理业务程序的核心地位。货代业务员要具有一定的营销知识。具体操作时，须及时向客户介绍本公司的业务范围、服务项目、各项收费标准，特别是向出口客户介绍本公司的优惠运价和服务优势等。

Contracting goods is at the core of the entire air cargo export transportation agency business procedure. The freight forwarder should have a certain knowledge of marketing. During the specific operation, the freight forwarder needs to introduce the company's business scope, the service items, the charging standards, especially the company's preferential freight rates and service advantages to the customer in a timely manner.

相关知识
Relevant Knowledge

一、空运的运价构成及询价信息
Air Freight Composition and Inquiry Information

（一）空运的运价构成
Composition of Air Freight Rates

空运费包括：空运费、燃油附加费、战争附加费（战险）。

Air freight includes: air freight, fuel surcharge, war surcharge (war risk).

港前费包括：报关费、文件费、舱单费、机场操作费等。

Pre-port charges include: declaration fees, document fees, manifest fees, airport operating fees, etc.

所有费用均为人民币计费；运费按等级分类，等级越高价格越低。

All fees are in RMB. Freight is classified by grade, the higher the grade, the lower the price.

等级分为：MIN、N 级、+45KG、+100KG、+300KG、+500KG、+1000KG。

The grades are divided into：MIN，N，+45KG，+100KG，+300KG，+500KG，+1000KG.

空运计算公式：1CBM ＝ 167KG，例：0. 7CBM×167≈117KG。

Air freight formula：1CBM ＝ 167KG，case：0. 7CBM×167≈117KG.

（二）询价信息

Information Involved in Inquiry

询价需提供：件数、重量、体积、品名。

Enquiries need to be supplied：quantity，weight，volume and name.

问品名原因：避免是需要做非危鉴定的货物，如粉末、液体、磁类、泵类等。

The reason for inquiring the product name is to avoid goods that need to be identified as non-hazardous，such as powders，liquids，magnetics，and pumps.

二、空运货型的介绍

Introduction of Air Cargo

（一）平货例：5CTNS 350KG 2CBM 汽车配件

The Example of Dry Cargo：5CTNS 350KG 2CBM Auto Parts

算法：总毛重/总体积的比例结果在 100—200 多的数值，即平货。

Algorithm：the ratio of gross weight/total volume results in values between 100 and 200，that is，dry cargo.

如：350 / 2 ＝ 175，即平货（也称之为 1 ∶ 1 的货），则运费按实际毛重计费。

For example，350 / 2 ＝ 175，that is，the freight of dry cargo（also known as 1 ∶ 1）is charged according to the actual gross weight.

（二）重货例：5CTNS 350KG 1CBM 阀门

Deadweight Cargo：5CTNS 350KG 1CBM valve

算法：总毛重/总体积的比例结果在 300 以上的数值，即重货。

Algorithm：the ratio of total gross weight to total volume is over 300，that is，deadweight cargo.

如：350 / 1 ＝ 350，即重货（也称之为 1 ∶ 300 重货），则按实际毛重计费。

For example, 350 / 1 = 350, that is, the freight of deadweight cargo (also known as 1 : 300 heavy cargo) is charged according to the actual gross weight.

（三）泡货例：5CTNS 350KG 3CBM 服装

Measurement Cargo: 5CTNS 350KG 3CBM clothing

算法：体积×167 =501KG，即泡货，则空运费按501KG计费。

Algorithm: Volume ×167 = 501KG, that is, the air freight of measurement cargo is charged by 501KG.

任务实施
Task Implementation

一、空运出口流程及行程时间

Air Export Process and Travel Time

（一）空运出口流程

Air Export Process

订舱—确认送/提货时间—安排航班—送/提货—机场交货—出航运货物运单（即提单）—报关—放行—起飞。

Booking cargo space, confirmation of delivery time, arrangements of flights, delivery, delivery at the airport, shipping freight waybill (bill of lading), customs clearance, release, taking off.

（二）航运货物运单的周转过程

Turnover of Shipping Cargo Waybill

放行后提供航运货物运单复印件给发货人—发货人转给收货人—到港后换单—清关—提货。

The copy of shipping cargo waybill should be given to the consignor, the consignor to the consignee, to change the order after arrival, customs clearance, delivery.

（三）行程时间

Schedule Time

一般天津直飞的空港：东南亚/日/韩等空港当天到；欧美加等空港一天到。

Direct flights to Tianjin：South East Asia / Japan / the Republic of Korea and other airports —the same day；Europe / America / Canada and other airports —one day.

一般天津转飞的空港：日/韩/中东 3 天左右到；欧美加 4 天左右到；南美/非洲等 1 周左右到。

Connecting flight in Tianjin：Japan / the Republic of Korea / the Middle East—about 3 days；Europe / America / Canada—about 4 days；South America / Africa—1 week or so.

二、空运出口询价要求

The Inquiry of Air Export

接受货主询价过程中，应向询价货主问明一些信息。

In accepting the owner's inquiry，you should figure out the following information.

1. 目的地

Destination

最好能知道港口的英文拼写及港口、国家的三字代码。有经验的货代可以根据客人提供的收货地址城市名称，知晓货物到达的机场。

It is best to know the English spelling and three-word code of the port and the country. Experienced freight forwarders can know the airport where the goods arrive according to the address of the city provided by the customer.

2. 起运港

Port of Departure

起运港，如国内的杭州、上海、北京、广州等；或者货物所在地，货代可以根据货物所在地选择合适的机场。

The port of departure，such as Hangzhou，Shanghai，Beijing，Guangzhou，etc.，or the location of the goods，the freight forwarder can choose the right airport based on the location of the goods.

3. 毛重和体积

Gross Weight and Volume

把毛重和体积转化为体积重量。还要注意询问货主，货物是否需用卡板进行装运。

如果需要卡板，就知道卡板的尺寸和单件重量。因为有些航班属于客机，不能选用较重的卡板。

Convert gross weight and volume to volume weight. In addition, we also need to make it clear if the goods are necessary for shipment by using pallets. If doing so, we had better know about the size of the pallet and the weight of the single piece. Some flights belong to passenger aircrafts, which cannot use heavier pallets.

4. 出运时间

Shipping Time

询问客户的出运时间或者送货的大概时间，明确其要求的时效性，以及对航程有无特殊要求等，如客户是否坚持选用直达航班等，以便考虑可供配载的航班。

Inquire the customer about the shipping time or the approximate time of delivery, clear the timeliness of customers requirements and the special requirements for the voyage, such as whether the customer insists on using direct flights, etc. , in order to consider the flights available for loading.

5. 运费支付方式

Type of Payment

运费预付还是到付，是否为门到门运输。如果是门到门运输，还需要提供收货人详细地址才能报价。

Freight can be classified into prepayment and collection. If door to door transportation is required, the consignee's detailed address must be provided before the price can be quoted.

(1) 到门 DDU/DAP 询价。

Inquiry to DDU/DAP.

需要客户名称、件重尺、品名、起运港、到门地址、运输条款等信息。

We need the following information, including customer name, weight, product name, departure port, arrival address, transportation terms and so on.

(2) 到门 DDP 询价。

Inquiry to the door DDP.

需要客户名称、件重尺、品名、税号、起运港、到门地址、运输条款等信息。

We need the following information, including customer name, weight, product name, tax number, departure port, arrival address, transportation terms and so on.

6. 货名

Name of the Goods

确定货物是否为危险品，是否需要商检。如磁钢需要做磁检，有些化工品要提供非危保函和化工品鉴定书（正本）。

Determine whether the goods are dangerous and need commodity inspection. For example, magnetic steel needs to do magnetic inspections, and some chemical products must provide non-endangered guarantee and chemical identification (original).

根据以上信息查询合适的航空公司运输，与货主确认价格。询价内容模板如图 3-1 所示。

According to the above information, check the appropriate airline transportation and confirm the price with the shipper. Inquiry content template, as shown in Figure 3-1.

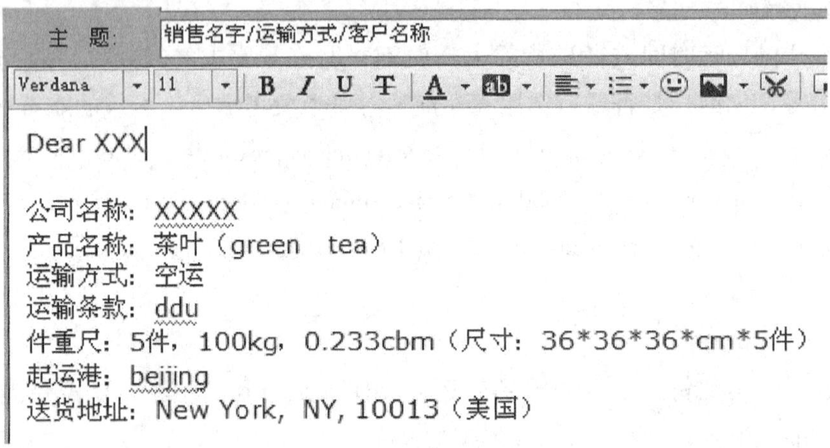

图 3-1　询价内容模板

思考题
Questions

1. 空运的运价构成要素有哪些？

What are the elements of the air freight rates?

2. 到门 DDU/DAP 询价时，需要哪些信息？

What information is required when asking for a DDU/DAP inquiry?

子任务之三　委托运输
Section Three: Entrusted Transportation

任务引入
Task Introduction

小张是某货运代理公司业务员。一位客户打算从中国天津到德国克内瑟贝克(Knesebeck) 空运一批货物（不锈钢连接件），销售合同如图 3-2 所示。请帮助小张接受货主委托，为客户办理订舱事宜。

Xiao Zhang worked as a freight forwarder in a freighting company. A customer intends to air a batch of goods (Stainless Steel Flexible Couplings) from Tianjin, China to Knesebeck, Germany. The sales contract is shown in Figure 3-2. Please help Xiao Zhang accept the consignment of the owner and arrange the booking for the client.

Sales Contract

Tel: 86-10-51. 02-8 45
Fax: 86-10-5 219
Email: marketing@h er.com
www. ho . on-w er.com

S/C No.:SC 1116-001
Date: 16/Nov/17
Project: "Sako" 200.000 m^3/d
Customer: H. Bu ing GmbH & Co. KG
Address: Gifhorner St. 5 ,2 79 Kn beck,Germany
Contact: Al er Sch ndt
Tel.: +49 58 . 50 310
Web: www.bu ing.com
Email: Al er.Sch dt@bu ing.de

Contact: Cameron
Email: ji. @ho er.com

Memline® Stainless Steel Flexible Pipe Couplings					
No.	**DESCRIPTION**	**MATERIAL**	**QTY.**	**UNIT PRICE (USD)**	**TOTAL PRICE(USD)**
1	MemLine® SS Flexible Couplings 2.5" 1200PSI	Housing: 316SS Bolts and washer: 316SS Nuts: 316SS Gasket: C Type, EPDM	3192	35.44	113,124.48
2	MemLine® SS Flexible Couplings 3" 1200PSI	Housing: 316SS Bolts and washer: 316SS Nuts: 316SS Gasket: C Type, EPDM	2240	42.19	94,505.60
3	MemLine® SS Flexible Couplings 3" 300PSI	Housing: 316SS Bolts and washer: 316SS Nuts: 316SS Gasket: C Type, EPDM	334	24.60	8,216.40
				Sub-total in USD	**215,846.48**

Remarks:

1 Payment Terms: Irrevocable L/C at sight
L/C has to be opened as following requests:
1st delivery : supplier has to receive the L/C not later than November 4th;
2nd delivery : supplier has to receive the L/C not later than November 6th;
3nd delivery : supplier has to receive the L/C not later than December 1st;
If supplier cannot receive the L/C as above-mentioned date,Supplier has the right to suspend the production

2 Delivery Terms : DAP Knesebeck/Germany,supplier doesn't assume any tariffs and other taxes incurred in Germany.

3 Delivery Time up :1st delivery by end of November, 2nd delivery by last week of December, 3nd delivery by end of January

4 Warranty: 24 months since commissioning or 30 weeks since Delivery

5 If customer ask for second and third delivery by air,the air freight costs will be calculated additionally.

6 This quote is valid for 1 month period from the above date

图 3-2　销售合同

任务分析
Assignment Analysis

发货人发货时，首先需填写委托书，并加盖公章，作为货主委托代理承办航空货物出口货运的依据。航空货运代理公司根据委托书要求办理出口手续，并据以结算费用。

When the consignor delivers the goods, he must first fill in the power of attorney and stamp with the official seal as the basis for the owner to entrust the agent to undertake the export of air cargo. The air freight forwarder handles the export formalities according to the power of attorney and charges the settlement.

相关知识
Relevant Knowledge

一、国际货物托运书
Shippers Letter of Instruction (SLI)

航空货运代理公司与出口单位（发货人）就出口货物运输事宜达成意向后，可以向发货人提供所代理的有关航空公司的《国际货物托运书》。

After the air freight forwarding company and the exporting company (consignor) have reached an agreement on the export goods, they may provide the consignor with the Shippers Letter of Instruction of the relevant airline.

托运书是托运人用于委托承运人或其代理人填开航空货运单的一种表单，表单上列有填制货运单所需的各项内容，并印有授权于承运人或其代理人代其在货运单上签字的文字说明。

Shippers Letter of Instruction is a form used by the shipper to entrust the carrier or his agent to fill out the air waybill. The form contains all the contents required to fill in the waybill and is printed a written description authorized to sign the waybill on behalf of the carrier or his agent.

二、国际货物托运书的内容
The contents of Shippers Letter of Instruction

国际货物托运书包括下列内容栏，如表 3-4 所示。

The Shippers Letter of Instruction includes the following columns, as shown in Table 3-4 below.

表 3-4　　**国际货物托运书**

××物流有限公司
国际货物托运书

<table>
<tr><td colspan="4">至:</td><td colspan="2">进仓编号:</td></tr>
<tr><td>发货人</td><td colspan="5">NANJING ×× CO. , LTD.
HUARONG MANSION RM2× NO. ×× GUANJIAQIAO,
NANJING 210005, CHINA</td></tr>
<tr><td>收货人</td><td colspan="5">FASHION FORCE CO. , LTD.
P. O. BOX 8935 NEW TERMINAL, ALTA,
VISTA OTTAWA, CANADA</td></tr>
<tr><td>通知人</td><td colspan="5">×× CO. , LTD.
P. O. BO××× NEW TERMINAL, ALTA,
VISTA OTTAWA, CANADA</td></tr>
<tr><td>起运港</td><td>SHANGHAI</td><td>目的港</td><td>MONTREAL</td><td>运费</td><td>PREPAID</td></tr>
<tr><td>标记唛头</td><td>件数</td><td colspan="2">中英文品名</td><td>毛重（公斤）</td><td>尺码（立方米）</td></tr>
<tr><td>FASHION FORCE
F01LCB05127
CTN NO.
MONTREAL
MADE IN CHINA</td><td>85 箱</td><td colspan="2">女式棉运动上衣
(100% COTTON, 40S×20/140×60)</td><td>19KGS</td><td>21</td></tr>
<tr><td colspan="3">1. 货单到达时间：3. 17 报关</td><td colspan="2">2. 航班：OZ/3. 18</td><td>3. 运价：29/KG+50</td></tr>
</table>

续表

电　话：842××××× 传　真：842××××× 联系人：×× 地　址：上海市××路 60 号××大厦 24×室 托运人签字：	★如改配航空公司请提前通知我司 （公章） 制单日期：20××年×月×日

Table 3-4　　SHIPPER'S LETTER OF INSTRUCTION

×× LOGISTICS CO. , LTD.

Shipper's Letter of Instruction

To：					Ware house entry Number：
Shipper	NANJING ×× CO. , LTD. HUARONG MANSION RM2× NO. ×× GUANJIAQIAO, NANJING 210005, CHINA				
Consignee	FASHION FORCE CO. , LTD. P. O. BOX 8935 NEW TERMINAL, ALTA, VISTA OTTAWA, CANADA				
Notify Party	×× CO. , LTD. P. O. BO××× NEW TERMINAL, ALTA, VISTA OTTAWA, CANADA				
Port of Shipment	SHANGHAI	Port of Discharge	MONTREAL	Freight	PREPAID
Marks	Number	Description of Goods		G. W（KGS）	Size
FASHION FORCE F01LCB05127 CTN NO. MONTREAL MADE IN CHINA	85 CARTONS	LADIES COTTON BLAZER （100% COTTON, 40S×20/140×60）		19KGS	21
1. Arrival Time of Manifest：3. 17			2. Flight：OZ/3. 18		3. Freight Rate： 29/KG+50

Continued

Telephone Number: 842××××× Fax Number: 842××××× Contacts: ×× Address: ROOM 24××, BUILDING××, NO. 60 ROAD××, SHANGHAI Signature of Shipper:	★ Please inform us in advance if you want to change the airline (Official Seal) Date:

1. 托运人

Shipper

填托运人的全称、街名、城市名称、国名，以及便于联系的电话号码、电传号码或传真号码。

Fill in the shipper's full name, street name, city name, country name, telephone number, telex number or fax number for easy contact.

2. 收货人

Consignee

填收货人的全称、街名、城市名称、国名（特别是在不同国家内有相同城市名称时，必须要填上国名）以及电话号码、电传号码或传真号码，本栏内不得填写“to order”或“to order of the shipper”（按托运人的指示）等字样，因为航空货运单不能转让。

Fill in the full name, street name, city name, country name of the consignee (especially when the same city name exists in different countries, the name of the country must be filled in) and the telephone number, telex number or fax number. In this column, the words “to order” or “to order of the shipper” (as indicated by the shipper) are not allowed to be filled out, because the air waybill cannot be transferred.

3. 始发站机场

Airport of Departure

填始发站机场的全称，若机场名称不明确，可填城市名称。

Fill in the full name of the airport. If the airport name is not clear, you can fill in the city name.

4. 目的地机场

Airport of Destination

填目的地机场（不知道机场名称时，可填城市名称），如果某一城市名称用于一个以上国家时，应加上国名。例如：LONDON UK 伦敦，英国；LONDON KY US 伦敦，肯塔基州，美国；LONDON TO CA 伦敦，安大略省。

Fill in the destination airport (you can fill in the city name if you don't know the airport name). If a city name is used in more than one country, you should add the country name. For example, LONDON UK London, UK. LONDON KY US London, Kentucky, USA. LONDON TO CA London, Ontario.

5. 要求的路线/申请订舱

Requested Routing/Requesting Booking

本栏在航空公司安排运输路线时使用，但如果托运人有特别要求，也可填入本栏。

This column is used by airlines when arranging transportation routes, but it can also be filled in if the shipper has special requirements.

6. 供运输用的声明价值

Declared Value for Carriage

填供运输用的声明价值金额，该价值即为承运人负赔偿责任的限额。承运人按有关规定向托运人收取声明价值费，但如果所交运的货物毛重每公斤不超过 20 美元（或其等值货币），无须填写声明价值金额，可在本栏内填入“NVD”（No Value Declared，未声明价值），如本栏未填写时，承运人或其代理人可视为货物未声明价值。

The declared value sum filled for transport is the limit of the carrier's liability for compensation. The carrier charges the shipper a declared value fee in accordance with the relevant regulations. However, if the gross weight of the delivered goods does not exceed US $ 20 per kilogram (or its equivalent currency), it is not necessary to fill in the declared value amount. In this situation, the carrier or its agent may fill in “NVD” (No Value Declared) in this column. If it is not filled out in this column, it can be regarded as undeclared value of goods.

7. 供海关用的声明价值

Declared Value for Customs

国际货物通常要受到目的站海关的检查，海关根据此栏所填数额征税。

International goods are usually subject to inspection by destination stations, and customs duties are levied on the basis of this column.

8. 保险金额

Insurance Amount Requested

中国民航各空运企业暂未开展国际航空运输代保险业务，本栏可空着不填。

The air transport companies of CAAC have not carried out international air transport insurance business, so this column can be left empty.

9. 处理事项

Handling Information

填附加的处理要求，例如另请通知（Also Notify）。除填收货人之外，如托运人还希望在货物到达的同时通知他人，请另填写通知人的全名和地址。

Fill in additional processing requirements, for example, please also notify. In addition to the consignee, if the shipper wishes to notify others at the same time as the arrival of the goods, please fill in the full name and address of the notifier.

10. 货运单所附文件

Document to Accompany Air Waybill

填随附在货运单上送往目的地的文件，应填上所附文件的名称，例如：托运人的动物证明（Shipper's Certification for Live Animals）。

Fill in the documents attached to the waybill to the destination with the name of the attached documents, such as the shipper's animal certificate (Shipper's Certification for Live Animals).

11. 件数和包装方式

Number and Kind of Packages

填该批货物的总件数，并注明其包装方法，例如包裹（Package）、纸板盒（Carton）、盒（Case）、板条箱（Crate）、袋（Bag）、卷（Roll）等，如货物没有包装时，就注明为散装（Loose）。

Fill in the total number of pieces of the goods and indicate the packaging method, such as Package, Carton, Case, Crate, Bag, Roll, etc. If the goods are not packaged, they are marked as Loose.

12. 实际毛重

Actual Gross Weight

本栏内的重量应由承运人或其代理人在称重后填入。如托运人已经填上重量，承运人或其代理人必须进行复核。

The weight in this column should be filled by the carrier or his agent after weighing. If the shipper has already filled in the weight, the carrier or his agent must review it.

13. 运价类别

Rate Class

本栏可空着不填，由承运人或其代理人填写。

This column can be left blank and filled in by the carrier or his agent.

14. 计费重量（公斤）

Chargeable Weight（kg）

本栏内的计费重量应由承运人或其代理人在量过货物的尺寸（以厘米为单位）后，由承运人或其代理人算出计费重量后填入，其代理人必须进行复核。

The charged weight in this column shall be filled in by the carrier or his agent after the size of the goods (in centimeters) is calculated and measured by the carrier or his agent. The agent must review the charged weight.

15. 费率

Rate/Charge

本栏可空着不填。

This column can be left blank.

16. 货物的品名及数量（包括体积及尺寸）

Nature and Quantity of Goods（Incl. Dimensions or Volume）

填货物的品名和数量（包括尺寸和体积）。

The name and quantity of the goods (incl. size and volume) should be filed in this column.

若一票货物包括多种物品时，托运人应分别申报货物的品名。需要注意的是，填写品名不能使用“样品”“部件”等这类比较笼统的名称。货物中的每一项均须分开填写，并尽量填写详细，如“9 筒 35 毫米的曝光动画胶片”“新闻短片”（美国制）等，本栏所属填写内容应与出口报关发票和进口许可证上所列明的相符，所填写的货物尺寸应注明计量单位，对于危险物品，则应注明其专用名称和包装级别。

If a shipment contains multiple items, the shipper should separately declare the name of the goods. It should be noted that the general names such as “sample” and “parts” cannot be used to fill as the name. Each item in the goods must be filled out separately and in detail as far as possible, such as “9 cylinders of 35mm exposure animation film” “news video” (made in the United States), etc. The contents of this column should be in accordance with those specified in the export declaration invoice and import license. The dimensions of the goods filled in should indicate the unit of measurement. For dangerous goods, the special names and packaging levels shall be marked.

17. 托运人签字

Signature of Shipper

托运人必须在本栏内签字。

This column should be filled in by the shipper.

18. 日期

Date

填托运人或其代理人交货的日期。在接受托运人委托后、单证操作前，货运代理公司的指定人员对托运书进行审核，可称之为合同评审。审核的主要内容包括价格、航班日期。目前，在审核起降航班的航空公司大部分采取自由销售方式。每家航空公司、每条航线、每个航班甚至每个目的港均有优惠运价，这种运价会因货源、淡旺季经常调整，而且各航空公司之间的优惠价格也不尽相同。所以有时候更换航班，运价也会随之更换。需要指出的是，货运单上显示的运价虽然与托运书上的运价有联系，但互相之间有很大区别。货运单上显示的是 TACT（空运货物运价表）上公布的适用运价和费率，托运书上显示的是航空公司优惠价加上杂费和服务费或使用协议价格。托运书的价格审核就是判断其价格是否被接受，预订航班是否可行。审核人员必须在托运书上签名和写上日期以示确认。

Fill in the date of delivery by the shipper or his agent. After accepting the consignor's entrustment, the designated agent of the freight forwarding company will examine the shipment document or refer to the contract review before operating the document. The main contents of the review are as follows: price and flight date. At present, the majority of the airlines that review flights are taking the form of free sales. Every airline, every route, every flight and even every destination port has a preferential tariff, which will be adjusted frequently due to the source of goods and the off-peak season, and the preferential prices among airlines are also different. So sometimes flights are changed and freight rates are also replaced. It should be pointed out that although the freight rates shown on the waybill are related to those on the shipping documents, they are quite different from each other. The applicable freight rates published on the TACT (The Air Cargo Tariff) are displayed on the waybill, and airline discount prices plus miscellaneous fees and service charges or agreement prices are shown the shipping documents. Checking the price of the consignment document is to determine whether the price is acceptable or not, and whether the flight is available. The auditor must sign and date the consignment for confirmation.

任务实施

Task Implementation

托运书应包括下列内容栏：托运人、收货人、始发站机场、目的地机场、要求的路线/申请订舱、供运输用的声明价值、供海关用的声明价值、保险金额、处理事项、货运单所附文件、实际毛重、运价类别、计费重量、费率、货物的品名及数量、托运人签字、日期等。

The consignment document should include the following contents: shipper, consignee, departure airport, destination airport, required route/application booking, value for shipping, value for customs declaration, insurance amount, matters to be handled, documents attached to the bill of lading, actual gross weight, freight rate category, chargeable weight, tariff rate, the name and quantity of the goods, the shipper's signature and date, etc.

缮制托运书时，应最大程度保证原始托单的数据正确，以减少后续过程的频繁更改，一般发货人、收货人（如详细名称、地址、电话等）和品名都要正确填写。

When making the consignment document, the data of original supporting documents should be guaranteed to the greatest extent to reduce frequent changes in the follow-up process. Generally speaking, the consignor, the consignee (such as the detailed name, address, telephone number, etc.) and the product name should be filled in correctly.

需要注意的是，收货人必须指明，不能是"to order"，托运书上显示的是航空公司优惠价加上杂费和服务费或使用协议价格，货运单上是 TACT 的公布运价。

It should be noted that the consignee must specify that it cannot be "to order", that the consignment document shows the airline discount prices plus miscellaneous fees and service charges or agreement prices, and that TACT's published rates are on the waybill.

货代业务员接到货主托运书后，需要仔细审核托运书，主要检查基本的信息是否齐全，确认取货时间和送货方式。

After receiving the consignment document from the shipper, the freight forwarder needs to examine the consignment document carefully, mainly checking whether the basic information is complete, confirming the time of delivery and the mode of delivery.

核对无误后，将托运书通过传真或邮件发给航空公司代理，并确认其是否收到。如有特殊要求，须再次叮嘱确认。

After checking, the consignment document will be sent to the airline agent by fax or mail to confirm whether they have been received. If there is any special requirement, it must be confirmed again.

在接到发货人的发货预报后，货代业务员须向航空公司吨控部门领取并填写订舱单，同时提供相应的信息：货物的名称、体积、重量、件数、目的地，以及要求出运的时间等。航空公司根据实际情况安排舱位。货运代理订舱时，可依照发货人的要求选择最佳的航线和承运人，同时为发货人争取合理的运价。订舱后，航空公司签发舱位确认书（即舱单），如图 3-3 所示。并将取得的进仓编号和进仓图发给货主。特别是由客户自己送进机场的，一般要提前给客户传进仓单，告知其进仓编号和进仓地址，单证随货的情况须告知承运方。

After receiving the shipper's delivery forecast, the freight forwarder shall collect and fill in the booking form from the airline's tonnage control department, and at the same time provide the corresponding information: the name, volume, weight, number of pieces, destination of the goods, and the time required for shipment. The airline arranges the cabin according to the actual situation. The freight forwarder may choose the best route and carrier according to the requirements of the shipper, and meanwhile strive for a low and reasonable freight rate for the shipper. After booking, the airline issues a confirmation of the space (i. e. the manifest), as shown in Figure 3-3. The acquired warehousing number and warehousing plan will be sent to the shipper. Especially when the customer sends the warehouse receipt to the airport by himself, it is generally necessary to inform the customer in advance of the warehouse number and the warehouse address, and inform the carrier of the documents along with the goods.

×××FREIGHT FORWARDING(TIANJIN) CO., LTD.

CONSOLIDATION MANIFEST

ORIGIN: BEIJING AIRPORT　　DEST: HAJ　　MAWB NO.:205-255××4　　FLIGHT/DATE: NH962 / 25-Nov-17

CNEE: Mu\ er+Partner G×H - International Logistics　　TEL: 022-231××5

FAX: 022-231××9

HAWB NO.	PCS.	G.WT.	DESCRIPTION	DEST.	SHIPPER	CONSIGNEE	CC/PP
HTA1711008TJ	1PALLET	288.0 KGS	SUPPLY OF FLEXIBLE COUPLING ACCORDING TO REVISED BUTTING PO NO.4500144997 DATED 02.11.2017	HAJ	HORIZON WATER CO.LTD. 5/F BLDG.C,TONGHUI MANSION,1132 HUIHE SOUTH ST., CHAOYANG DISTRICT BEIJING 100023, P.R.CHINA	H. BUTTING GMBH+CO. KG, GIFHORNER STR. 59,29379 WITTINGEN-KNESEBECK,GERMANY CONTACT:SEBASTIAN TEL.: +49 5834 50 - 329	PP
TOTAL: ONE (1) PALLET ONLY							

图 3-3　舱单

思考题
Questions

1. 若一票货物包括多种物品时，货物的品名和数量在填制过程中需要注意哪些事项?

If a batch of goods includes a variety of goods, what should be noted in filling out the name and quantity of the goods?

2. 以小组为单位，编制并模拟情景，填写国际货物委托书。

Simulate the scenario in groups, and fill out the Shipper's Letter of Instruction.

表 3-5　国际货物托运书

托运人姓名、地址、电话号码				航空货运单号码		
				安全检查		
收货人姓名、地址、电话号码				是否定妥航班日期吨位		
				预定一程航班/日期	预定二程航班/日期	预定三程航班/日期
				预付	到付	
				供运输用声明价值	供海关用声明价值	
始发站		目的港		另请通知		
储运注意事项及其他 1. 货物、单据交接时间： 2. 是否提货： 提货时间： 提货地点： 联系人及电话：				运　价　确　认 运价：　操作费： 提货费：　报关费： 商检费　制单费：		

续表

<table>
<tr><td colspan="5">3. 报关特殊要求：
4. 运输时间要求：
5. 分单要求：
6. 是否有随机文件：</td><td>鉴定费：换正本实报　　　　转关费：
其他费用：</td></tr>
<tr><td rowspan="2">件数</td><td rowspan="2">毛重
（千克）</td><td rowspan="2">海关编码</td><td rowspan="2">计费重量
（千克）</td><td rowspan="2">费率</td><td>货物品名（包括包装、尺寸或体积）：</td></tr>
<tr><td></td></tr>
<tr><td></td><td></td><td></td><td></td><td></td><td></td></tr>
<tr><td></td><td></td><td></td><td></td><td></td><td>中英文品名：</td></tr>
<tr><td></td><td></td><td></td><td></td><td></td><td></td></tr>
<tr><td></td><td></td><td></td><td></td><td></td><td></td></tr>
<tr><td></td><td></td><td></td><td></td><td></td><td>单件尺寸（长×宽×高厘米）：</td></tr>
<tr><td></td><td></td><td></td><td></td><td></td><td>货物总体积：</td></tr>
<tr><td colspan="5"></td><td>托运人（或代理人）名称：:</td></tr>
<tr><td colspan="5"></td><td>经办人签名：</td></tr>
</table>

Table 3-5 **The Shipper's Letter of Instruction**

Shipper's Name, Address & Telephone Number				Air Waybill Number		
				Safety Inspection		
Consignee's Name, Address & Telephone Number				Booked		
				Scheduled Flight / Date	Scheduled Flight / Date	Scheduled Flight / Date
				PP	CC	
				Declared Value for Transport	Declared Value for Customs	
Departure Station		Destination Port		Also Notify		
Precautions for storage & transportation and others Delivery Time of Goods and Documents: Pick Up or Not: Pickup Time: Pickup Location: Contact Person and Phone Number:				Freight Confirmation Freight Fee: Delivery Fee: Inspection Fee	Operation Fee: Customs Fee: Production Fee	

Continued

Special Requirements for Customs Declaration: Requirements for Transportation Time: Ordering Requirements: Random Documents:					Appraisal Fee:　　　　Transfer Fee: Other Fees:
No. of Pieces	Gross Weight (KG)	Customs Code	Chargeable Weight (KG)	Rate/kg	Nature and Quantify of Goods
					(Incl, Packaging, Dimensions or Volume):
					Product Name in Chinese and English:
					Single Size (length× width×height cm):
					Total Volume (CBM):
					Name of Shipper (or Agent):
					Signature of Operator:

子任务之四　货物报关
Section Four：Cargo Declaration

任务引入
Task Introduction

小张是某货运代理公司业务员。一位客户打算从中国天津向德国克内瑟贝克（Knesebeck）空运一批货物（不锈钢连接件/ Stainless Steel Flexible Couplings）。请帮助小张为客户办理报关事宜。

Xiao Zhang works in a freight forwarding company as a clerk. A customer intends to air a batch of goods（Stainless Steel Flexible Couplings）from Tianjin，China to Knesebeck，Germany. Please help Xiao Zhang to handle customs clearance for the client.

任务分析
Assignment Analysis

接受发货人的委托，预定舱位后，货代业务员需要从发货人处取得必要的出口单据，认真核对单证信息，安排运输工具取货或由发货人送货到指定地点。

After accepting the consignor's entrustment and booking the shipping space，the freight forwarder needs to obtain the necessary export documents from the consignor，check the document information carefully，and arrange the transportation means to pick up the goods or deliver the goods to the designated place by the consignor.

货代业务员还需要根据货物情况，与报关员和货主沟通如何报关。

The freight forwarder also needs to communicate with the customs declarers and the cargo owners according to the conditions of the goods.

报关单据一般为商业发票、装箱单、商检证、出口货物报关单，有的商品则需要动植物检疫证书或产地证、出口外汇核销单、外销合同等。

Customs declaration documents generally consist of the following items：commercial invoices，packing lists，commodity inspection certificates，customs declarations for export goods，animal and plant quarantine certificates，certificates of origin，export foreign exchange verification sheets，and export contracts，etc.

相关知识
Relevant Knowledge

一、报关行
Customs Broker

（1）接单、送单：客户可自行选择报关行，也可委托货运代理公司进行报关，但都需要将发货人准备好的所有报关资料，连同货站的“可收运书”，航空公司的正本运单及时交给报关行，以便及时报关，方便货物及早通关以及运输。

Receiving and delivering orders: Customers can choose the customs broker by themselves or entrust the freight forwarding company to declare the goods. However, all the customs declaration materials prepared by the consignor, together with the "receivable document" of the terminal, should be submitted to the customs broker in time to facilitate timely customs declaration and goods transportation.

（2）预录入：报关行将根据以上文件，整理并完善所有报关文件，将数据录入海关系统，进行预先审核。

Pre-input: According to the above documents, the customs broker will organize as well as improve all customs declaration documents, and input the data into the customs system for pre-examination.

（3）申报：预录通过后，可进行正式申报程序，将所有单证交由海关审核。

Declaration: After the pre-record is passed, the formal declaration procedure can be carried out, and all documents will be submitted to the customs for examination.

（4）送单时间：根据航班时间，要在中午报关通过的货物单证最迟需要在10：00前交接给报关行；需在下午报关通过的货物单证最迟在15：00前交接给报关行。否则将加重报关行报关速度的负担，也可能导致货物不能进入预计航班，或因情况紧急而造成货站收取超时费用（0.5元/千克）。

Delivery time: According to flight time, cargo documents that need to be declared at noon should be handed over to the customs broker by 10: 00 at the latest; cargo documents that need to be declared in the afternoon should be handed over to the customs broker by 15: 00 at the latest. Otherwise, it will aggravate the burden of customs declaration speed, and may also lead to the goods not being able to enter the scheduled flights, or result in the freight stations charging overtime fees (0.5yuan/kg) due to emergency.

（5）报关行工作时间：8：30—17：30，但可根据客户需要随时上班。

Customs broker working hours：8：30-17：30，but can work at any time according to customer needs.

空运货物要提前一天中午送到仓库，而且货物到仓库以后才能报关。

Air cargo should be delivered to the warehouse at noon one day in advance, and the goods can be declared after their arrival.

二、海关

Customs

（1）审单：海关将根据报关资料审核货物以及单证。

Review：The customs will review the goods and documents according to the customs declaration materials.

（2）查验：抽查或者由货运代理自查（后果自负）。

Check：Random inspection or self-examination by the freight forwarder（consequence at your own risk）.

（3）征税：海关根据货物的类别，按照国家法律的规定收取税收，并填写核销单（以便货物出口后，货主退税用）。

Tax：According to the category of the goods, the customs collects the tax in accordance with the provisions of the national laws, and fills in the verification form（for the purpose of tax refund by the shipper after the export of goods）.

（4）放行：以上手续完备后，海关将对货物进行放行，在相关单证上加盖海关放行章，交给相关的报关行。

Release：After the above procedures are completed, the customs will release the goods, stamp the customs clearance on the relevant documents, and hand it over to the customs broker.

注：空运货物的通关时间一般情况下为半个工作日。

Note：Customs clearance time for air cargo：usually half a working day.

任务实施

Task Implementation

本任务中某货运代理公司和客户签订了《代理报关委托书》（如表 3-6 所示）和委托报关协议（如表 3-7 所示）。

In this task, a freight forwarding company and the customer signed the Declaration Entrustment Letter (as shown in Table 3-6) and the Declaration Entrustment Agreement (as shown in Table 3-7).

表 3-6　　代理报关委托书

编号：□□□□□□□□□□□□□□□□

我单位现　　　（A. 逐票、B. 长期）委托贵公司代理　　　　等通关事宜。（A. 报关查验　B. 垫缴税款　C. 办理海关证明联　D. 审批手册　E. 核销手册　F. 申办减免税手续　G. 其他）详见《委托报关协议》。

我单位保证遵守《海关法》和国家有关法规，保证所提供的情况真实、完整、单货相符。否则，愿承担相关法律责任。

本委托书有效期自签字之日起至 2017 年 12 月 30 日止。

委托方（盖章）：

法定代表人或其他授权签署《代理报关委托书》的人（签字）

2017 年 11 月 21 日

Table 3-6　　Declaration Entrust Letter

Our company (A. vote, B. long-term) entrust your agency to deal with the following customs clearance matters. (A. declaration inspection　B. tax payment　C. customs certification　D. approval manual　E. verification manual　F. application for tax reduction and exemption　G. others). For details, please refer to the Agreement on Entrusted Customs Declaration.

Our company guarantees to abide by the Customs Law and relevant national regulations, and to ensure that the information provided is true, complete and consistent with the goods. Otherwise, we are willing to bear relevant legal responsibilities.

This Power of Attorney shall be valid from the date of signature to December 30, 2017.

Client (seal):

Legal representative or other person authorized to sign the "Power of Attorney for Customs Declaration" (signature)

November 21, 2017

表 3-7　　委托报关协议

为明确委托报关具体事项和各自责任，双方经平等协商签订协议如下：

<table>
<tr><td>委托方</td><td>××××（北京）
环境技术股份有限公司</td><td>被委托方</td><td colspan="2"></td></tr>
<tr><td>主要货物名称</td><td>卡箍</td><td>报关单编码</td><td colspan="2">NO.</td></tr>
<tr><td>HS 编码</td><td>73071900</td><td>收到单证日期</td><td colspan="2">年　月　日</td></tr>
<tr><td>进出口日期</td><td>20××-11-21</td><td rowspan="4">收到单证
情况</td><td>合同□</td><td>发票□</td></tr>
<tr><td>提单号</td><td></td><td>装箱单□</td><td>提（运）单□</td></tr>
<tr><td>贸易方式</td><td>一般贸易</td><td>加工贸易手册□</td><td>许可证件□</td></tr>
<tr><td>原产地/来源地</td><td>北京</td><td colspan="2">其他</td></tr>
<tr><td>传真电话</td><td>010-5165××××</td><td>报关收费</td><td colspan="2">人民币：　　元</td></tr>
<tr><td colspan="2">其他要求：</td><td colspan="3">承诺说明：</td></tr>
<tr><td colspan="2">背面所列通用条款是本协议不可分割的一部分，对本协议的签署构成了对背面通用条款的同意</td><td colspan="3">背面所列通用条款是本协议不可分割的一部分，对本协议的签署构成了对背面通用条款的同意</td></tr>
<tr><td colspan="2">委托方业务签章：

经办人签章：孟宪芝
联系电话：51659602-8040
2017 年 11 月 21 日</td><td colspan="3">被委托方业务签章：

经办报关员签章：
联系电话：
年　月　日</td></tr>
</table>

Table 3-7　　The Declaration Entrustment Agreement

In order to clarify the specific matters and respective responsibilities of the entrusted customs declaration, both parties sign the following agreement through equal consultation:

<table>
<tr><td>Entrusting Party</td><td>×××× Environmental Technology Co., Ltd.</td><td>Entrusted Party</td><td colspan="2"></td></tr>
<tr><td>Cargo Name</td><td></td><td>Customs Declaration Code</td><td colspan="2">No.</td></tr>
<tr><td>HS Encoding</td><td>73071900</td><td>Receipt Date</td><td colspan="2"></td></tr>
<tr><td>Date of Import and Export</td><td>20××-11-21</td><td rowspan="4">Documents</td><td>Contract□</td><td>Invoice□</td></tr>
<tr><td>Bill of Lading Number</td><td></td><td>Packing List□</td><td>Bill of Lading□</td></tr>
<tr><td>Trade Mode</td><td>General Trade</td><td>Processing Trade Manual□</td><td>Permit□</td></tr>
<tr><td>Origin / Source:</td><td>Beijing</td><td colspan="2">Others</td></tr>
<tr><td>Fax Number</td><td>010-5165××××</td><td>Customs Charges:</td><td colspan="2">RMB</td></tr>
<tr><td colspan="2">Other Requirements:</td><td colspan="3">Commitment Statement:</td></tr>
<tr><td colspan="2">The general terms and conditions listed on the back are an integral part of this agreement, to which the signing of this Agreement constitutes the consent.</td><td colspan="3">The general terms and conditions listed on the back are an integral part of this agreement, to which the signing of this Agreement constitutes the consent.</td></tr>
<tr><td colspan="2">Signature and seal of the entrusting party:

Signature and seal of operator: Meng Xianzhi
Contact Number: 51659602-8040
November 21, 2017</td><td colspan="3">Signature and seal of the entrusted party

Signature and seal of the customs broker:
Phone Number:
Specific Date:</td></tr>
</table>

确定本任务的海关申报要素，具体内容如下：

The customs declaration elements for this task have been determined. The details are as follows：

73071900

73071900

（1）品名：不锈钢连接件

Name：Stainless Steel Flexible Couplings

（2）用途（用于管子之间连通）：用于管道之间连接

Use（for interconnection between pipes）：for connection between pipes

（3）材质（铁、非合金钢、不锈钢、合金钢）：不锈钢

Material（iron，non-alloy steel，stainless steel，alloy steel）：stainless steel

（4）种类（法兰、管套、十字接头、对焊件等）：管套

Type（flange，sleeve，cross joint，butt welds，etc.）：pipe sleeve

（5）加工方法（铸造、锻造等）：铸造

Process（casting，forging，etc.）：casting

货代操作员将发货人提供的出口货物报关单的各项内容输入电脑，完成信息预录入。报关单上加盖报关单位的报关专用章后，装箱单（见图 3-4）、将报关单（见图 3-5）与有关的发票和货运单综合在一起，根据需要随附有关的证明文件。以上报关单证齐全后，由持有报关证的报关员正式向海关申报。海关审核无误后，海关官员即在运单正本上加盖放行章，同时在出口收汇核销单和出口报关单上加盖放行章，在发货人用于产品退税的单证上加盖验讫章，粘上防伪标志，完成出口报关手续。

The freight forwarder operator inputs the contents of the export declaration form provided by the consignor into the computer and completes the pre-entry of the information. After the customs declaration form is stamped with the special seal，the customs declaration is combined with the relevant invoices（as shown in Figure 3-5），the packing list（as shown in Figure 3-6）and the freight bill，accompanied by relevant supporting documents as required. After the above documents are complete，the customs declarer who holds the certificate shall formally declare to the customs. After the customs examination is correct，the customs officers affix the release stamp to the original of the shipping documents used for shipment，at the same time affix the release stamp to the export receipt verification form together with export declaration form，affix the inspection stamp to the documents used for product tax refund by the shipper，affix the anti-counterfeiting mark，and complete the export declaration formalities.

HORIZON

Commercial Invoice

Invoice No.:INV171116-001
Date: 16/Nov/17
Project: "Sako" 200.000 m^3/d
Customer: H. Butting GmbH & Co. KG
Address: G█████Strasse 59,29379 K█████,Germany
Contact: █████
Tel.: +49 5834 50 310
Web: www.butting.com
Email: █████@butting.de

HORIZON WATER CO., LTD.

Tel: 86-10-51█████045
Fax: 86-10-█████
Email: marketing@ho█████.com
www. ho█████.com

Contact: Cameron
Email: █████@█████.com

Memline® Stainless Steel Flexible Pipe Couplings					
No.	DESCRIPTION	MATERIAL	QTY.	UNIT PRICE (USD)	TOTAL PRICE(USD)
1	MemLine® SS Flexible Couplings 2.5" 1200PSI	Housing: 316SS Bolts and washer: 316SS Nuts: 316SS Gasket: C Type, EPDM	228	35.44	8,080.32
				Total CIP/HANNOVER in USD	8,080.32

Remarks:

1 Payment Terms: Irrevocable L/C at sight
L/C has to be opened as following requests:
1st delivery : supplier has to receive the L/C not later than November 4th;
2nd delivery : supplier has to receive the L/C not later than November 6th;
3nd delivery : supplier has to receive the L/C not later than December 1st;
If supplier cannot receive the L/C as above-mentioned date,Supplier has the right to suspend the production

2 Delivery Terms : DAP Knesebeck/Germany,supplier doesn't assume any tariffs and other taxes incurred in Germany.

3 Delivery Time up :1st delivery by end of November, 2nd delivery by last week of December, 3nd delivery by end of

4 Warranty: 24 months since commissioning or 30 weeks since Delivery

5 If customer ask for second and third delivery by air,the air freight costs will be calculated additionally.

6 This quote is valid for 1 month period from the above date

Packing List

Invoice No.: INV█████6-001
Date: 2017/11/16
Consignee: H.█████H & Co. KG
Gifhorner Strasse 59,29379 Knesebeck,Germany
Tel.: +49 5834 50 310
Email: s█████@b█████.de

HORIZON WATER CO., LTD.

Tel: 86-10-█████2/03
Fax: 86-10-84466118
www. horizon-█████.com

Contact: Cameron

Memline® Stainless Steel Flexible Pipe Couplings							
NO.	Mark	Pressure	DESCRIPTION	QTY(PCS)	N.W. (Kg)	G.W. (Kg)	Net Size L×W×H (m3)
1	N/M	1200PSI	Memline® SS Flexible Couplings 2.5"	228PCS	275.75	288.75	0.90*0.77*0.67
		Total:	1PALLET（18CTNS）		275.75	288.75	0.46

图 3-4　装箱单

中华人民共和国海关出口货物报关单

预录入编号：　　　　　　　　　　海关编号：

出口口岸 北京	备案号	出口日期	申报日期	
经营单位 110. 53206…（北京）…技术有限公司	运输方式 空运	运输工具名称	提运单号	
发货单位 110 63206…（北京）…技术有限公司	贸易方式 一般贸易	征免性质	结汇方式 电汇	
许可证号	运抵国（地区） 德国	指运港 汉诺威	境内货源地 北京朝阳	
批准文号	成交方式 CIP	运费	保费 RMB100	杂费
合同协议号 INV 111 -001	件数 1	包装种类 木托	毛重（公斤） 275.75	净重（公斤） 288.75
集装箱号	随附单据		生产厂家	
标记唛码及备注 贸易国：德国 三种特殊关系：否				

项号	商品编号	商品名称、规格型	数量及单位	最终目的国（地区）	单价	总价	币制	征免
1	73071900	卡箍	228 PCS	德国	35.44	8080.32	USD	

税费征收情况		
录入员　　录入单位	兹声明以上申报无讹并承担法律责任	海关审单批注及放行日期（签章）
报关员		审单　　审价
单位地址	申报单位（签章）	征税　　统计
邮编　　电话	填制日期	查验　　放行

图 3-5　报关单

思考题
Questions

1. 航空货物的送单时间有哪些要求？

What are the requirements for the delivery time of air cargo?

2. 空运货物的通关步骤是什么？有何注意事项？

What are the steps for customs clearance of air cargo? What are the precautions?

子任务之五　航空运单缮制
Section Five: Air Waybill Completion

任务引入
Task Introduction

小刘是某货运代理公司操作员。一位客户打算从中国天津向德国克内瑟贝克（Knesebeck）空运一批货物（不锈钢连接件/ Stainless Steel Flexible Couplings）。请帮助小刘为客户缮制航空运单。

Xiao Liu works in a freight forwarding company as a clerk. A customer intends to air a batch of goods (Stainless Steel Flexible Couplings) from Tianjin, China to Knesebeck, Germany. Please help Xiao Liu to complete the air waybill for the client.

任务分析
Assignment Analysis

海关验收完货物，在报关单上盖验收章后，即可缮制航空运单。不过，现在很多航空公司也会采用“先出提单，后报关”的形式。

The customs can stamp on the customs declaration form and complete the air waybill after the goods are checked and accepted. However, many airlines will adopt the form of "first bill of lading, then customs declaration".

货代业务员接受托运人或其代理人送交的已经审核确认的托运书及报关单证和收货凭证。将收货记录与收货凭证核对，制作操作交接单，填上所收到的各种报关单证份数，给每份交接单配一份总运单或分运单。将制作好的交接单、配好的总运单或分运单、报关单证移交操作员。

The freight forwarder accepts the checked and confirmed shipping documents, customs declaration documents and receipt certificate delivered by the shipper or its agent. Check the receipt record with the receipt certificate, create the operation delivery order, fill in the number of various customs declaration documents received, and assign each delivery order with a total waybill or a consignment note. Transfer the completed delivery orders, the completed total waybill or the distribution order and the customs declaration documents to the operator.

航空货运单包括总运单和分运单，填制航空货运单的主要依据是发货人提供的国际货物委托书，委托书上的各项内容都应体现在货运单上，一般用英文填写。填制航空货运单是空运出口业务中重要的环节，货运单填写的准确与否直接关系到货物能否及时、准确地运达目的地，货运单也是发货人结汇的主要有效凭证，因此必须单货一致、单单一致。

The air waybill includes the total waybill or the distribution order. The main basis for filling out the air waybill is the international cargo power of attorney provided by the consignor. The contents of the power of attorney should be reflected in the freight bill, which is usually filled in English. Filling in the air waybill is an important part of the air export business. The accuracy of the filling in the air waybill is directly related to whether the goods can be delivered to the destination in a timely and accurate manner. The freight waybill is also the main valid certificate for the consignor to settle the foreign exchange. Therefore, it is necessary that the waybill should be consistent with the cargo.

相关知识
Relevant Knowledge

一、航空运单
Air Waybill

航空运单（简称 AWB），是航空运输公司及其代理人（即承运人签发给发货人表示已收到货物并接受托运的货物收据，航空运单也是承运人与托运人之间的运输合同，但它不是物权凭证，既不能背书转让（运单右上方即有“NON NEGOTIABLE”字样），也不能凭其提货。航空运单样本，如表 3-8 所示。

The Air Waybill (AWB) is a receipt issued by the Air Transport Company and its agents (i. e. the carrier) to the consignor indicating that the goods have been received and accepted for consignment. The Air Waybill is also the contract of carriage between the carrier and the shipper. However, it is not a document of property rights; neither can be transferred by endorsement. (the word “NON NEGOTIABLE” on the top right of the waybill), nor can be taken for delivery. Air waybill samples, as shown in Table 3-8.

航空运输货物托运要先填写“国际货物托运书”，连同出口明细表、发票、装箱单及海关发票、商检需要的单证，办妥报关手续；当货物运抵目的地后，收货人凭航空公司的到货通知及有关证明即可提取货物并在货单上签收。

For air cargo consignment, the customs declaration formalities should be completed first by filling in the "International Cargo Consignment Document", together with export details, invoices, packing lists, customs invoices and documents needed for commodity inspection. When the cargo arrives at the destination, the consignee can withdraw the cargo and sign on the cargo list with the arrival notification of the airline and the relevant certificate.

表 3-8　　空运单样本

<table>
<tr><td colspan="6">托运人名称及地址

MATSUDA TELEVISION SYSTEMS CO.
LOT5, PRESIAN TENKU APUAN
SITE 400 SHA ALAM
SELANG DE MALAYSIA</td><td colspan="3">不可转让航空运单
签发人
BEIJING KINTE WORLD EXPRESS CO., LTD.</td></tr>
<tr><td colspan="6">收货人名称及地址

MATSUDA QINGDAO CO., LTD.
NO. 128 WUHAN ROAD
QINGDAO
CHINA</td><td colspan="3" rowspan="3">经双方同意，本合同所述货物在外观良好的情况下被接受（除注明的情况外），运输条件须符合本合同背面的合同条件，所有货物均可通过其他方式进行运输。允许通过道路或其他承运人完成运输，除非托运人在此明确地做出特殊指示。并请托运人注意有关承运人责任限制的相关规定。

托运人可以通过申报较高的运费并在必要时支付附加费来提高对承运人的责任限制。</td></tr>
<tr><td colspan="6">签发运单的承运人代理人的名称和城市
BEIJING KINTE WORLD EXPRESS CO., LTD.</td></tr>
<tr><td colspan="2">代理人的 IATA（国际航空运输协会）代码（非必填）</td><td colspan="4">收货人账号（非必填）</td></tr>
<tr><td colspan="6">起飞机场和指定航线
K. LUMPUR, MALAYSIA</td><td colspan="3">会计事项
FREIGHT COLLECT</td></tr>
<tr><td>至
QAO</td><td>第一承运人
KE</td><td>至</td><td>承运人</td><td>至</td><td>承运人</td><td>货币</td><td>运费申报价值
NVD（NVD 指无申报价值）</td><td>海关申报价值
NCV</td></tr>
<tr><td colspan="3">目的地机场
QINGDAO, CHINA</td><td colspan="2">KE855/17JUN</td><td>保险金额</td><td colspan="3">如果承运人提供保险等保险是依照条件要求所显示的数据量为被保险人在盒中注明的"保险金额"</td></tr>
<tr><td colspan="9">受理情况
"NOTIFY PARTY-SAME AS CONSIGNEE"</td></tr>
</table>

续表

件数	毛重	费率等级	计费重量	费率/费用	总计	货物的性质和数量
52	510. 00KGS		211KGS	AS ARRANGED		TV-PARTS 12. 638m^3

预付重量费用汇总　AS ARRANGED	其他费用
申报价值	
税	
因代理人需要而产生的费用	托运人保证本合同所列各项内容正确无误，且只要托运货物的任何部分含有危险货物，该部分应按有关危险货物条例的规定，正确描述名称，并在适宜的航空运输环境下进行运输。
因承运人需要而产生的费用	
	________________ 发货人及其代理人签字

预付费用总额	代付费用总额	于________签发日期________年________月________日签署 承运人或代理人	
汇率	到付货物运费		
仅供承运人在目的地使用 37/5000	目的地的收费	收取费用总额	航空运单编号 KEW-51000788

Table 3-8　　The Airway Bill

Shipper's name and address MATSUDA TELEVISION SYSTEMS CO. LOT5, PRESIAN TENKU APUAN SITE 400 SHA ALAM SELANG DE MALAYSIA		NOT NEGOTIABLE Air Waybill Issued by BEIJING KINTE WORLD EXPRESS CO. , LTD.
Consignee's name and address MATSUDA QINGDAO CO. , LTD. NO. 128 WUHAN ROAD QINGDAO CHINA		It is agreed that the goods described herein are accepted in apparent good order and condition (exceptas noted) for carriage subject to the conditions of contract on the reverse hereof, all goods may be carried by any other means. including road or any other carrier unless specific contrary instructions are given hereon by the shipper. the shipper's attention is drawn to the notice concerning carrier's limitation of liability. shipper may increase such limitation of liability by declaring a higher value of carriage and paying a supplemental charge if required.
Issuing Carrier's Agent Name and City BEIJING KINTE WORLD EXPRESS CO. , LTD.		
Agents IATA Code	Account No.	

Continued

Airport of Departure (Add. of First Carrier) and Requested Routing K. LUMPUR, MALAYSIA	Accounting Information FREIGHT COLLECT

To QAO	By first carrier KE	To	By	To	By	Currency USD	Declared Value for Carriage NVD (No Value Declaration)	Declared Value for Customs NCV (No Value Declaration)

Airport of Destination QINGDAO, CHINA	Flight/Date KE855/17JUN	Amount of Insurance	If carrier offers insurance and such insurance is requested in accordance with the conditions thereof indicate amount to be insured in figures in box marked "Amount of Insurance"

Handling Information
"NOTIFY PARTY-SAME AS CONSIGNEE"

No. of Pieces	Gross Weight	Rate Class	Chargeable Weight	Rate/Charge	Total	Nature and Quantity of Goods
52	510.00 KGS		211KGS	AS ARRANGED		TV-PARTS 12.638m^3

Prepaid Weight Charge Collect AS ARRANGED	Other Charges
Valuation Charge	
Tax	

Continued

<table>
<tr><td colspan="2">Total Other Charges Due Agent</td><td colspan="2" rowspan="3">Shipper certifies that the particulars on the face hereof are correct and that insofar as any part of the consignment contains dangerous goods, such part is properly described by name and is in proper condition for carriage by air according to the applicable Dangerous Goods Regulations.

____
Signature of Shipper or his agent</td></tr>
<tr><td colspan="2">Total Other Charges Due Carrier</td></tr>
<tr><td colspan="2"></td></tr>
<tr><td>Total Prepaid</td><td>Total Collect as Arranged</td><td colspan="2" rowspan="2">Executed on ________ at ________ Signature of issuing
Carrier or as Agent</td></tr>
<tr><td>Currency
Conversion Rates</td><td>CC Charges in des.
Currency</td></tr>
<tr><td>For Carrier's Use Only at Destination</td><td>Charges at Destination</td><td>Total Collect Charges</td><td>Air Waybill Number
KEW-51000788</td></tr>
</table>

二、航空运单的内容及缮制

Contents and Completion of Air Waybill

（1）航空运单编号，航空运单最上方的编号由航空公司填写。编号前三位一般是各国航空公司的代号，如中国民航的代号为 999，日本航空公司的代号为 131 等。

Air Waybill Number, the number at the top of the air waybill is filled in by the airline. The top three numbers are generally the codes of national airlines. For example, the code name of China Civil Aviation is 999, and the code name of Japan Airlines is 131.

（2）承运人，即航空公司。UCP600 第 27 条规定，若信用证要求空运单据，银行将接受表面标明承运人名称的单据。

Carrier, which is the airline. Article 27 of UCP600 stipulates that if a letter of credit requires an air transport document, the bank will accept a document indicating the name of the carrier.

（3）发货人名称及地址，发货人名称及地址，信用证结算方式一般填写受益人名称；托收结算方式一般填写合同卖方的名称地址。如信用证另有规定则按信用证要求填写。

Shipper's Name and Address. The name of the beneficiary is generally filled in by the name and address of the shipper as well as the letter of credit settlement method, and the name and address of the contract seller is usually filled in by the collection & settlement method. If the credit stipulates otherwise, it will be completed in accordance with the letter of credit.

（4）发货人账号，一般可以不填。

Shipper's Account Number, which generally cannot be filled.

（5）收货人名称及地址，此栏在托收结算中一般填写合同中的买方。信用证结算方式，有的是以买方为收货人，有的是以开证行为收货人，根据信用证的规定填写。

Consignee's Name and Address, which is usually filled in by the buyer in the contract in the collection settlement. Letter of Credit is settled by the buyer or by the certificate issuer as consignee, according to the provisions of the letter of credit.

（6）收货人账号，一般可不填。

Consignee's Account Number, which generally cannot be filled.

（7）签发运单的承运人的代理人名称及城市。本栏若运单由承运人的代理人签发时，可填写实际代理人名称及城市名。如果运单直接由承运人本人签发，此栏则可空白不填。

The Name and city of issuing carrier's agent. If the waybill is issued by the carrier's agent, the actual agent name and city name can be filled in in. If the waybill is directly issued by the carrier himself, the column can be blank.

（8）代理人国际航空运输协会代号，一般可不填（IATA 系 "International Air Transport Association" 的缩写）。

Agent International Air Transport Association Code, generally cannot be filled (IATA is the abbreviation of "International Air Transport Association").

（9）代理人账号（Accoount Number），可填写代理人账号，供承运人结算时使用。一般不填。

Accoount Number, which can be filled in the agent account number for the settlement by the carrier.

（10）起飞机场和指定航线，一般仅填写起航机场名称即可。

Airport of Departure and Requested Routing, which usually can just be filled in the name of the departure airport.

（11）会计事项，指与费用结算的有关事项。如运费预付、到付或发货人结算使用信用卡号、账号以及其他必要的情况。

Accounting Information refers to matters related to the settlement of expenses. Such as freight prepayment, credit card number used for settlement, account number and other necessary information.

（12）转运机场、首程船、路线及目的地，货物运输途中需转运时按实际情况填写。

Routing and Destination Transshipment airport/first vessel/route and destination should be filled in according to the actual situation when transshipment is required in the course of cargo transportation.

（13）目的地机场，即货物运输的最终目的地机场。

Airport of Destination, the final destination airport for cargo transportation.

（14）航班/日期（仅供承运人使用）。

Flight/Date For (Carrier's Use Only).

即飞机航班号及其实际起飞日期。但本栏所填内容只能供承运人使用，因而该起飞日期不能视为货物的装运日期（一般以航空运单的签发日期作为装运日期）。UCP600 第 27 条规定，就本条款而言，在空运单据的方格内（注有“仅供承运人使用”或类似意义的词语）所表示的有关航班和起飞日期的信息，将不视为发运日期的专项批注”。

That is, the flight number and actual departure date. However, the contents of this column can only be used by the carrier, so the date of departure cannot be regarded as the date of shipment of the goods (generally the date of issue of the air waybill as the date of shipment). Article 27 of UCP600 stipulates that for the purposes of this article, information on flights and departure dates expressed in the column of the air transport document (marked with the words "for the use of the carrier only" or similar meaning) will not be considered as a special annotation of the date of shipment.

（15）货币及费用代码。

Currency And CHGS Code.

货币及费用代码即支付费用使用的货币的货币国际标准电码表示，如 USD、HKD 等，费用代码可以不填。

Currency and expense code is the international standard code of currency used to pay expenses, such as USD, HKD and so on. The expense code cannot be filled in.

（16）运费/声报价值及其他费用。

WT/VAL and Other.

“声报价值费”是指下列第17栏向承运人声报了价值时，必须与运费一起交付声报价值费。若该栏费用是预付，则在“PPD”（Prepaid）栏下打“×”。若是待付，则在“Collect”栏下打“×”。此栏应注意与第11栏保持一致。

"Valuation Charge" means that when the value is reported to the carrier in column 17 below, the valuation charge must be paid together with the freight. If the cost is prepaid, "×" will be filled out under the "PPD" (Prepaid) column. If it is to be paid, "×" should be filled in under the "Collect" column. This column must be consistent with column 11.

（17）运费申报价值。

Declared Value For Carriage.

填写托运货物总价值，一般可按发票额填列，如不愿申报，则填“NVD”（No Value Declared），即无申报价值。

Fill in the total value of the consignment, which can generally be filled in according to the invoice amount. If you are unwilling to declare, fill in "NVD", that is, No Value Declaration.

（18）海关申报价值。

Declared Value For Customs.

此栏所填价值是提供给海关的征税依据。当以出口货物报关单或商业发票作为征税时，本栏可空白不填或填“As Per Invoice”，如果货物系样品等数量少且无商业价值，可填“NCV”（No Commercial Value）。

The value added in this column is the basis for taxation provided to the customs. When tax is levied on customs declarations or commercial invoices for export goods, this column may be blank or could be filled in "As Per Invoice"; if the goods are small in quantity and are little in commercial value, this column could be filled in "NCV" (No Commercial Value).

（19）保险金额。

Amount of Insurance.

如发货人根据本运单背面条款要求保险，则在本栏内注明保险金额，若无，可填“NIL”。

If the consignor requires insurance in accordance with the terms of the back of this waybill, the insurance amount should be indicated in this column. If not, the NIL can be filled.

（20）处理情况。

Handling Information.

可利用本栏填所需要注明的内容。如 A，被通知人；B，飞机随带的有关商业单据名称；C，包装情况；D，发货人对货物在途时的某些特别指示等；E，对第二承运人的要求等。

This column could be filled in the contents you need to indicate. Such as A, the notified person; B, the name of the relevant commercial document accompanying the aircraft; C, packaging situation; D, the shipper's special instructions on the way of the goods; E, requirements for the second carrier, etc.

任务实施
Task Implementation

货代操作员须将收货人提供的货物随行单据订在运单后面。如果是集中托运的货物，要制作集中托运清单，并将清单、所有分运单及随行单据装入一个信袋，订在运单后面。

The freight forwarder shall place the accompanying documents provided by the consignee behind the waybill. In case of centralized consignment, a centralized consignment list should be made. Finally, the centralized consignment list, all the distribution orders and accompanying documents should be packed into an envelope and placed at the back of the waybill.

货代业务员将制作好的运单标签贴在每一件货物上。如果是集中托运的货物，还必须有分运单标签。

The freight forwarder will attach the produced waybill labels to each item. If it is a centralized consignment, it must also have a distribution note.

报关放行后，承运方出具主运单（见图 3-6）和分运单（见图 3-7 ）。

After the customs clearance is released, the carrier will issue the total waybill (as shown in Figure 3-6) and the distribution order (as shown in Figure 3-7).

航空运单生成后，即可生成正式保回单。经委托人确认后，则正式保险单（如图 3-8所示）及货运险生效，由代理人出具正本保单邮寄委托人。

After the air waybill is created, the official insurance policy can be generated and confirmed by the client. The official insurance policy (Figure 3-8) and the cargo insurance will take effect. The agent issues the original policy to the client by mail.

Shipper's Name and Address | Shipper's Account Number

205 PEK 25 5154

HO ... N W R CO.LTD.
[redacted] SION, 32 HUIHE SOUTH
ST., CHAOYANG DISTRICT BEIJING 100023,
P.R.CHINA

Not negotiable
Air Waybill
issued by

HAWB:HTA1711008TJ

HI-TRUST
FREIGHT FORWARDING CO., LTD.

Consignee's Name and Address | Consignee's Account Number

H. BU ING GMBH+CO. KG,
GIFHORNER STR. ,29. 9 WI EN-
KNESEBECK,GERMANY
CONTACT:SE TIAN
TEL:+49- -50-3

Copies 1, 2 and 3 of this Air Waybill are originals and have the same validity.

It is agreed that the goods described herein are accepted in apparent good order and condition (except as noted) for carriage SUBJECT TO THE CONDITIONS OF CONTRACT ON THE REVERSE HEREOF. ALL GOODS MAY BE CARRIED BY ANY OTHER MEANS INCLUDING ROAD OR ANY OTHER CARRIER UNLESS SPECIFIC CONTRARY INSTRUCTIONS ARE GIVEN HEREON BY THE SHIPPER, AND SHIPPER AGREES THAT THE SHIPMENT MAY BE CARRIED VIA INTERMEDIATE STOPPING PLACES WHICH THE CARRIER DEEMS APPROPRIATE. THE SHIPPER'S ATTENTION IS DRAWN TO THE NOTICE CONCERNING CARRIER'S LIMITATION OF LIABILITY. Shipper may increase such limitation of liability by declaring a higher value for carriage and paying a supplemental charge if required.

Issuing Carrier's Agent Name and City

Accounting Information

Agent's IATA Code | Account No.

Airport of Departure (Addr. of first Carrier) and requested Routing

BEIJING AIRPORT

FREIGHT PREPAID

To	By First Carrier (Routing and Destination)	to	by	to	by	Currency	Chgs Code	WT/VAL PPD	WT/VAL COLL	Other PPD	Other COLL	Declared Value for Carriage	Declared Value for Customs

Airport of Destination	Flight/Date	For Carrier Use Only / Flight/Date	Amount of Insurance	INSURANCE
HAJ NH HANNOVER	NH962	25-Nov	NIL	If carrier offers insurance and such insurance is requested in accordance with conditions on reverse hereof indicate amount to be insured in figures in box marked Amount of Insurance.

Handling Information

These commodities, technology or software were exported from the United States in accordance with the Export Administration Regulations. Ultimate destination　　Diversion contrary to U.S. law prohibited.　　SCI

No. of Pieces RCP	Gross Weight	kg lb	Rate Class / Commodity Item No.	Chargeable Weight	Rate / Charge	Total	Nature and Quantity of Goods (incl. Dimensions or Volume)
1	288.0 KGS	K	Q	288.0 KGS		AS ARRANGED	SUPPLY OF FLEXIBLE COUPLING ACCORDING TO REVISED BUTTING PO NO.4500144997 DATED 02.11.2017 CIF HAMBURG SEAPORT GERMANY AS PER INCOTERMS 2010 OR CIP HANNOVER AIRPORT GERMANY AS PER INCOTERMS 2010 VAT-NO [redacted]

MULLER+PARTNER GMBH - INTERNATIONAL LOGISTICS
GEORG-WULF-STRASSE 1 AIRCARGOCENTER
BERLIN, 12529 SCHOENEFELD, GERMANY
PHONE: [redacted]
FAX:
E-MAIL:
SEBASTIAN.POEK@MNP.DE
INTERNET: WWW.MNP.DE

Prepaid / Weight Charge / Collect	Other Charges
AS ARRANGED	AS ARRANGED
Valuation Charge	
Tax	
Total other Charges Due Agent	Shipper certifies that the particulars on the face hereof are correct and that insofar as any part of the consignment contains dangerous goods such part is properly described by name and is in proper condition for carriage by air according to the applicable Dangerous Goods Regulations.
Total other Charges Due Carrier AS ARRANGED	HI- FREIGHT FORW (TIANJIN) CO.,LTD.
	Signature of Shipper or His Agent
Total prepaid: AS ARRANGED / Total collect	
Currency Conversion Rates / cc Charges in Dest. Currency	Executed on (Date) at (Place) HAWB:HTA1711008TJ Signature of Issuing Carrier or its Agent
For Carriers Use only at Destination / Charges at Destination	Total Collect Charges

ORIGINAL 3(FOR SHIPPER)

图 3-6　主运单

205 | PEK | 25555154 HAWB:HTA1711008TJ

Shipper's Name and Address	Shipper's Account Number	Not negotiable **Air Waybill** * issued by **HI-TRUST FREIGHT FORWARDING CO., LTD.**
CO.LTD. 5/F BLDG.C,TONGHUI M HE SOUTH ST., CHAOYANG DISTRICT BEIJING 100023, P.R.CHINA		Copies 1, 2 and 3 of this Air Waybill are originals and have the same validity.
Consignee's Name and Address	Consignee's Account Number	It is agreed that the goods described herein are accepted in apparent good order and condition (except as noted) for carriage SUBJECT TO THE CONDITIONS OF CONTRACT ON THE REVERSE HEREOF. ALL GOODS MAY BE CARRIED BY ANY OTHER MEANS INCLUDING ROAD OR ANY OTHER CARRIER UNLESS SPECIFIC CONTRARY INSTRUCTIONS ARE GIVEN HEREON BY THE SHIPPER, AND SHIPPER AGREES THAT THE SHIPMENT MAY BE CARRIED VIA INTERMEDIATE STOPPING PLACES WHICH THE CARRIER DEEMS APPROPRIATE. THE SHIPPER'S ATTENTION IS DRAWN TO THE NOTICE CONCERNING CARRIER'S LIMITATION OF LIABILITY. Shipper may increase such limitation of liability by declaring a higher value for carriage and paying a supplemental charge if required.
H. BUTTING GMBH+CO. KG, GIFHORNER WITTINGEN-KNESEBECK,GERMANY CONTACT:SEBASTIAN TEL.: +49		
Issuing Carrier's Agent Name and City		Accounting Information
Agent's IATA Code	Account No.	
Airport of Departure (Addr. of first Carrier) and requested Routing BEIJING AIRPORT		FREIGHT PREPAID

To	By first Carrier	Routing and Destination	to	by	to	by	Currency	Chgs Code	WT/VAL PPD	WT/VAL COLL	OTHER PPD	OTHER COLL	Declared Value for Carriage	Declared Value for Customs
HAJ	NH						CNY		P		P		N.V.D.	N.C.V.

Airport of Destination	Flight/Date	For Carrier Use Only Flight/Date	Amount of Insurance	INSURANCE - If carrier offers insurance and such insurance is requested in accordance with conditions on reverse hereof indicate amount to be insured in figures in box marked Amount of Insurance.
HANNOVER	NH962	25-Nov		

Handling Information

These commodities, technology or software were exported from the United States in accordance with the Export Administration Regulations. Ultimate destination Diversion contrary to U.S. law prohibited. SCI

No. of Pieces RCP	Gross Weight	kg lb	Rate Class Commodity Item No.	Chargeable Weight	Rate / Charge	Total	Nature and Quantity of Goods (Incl. Dimensions or Volume)
1	288.0 KGS	K	Q	288.0 KGS		AS ARRANGED	SUPPLY OF FLEXIBLE COUPLING ACCORDING TO REVISED BUTTING PO NO. DATED 02.11.2017

MULLER+PARTNER GMBH - INTERNATIONAL LOGISTICS
GEORG- AIRCARGOCENTER
BERLIN, 12529 SCHOENEFELD, GERMANY
PHONE:
FAX:
E-MAIL:
SEBASTIAN.FOERSTER@MNP.DE
INTERNET: WWW.MNP.DE

Prepaid / Weight Charge / Collect	Other Charges
AS ARRANGED	AS ARRANGED
Valuation Charge	
Tax	
Total other Charges Due Agent	Shipper certifies that the particulars on the face hereof are correct and that insofar as any part of the consignment contains dangerous goods such part is properly described by name and is in proper condition for carriage by air according to the applicable Dangerous Goods Regulations.
Total other Charges Due Carrier AS ARRANGED	Signature of Shipper or His Agent
Total prepaid / Total collect AS ARRANGED	
Currency Conversion Rates / cc Charges in Dest. Currency	Executed on (Date) at (Place) Signature of Issuing Carrier or its Agent
For Carriers Use only at Destination / Charges at Destination	Total Collect Charges

HAWB:HTA1711008TJ

图 3-7 分运单

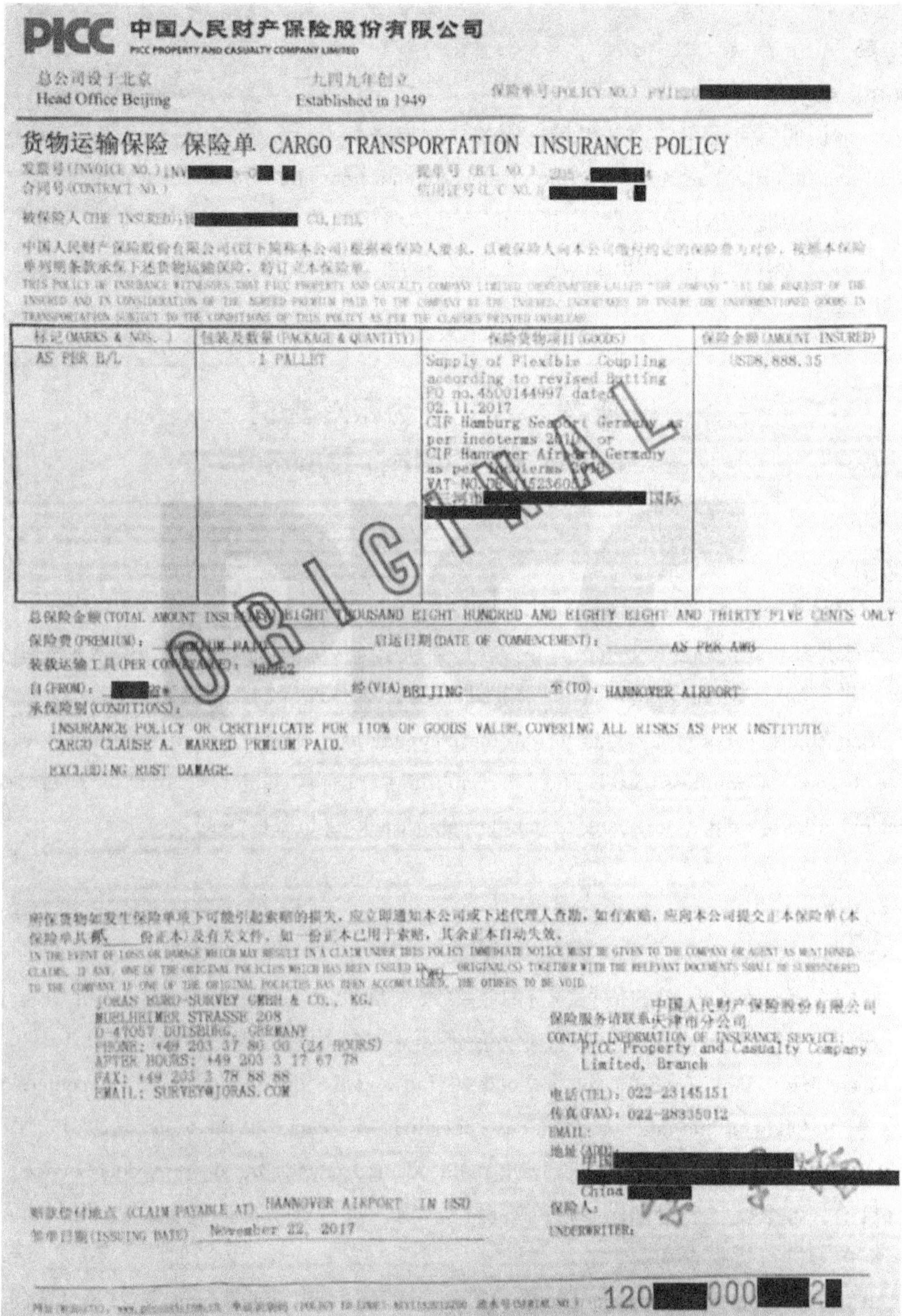

PICC 中国人民财产保险股份有限公司
PICC PROPERTY AND CASUALTY COMPANY LIMITED

总公司设于北京　Head Office Beijing　　一九四九年创立　Established in 1949　　保险单号(POLICY NO.)

货物运输保险 保险单 CARGO TRANSPORTATION INSURANCE POLICY

发票号(INVOICE NO.)　　提单号(B/L NO.)
合同号(CONTRACT NO.)　　信用证号(L/C NO.)

被保险人(THE INSURED)：CO.,LTD.

标记(MARKS & NOS.)	包装及数量(PACKAGE & QUANTITY)	保险货物项目(GOODS)	保险金额(AMOUNT INSURED)
AS PER B/L	1 PALLET	Supply of Flexible Coupling according to revised Batting PO no.4500144997 dated 02.11.2017 CIF Hamburg Seaport Germany as per incoterms 2010 or CIF Hannover Airport Germany as per incoterms 2010	USD8,888.35

总保险金额(TOTAL AMOUNT INSURED)：EIGHT THOUSAND EIGHT HUNDRED AND EIGHTY EIGHT AND THIRTY FIVE CENTS ONLY

保险费(PREMIUM)：AS ARRANGED　启运日期(DATE OF COMMENCEMENT)：AS PER AWB

装载运输工具(PER CONVEYANCE)：

自(FROM)：　经(VIA) BEIJING　至(TO)：HANNOVER AIRPORT

承保险别(CONDITIONS)：

INSURANCE POLICY OR CERTIFICATE FOR 110% OF GOODS VALUE,COVERING ALL RISKS AS PER INSTITUTE CARGO CLAUSE A. MARKED PREMIUM PAID.

EXCLUDING RUST DAMAGE.

所保货物如发生保险单项下可能引起索赔的损失，应立即通知本公司或下述代理人查勘。如有索赔，应向本公司提交正本保险单(本保险单共有 ___ 份正本)及有关文件。如一份正本已用于索赔，其余正本自动失效。

IN THE EVENT OF LOSS OR DAMAGE WHICH MAY RESULT IN A CLAIM UNDER THIS POLICY IMMEDIATE NOTICE MUST BE GIVEN TO THE COMPANY OR AGENT AS MENTIONED. CLAIMS, IF ANY, ONE OF THE ORIGINAL POLICIES WHICH HAS BEEN ISSUED IN TWO ORIGINAL(S) TOGETHER WITH THE RELEVANT DOCUMENTS SHALL BE SURRENDERED TO THE COMPANY. IF ONE OF THE ORIGINAL POLICIES HAS BEEN ACCOMPLISHED, THE OTHERS TO BE VOID.

JORAS EURO-SURVEY GMBH & CO., KG.
MUELHEIMER STRASSE 208
D-47057 DUISBURG, GERMANY
PHONE: +49 203 37 80 00 (24 HOURS)
AFTER HOURS: +49 203 3 17 67 78
FAX: +49 203 3 78 88 88
EMAIL: SURVEY@JORAS.COM

中国人民财产保险股份有限公司天津市分公司
保险服务请联系
CONTACT INFORMATION OF INSURANCE SERVICE:
PICC Property and Casualty Company Limited, Branch
电话(TEL)：022-23145151
传真(FAX)：022-28335012
EMAIL:
地址(ADD)：
China

赔款偿付地点(CLAIM PAYABLE AT) HANNOVER AIRPORT IN USD
签单日期(ISSUING DATE) November 22, 2017

保险人：
UNDERWRITER:

120 000 2

图 3-8　保险单

思考题
Questions

1. 请说明航空运单中海关申报价值的填制方法。

Please describe how to fill out the customs declaration value in the air waybill.

2. 请说明航空运单中运费/声报价值及其他费用项目的填制方法。

Please illustrate how to fill in the freight / valuation and other expenses items in the air waybill.

子任务之六　货物跟踪查询
Section Six：Cargo Query

任务引入
Task Introduction

小张是某货运代理公司业务员。一位客户要从中国天津向德国克内瑟贝克（Knesebeck）空运一批货物（不锈钢连接件）。请帮助小张为客户办理货物跟踪查询。

Xiao Zhang works in a freight forwarding company as a clerk. A customer intends to air a batch of goods（Stainless Steel Flexible Couplings）from Tianjin，China to Knesebeck，Germany. Please help Xiao Zhang to handle cargo tracking for customers.

任务分析
Assignment Analysis

根据主运单和分运单的信息，有时还要跟进货物起飞情况和联程中转机场起飞情况。若涉及 DDU、DDP 条款，货代业务员还要跟进货物完成到门运输。

According to the information of the total waybill and the distribution order，sometimes it is necessary to follow up the take-off situation of the flight and cargo. If the terms of DDU and DDP are involved，the freight forwarder will track the goods and provide the door-to-door service.

目前，各个航空公司都已通过网络提供货物追踪、货物查询服务。收/发货人可凭空运提单号进行货物查询。

At present，various airlines have offered cargo tracking and cargo inquiry services through the network. The consignee or consignor can conduct cargo inquiries with the air waybill number.

所以货物收发人务必保存好空运货物的运单号，输入运输单号后，可以进行空运货物追踪、查询。

Therefore, the consignor and consignee must keep the shipping number of the air cargo well. After inputting the shipping number, they can track and inquire the air cargo.

相关知识
Relevant Knowledge

一、出仓单
Compiling the Warehouse Receipt

配舱方案制定后就可着手编制出仓单（见表3-9）：出仓单的日期、承运航班的日期、装载板箱形式及数量、货物进仓顺序编号、总运单号、件数、重量、体积、目的地三字代码和备注。

The warehouse receipt (as shown in Table 3-9) can be compiled after the formulation of the cargo allocation plan: the date of the warehouse receipt, the date of the carrier flight, the form and quantity of the loading containers, the serial number of the goods entering the warehouse, the number of the total waybill, the number of pieces, the weight, the volume, the destination codes and remarks.

表3-9　　　　**出仓通知单**

发货单位：　　　　发货仓库：　　　　NO.
业务负责人：　　　　出仓日期：
销售合同号：

<table>
<tr><td>序号</td><td colspan="2">商品描述</td><td colspan="2">数量</td><td>件数</td><td>实发情况</td></tr>
<tr><td></td><td colspan="2"></td><td colspan="2"></td><td></td><td></td></tr>
<tr><td></td><td colspan="2"></td><td colspan="2"></td><td></td><td></td></tr>
<tr><td></td><td colspan="2"></td><td colspan="2"></td><td></td><td></td></tr>
<tr><td></td><td colspan="2"></td><td colspan="2"></td><td></td><td></td></tr>
<tr><td></td><td colspan="2"></td><td colspan="2"></td><td></td><td></td></tr>
<tr><td></td><td colspan="2"></td><td colspan="2"></td><td></td><td></td></tr>
<tr><td colspan="2">提货人及证件号</td><td colspan="2"></td><td>提货车号</td><td colspan="2"></td></tr>
<tr><td rowspan="2">备注</td><td colspan="6">××公司</td></tr>
<tr><td colspan="6">货物限于　年　月　日前提完</td></tr>
</table>

审核：　　　　用章人：　　　　仓管员：　　　　提货人：

Table 3-9 **The Warebouse Receipt**

Consignor: Delivery Warehouse: No. :

Business Operator: Delivery Date: Sales Contract Number:

<table>
<tr><td>Serial Number</td><td>Commodity Description</td><td>Quantity</td><td>Number of Pieces</td><td>Actual Situation</td></tr>
<tr><td></td><td></td><td></td><td></td><td></td></tr>
<tr><td></td><td></td><td></td><td></td><td></td></tr>
<tr><td></td><td></td><td></td><td></td><td></td></tr>
<tr><td></td><td></td><td></td><td></td><td></td></tr>
<tr><td></td><td></td><td></td><td></td><td></td></tr>
<tr><td></td><td></td><td></td><td></td><td></td></tr>
<tr><td>Shipper and Certificate Number</td><td colspan="2"></td><td>Vehicle Number</td><td></td></tr>
<tr><td rowspan="2">Remarks</td><td colspan="4">×× Company</td></tr>
<tr><td colspan="4">The goods shall be completed before mm/dd/yy</td></tr>
</table>

Reviewer: Seal User: Warebouse Keeper: Consignee:

二、提板箱

Lifting the Board or Container

向航空公司申领板、箱并办理相应的手续。提板、箱时，应领取相应的塑料薄膜和网。对所使用的板、箱要登记、销号。

Apply to the airline for the board, the container and go through the corresponding procedures. When lifting the board or container, you should receive the corresponding plastic film and net. Register and eliminate the number of boards and containers used.

三、货物装箱装板

Packing the Board or Container

不要用错集装箱、集装板；不要用错板型、箱型；不要超装箱板尺寸；要垫衬，封盖好塑料纸，防潮、防雨淋；集装箱、板内货物尽可能配装整齐，结构稳定，并接紧网索，防止运输途中倒塌；对于大宗货物、集中托运货物，尽可能将整票货物装一个或几个板、箱内运输。

Do not use the wrong container or board; do not use the wrong board type or container type; do not oversize the container or board. In addition, cover the plastic paper to prevent moisture and rain; keep tidy in the container, stable in structure, and connected to the net as far as possible to prevent collapse during transportation. For bulk cargo and concentrated consignment, the whole package should be transported in one or several containers and boards as much as possible.

四、签单

Signing the Bill

货运单在盖好海关放行章后还需要到航空公司签单，只有签单确认后才允许将单、货交给航空公司。

The waybill needs to be signed by the airline after the customs release stamp is sealed. Only after the confirmation can the waybill and cargo be delivered to the airline.

五、交接发运

Delivering the Cargo

交接是向航空公司交单交货，由航空公司安排航空运输。

The handover is to deliver the goods to the airline, and the airline arranges the air transportation.

交单就是将随机单据和应有承运人留存的单据交给航空公司。随机单据包括第二联航空运单正本、发票、装箱单、产地证明、品质鉴定证书。

The delivery of the waybill is to hand over the random document and the documents retained by the carrier to the airline. The random documents include the original copy of air waybill, invoice, packing list, certificate of origin, and certificate of quality appraisal.

交货即把与单据相符的货物交给航空公司。交货前必须粘贴或拴挂货物标签、清点和核对货物、填制货物交接清单。大宗货、集中托运货，以整板、整箱称重交接。零散小货按票称重，计年交接。

The goods are delivered to the airline in conformity with the documents. Before delivery, the goods must be labeled, counted as well as checked, and cargo handover list should be completed. Bulk cargo and centralized consignment shall be transferred to the whole board and the whole container. Scattered goods are weighed according to the package and are transferred annually.

任务实施
Task Implementation

需要联程中转的货物，在货物运出后，要求航空公司提供二程、三程航班中转信息，确认中转情况。及时将上述信息反馈给客户，以便遇到有不正常情况及时处理。

After the goods are shipped out, the airlines are required to provide two-way and three-way flight transit information to confirm the transit situation. Timely feedback the above informationto the customer in order to deal with abnormal situations in time.

一、空运货物查询
Air Cargo Enquiry

1. 查询网站
Query Website Redberrytrack

查询航空公司网站，如图 3-9 所示。

Query airline website, as shown in Figure 3-9.

图 3-9　航空公司网站截图

2. 单击“船期查询”按钮，在 AWB PREFIX 处输入提单号前三位

Click the“SHIPPING INQUIRIES”Button, and Enter the First Three Digits of the Bill of Lading at AWB PREFIX

如“999”。这三位数代表不同的航空公司，单击“SERCH”按钮，如图3-10所示。

Such as “999” . These three digits represent different airlines. Click the “SERCH” button, as shown in Figure 3-10.

图3-10　船期查询

3. 单击“AIR CHINA”按钮，如图3-11所示

Click the “AIR CHINA” Button, As Shown in Figure 3-11

图3-11　地区查询

4. 输入航空运单号后 8 位及验证码，单击“SEARCH”按钮，如图 3-12 所示

Enter the 8 Digits after the Air Waybill Number as well as the Verification Code, and Click the “SEARCH” Button, as Shown in Figure 3-12

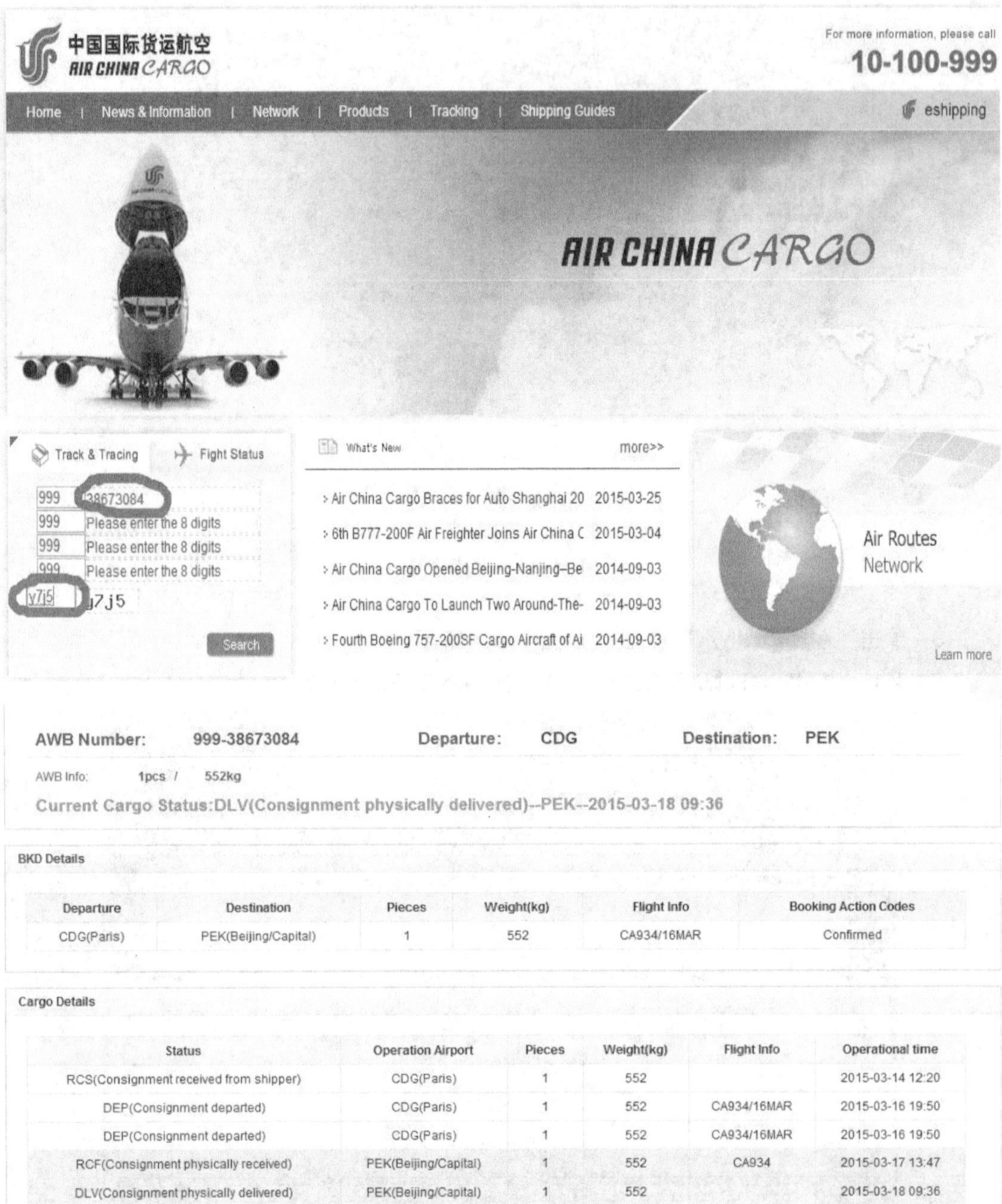

图 3-12 航空运单号查询

思考题
Questions

1. 货物装箱装板时，有哪些注意事项？

What are the precautions when loading and unloading the goods?

2. 请说明获得资格证书 CIFA 考试的成绩合格标准。

Please indicate the eligibility criteria for the CIFA qualification examination.

任务四　多式联运
Task Four: Multimodal Transport

【知识目标】
Knowledge Goals

1. 能说明多式联运的优势。
   To be able to illustrate the advantages of multimodal transport.
2. 能说明多式联运业务的内容。
   To be able to explain the contents of the multimodal transport business.

【技能目标】
Skill Goals

1. 能模拟货运代理公司的多式联运经营人，为客户审单。
   To be able to act as the multimodal transport operator of the freight forwarding company and check the bill for the customers.
2. 能模拟货运代理公司的多式联运经营人，为客户订舱。
   To be able to act as the multimodal transport operator of the freight forwarding company and book the shipping space for the customers.

子任务之一　多式联运业务培训
Section One: Multimodal Transport Training

任务引入
Task Introduction

小张刚入职某货运代理公司业务员岗位。今天，他主要负责多式联运业务。请为小张讲解一下多式联运经营都有哪些类型吧。

Xiao Zhang has just joined in a freighting company and worked as a freight forwarder. Today, he is mainly responsible for the multimodal transport business. Please explain to Xiao Zhang what types of multimodal transport operations are available.

任务分析
Assignment Analysis

多式联运的货物主要集装箱货物，具有集装箱运输的特点。多式联运是一票到底，实行单一运费率的运输。发货人只要订立一份合同，一次付费，一次保险，通过一张单证即可完成全程运输。

The main container cargo of multimodal transport is characterized by container transportation. Multimodal transport is the transportation of a single shipment. As long as the shipper concludes a contract for one payment, one insurance and one document, the whole transportation can be completed.

相关知识
Relevant Knowledge

一、多式联运的定义
Definition of Multimodal Transport

多式联运是指由一个多式联运经营人控制或所有由一个承运人运营的使用两个或两个以上的运输方式的运输系统。

Multimodal transport refers to a transport system usually operated by a carrier with more than one mode of transport under the control or ownership of one operator.

货物运输在国际贸易中通常会经手几个承运人并且要通过两个以上的运输方式才能完成。

Goods moving in international trade often have to pass through the hands of more than one carrier and over more than one mode of transport.

在传统的分段运输中，发货人/托运人需要与每个区段的承运人签订单独的运输合同，各区段承运人所承担的责任又受限于该承运人实际履行的情况。

Under the conventional system of segmented transport, the consignor enters into separate contracts with each carrier, the liability of each carrier being limited to the carriage performed by him.

如果必要，发货人或者其代理人还要负责货物在转运点的仓储。

The consignor or his agent has also to attend to another, including, if necessary, warehousing of the goods at any transshipment point.

二、多式联运的优势

The Advantages of Multimodal Transport

1. 多式联运将货物在转运地损失的时间减到最小

Minimizing Time Loss at Transshipment Points

多式联运是单独营运计划协调的，大大减少了货物在转运地时间上的损失以及灭失的风险、盗窃和货物的损害。

Multimodal transport, which is planned and coordinated as a single operation, minimizes the loss of time and the risk of loss, pilferage and damage to cargo at transshipment points.

多式联运经营人在转运点有自己的通信网络，保证货物在转运点能顺利转移并继续往前运输。

The multimodal transport operator maintains his own communication links and co-ordinates interchange and onward carriage smoothly at transshipment points.

2. 多式联运提供更快捷的货物运输方式

Providing Faster Transit of Goods

更快捷的运输方式可以减少市场距离相隔较远和资金紧张带来的不利因素。

The faster transit of goods made possible under multimodal transport reduces the disadvantages of distance from markets and the tying-up of capital.

3. 减少了文件和手续上的麻烦

Reducing the Burden of Documentation and Formalities

将分段运输中涉及的文件和其他手续上的麻烦减少到最小。

The burden of documentation and other formalities connected with segmented transport is reduced to a minimum.

4. 节约成本

Saving Cost

多式联运可以节约运输成本，这是由于它在费用方面占有优势，这些优势表现在多式联运人收取的联运货运价格和货物的保险费较低。

The savings in costs resulting from these advantages are usually reflected in the through freight rates charged by the multimodal transport operator and also in the cost of cargo insurance.

5. 只与一个代理打交道

Establishing Only One Agency to Deal With

托运人只与多式联运经营人联系处理所有与货物运输相关的问题，包括货物灭失，或者损失以及在目的地延迟交货所带来的损失赔偿的处理。

The consignor has to deal with only the multimodal transport operator in all matters relating to the transportation of his goods, including the settlement of claims for loss of goods, or damage to them, or delay in delivery at destination.

6. 减少出口成本

Reducing Cost of Exports

多式联运系统内在的优势有利于降低出口成本和增强其在国际市场上的竞争力。

The inherent advantages of multimodal transport system will help to reduce the cost of exports and improve their competitive position in the international market.

任务实施

Task Implementation

当前，不同类型的多式联运营运包括了不同类型的运输组合方式。这些方式有海运/空运，空运/公路运输，铁路运输/公路运输/内陆水路运输—海运—铁路运输/公路运输/内陆水路运输，小陆桥运输，陆桥运输，驮运联运和火车车厢运输船。

Currently, different types of multimodal transport operations involving different combinations are taking place. These are sea/air, air/road, rail/road/inland waterways-sea-rail/road/inland waterways, mini-bridge, land bridge, piggyback and sea train.

一、海/空联合运输

Sea/Air

海空联运结合了海运自身的经济实惠和空运快速的特点。

Sea/air combines in itself the economy of sea transport and the speed of air transport.

这种组合运输模式适合运输诸如电子电器产品、计算机和照相设备等高价值的物品。

The economics of this combination mode favor high value items like electronics, electrical goods, computers and photographic equipment.

二、空运/公路联合运输

Air/Road

在空运/公路联合运输中，公路运输现在越来越多地被用于远距离的货车空运运输中，有时需要穿过国界，与主要的航空公司本部联系提供长途运输服务，像横渡太平洋，横渡大西洋以及洲际间的运输。

In air/road, road transport is now being increasingly used for trucking air freight over long distances, sometimes across national boundaries, to connect with the main bases of airlines operating long haul services such as transpacific, transatlantic and intercontinental.

三、铁路/公路/内陆水路—海运—铁路/公路/内陆水路联合运输

Rail/Road/Inland Waterways-sea-rail/Road/Inland Waterways

铁路/公路/内陆水路—海运—铁路/公路/内陆水路联合运输方式通常用于当货物需要通过海运从一个国家运输到另外一个国家，并且货物从内陆中心运输至原产地港口或者从港口运至目的地国家的一个内陆中心采用一个或者更多的内陆运输方式，如铁路、公路或者内陆水路运输等方式。

Rail/road/inland waterways - sea - rail/road/inland waterways mode is in common use when goods have to be moved by sea from one country to another and one or more inland modes of transport such as rail, road or inland waterways have to be used for moving goods from an inland center to the seaport in the country of origin or from the seaport to an inland center in the country of destination.

四、小陆桥运输

Mini-bridge

小陆桥运输涉及集装箱运输，由海运承运人签发多式联运提单，通过船舶将货物从一个国家的港口运往另外一个国家的港口，并且再通过铁路运输运往二级国家的二级港口城市，在二级港口城市的终点站结束于铁路承运人。

Mini-bridge involves the movement of containers, under a through bill of lading issued by an ocean carrier, by a vessel from a port in one country to a port in another country and then by rail to a second port city in the second country, terminating at the rail carrier terminal in the second port city.

五、陆桥运输

Land Bridge

陆桥运输系统用于海陆或者海—陆—海路线部分的陆路集装箱运输。在这种情况下，海运承运人支付含铁路运输部分的统一运费并签发联运提单。这一运输系统主要用于某一个特定的重要的国际航线的集装箱运输。

Land bridge system concerns itself with shipment of containers overland as a part of a sea-land and or a sea-land-sea route. In this case, the railways are paid a flat rate by the ocean carrier who issues the through bill of lading. This system is in operation for the movement of containers on certain important international routes.

六、驮运联运

Piggyback

驮运联运是通过公路和铁路运输组合成为的多式陆上运输系统。它联合了铁路的快速和可靠性用于长途运输，与公路运输的门到门的灵活性用于货物的取送。

Piggyback is a system of unitized multimodal land transportation of transport by road and rail. It combines in itself the speed and reliability of rail on long truck hauls with door-to-door flexibility of road transport for collection and delivery.

七、火车车厢运输船

Sea Train

火车车厢运输船是另一个多式联运系统的创新，它联合了铁路和海洋运输。它类似于滚装装运系统，除此之外，在滚装运载工具的地方使用机动轨道车，使得地理上与海运分离的铁路运输系统能够被海运承运人联合起来使用。

Sea train is another innovation in the multimodal transport system involving the use of rail and ocean transport. It is similar to the roll-on, roll-off system except that in the place of the ro-ro vehicle a rail car is used so that geographically separated rail systems can be connected by the use of an ocean carrier.

思考题
Questions

1. 多式联运的好处有哪些？

What are the advantages of multimodal transport?

2. 请说明多式联运的类型。

Please indicate the types of multimodal transport.

子任务之二　多式联运业务操作
Section Two：Multimodal Transport Operation

任务引入
Task Introduction

小张刚入职某货运代理公司做业务员。今天，他接待了一位客户。该客户打算从澳大利亚往蒙古国运输一批货物，具体信息参见商业发票，如图 4-1 所示。请帮助小张为客户办理该项多式联运业务。

Xiao Zhang has just joined in a freighting company and worked as a freight forwarder. Today, he received a client. The client intends to ship a batch of goods from Australia to Mongolia. See the commercial invoice for details, as shown in Figure 4-1. Please help Xiao Zhang to handle the multimodal transport business for his client.

任务分析
Assignment Analysis

多式联运是不同方式的综合组织，全程运输均是由多式联运经营人组织完成的。无论涉及几种运输方式，分为几个运输区段，由多式联运经营人对货运全程负责。

Multimodal transport is a comprehensive organization of different modes, and the entire transport is organized by multimodal transport operators. Regardless of the several modes of transport involved and several transport sections divided, and the multimodal transport operator is responsible for the whole process of freight transportation.

COMMERCIAL INVOICE

EXPORTER	COMMERCIAL INVOICE NO.	EXPORT AGENT'S REF.	PAGE NO.
CUMMINS FILTRATION 31 GARDEN ST KILSYTH VIC 3137 AUSTRALIA	18673188 & 18873187	S00001622	1 of 1
	HOUSE BILL S00001622	**OWNER'S REFERENCE**	
	L/C NUMBER & DATE	**ORDER NUMBERS** E170227	

CONSIGNEE / BUYER	BUYER (IF NOT CONSIGNEE)
CUMINS MONGOLIA INVESTMENT LLC UNIT 413, LEVEL 4 CENTRAL TOWER 2 SUKHBAATAR SQUARE 8TH KHOROO SUKHBAATAR DISTRICT ULAANBATAR 14200 MONGOLIA	

NOTIFY PARTY	EXPORTER'S BANK	
TIANJIN HUAHENG INTL FORWARDING CO LTD RM 713, JIEFANGBEI RD JINGONG BUILDING, NO 72 ATT MR WANG HENG PH 86 22 23300529 TIANJIN 300010 CHINA	**ACCOUNT NUMBER**	**SWIFT CODE**
	TERMS / METHOD OF PAYMENT CFR - Cost And Freight	

PORT OF ORIGIN	DATE		
AUMEL - Melbourne	15-APR-17		
FINAL DESTINATION	**DATE**	**INSURANCE POLICY NUMBER**	**INSURED VALUE**
MNULN - Ulaanbaatar	17-APR-17		72416.80 USD

LEG 1 VESSEL / VOYAGE / IMO(LLOYDS)	LEG 1 PORT OF LOADING	DATE	LEG 1 PORT OF DISCHARGE	DATE
OOCL LE HAVRE 0082N	AUMEL - Melbourne	17-APR-17	Port Kelang	01-MAY-17
LEG 2 VESSEL / VOYAGE / IMO(LLOYDS)	**LEG 2 PORT OF LOADING**	**DATE**	**LEG 2 PORT OF DISCHARGE**	**DATE**
TRANSHIP	Port Kelang	10-MAY-17	CNTXG - Tianjin New Pt	25-MAY-17
LEG 3 VESSEL / VOYAGE / IMO(LLOYDS)	**LEG 3 PORT OF LOADING**	**DATE**	**LEG 3 PORT OF DISCHARGE**	**DATE**
RAIL	CNTXG - Tianjin New Pt	05-JUN-17	MNULN - Ulaanbaatar	20-JUN-17

MARKS & NUMBERS	DESCRIPTION OF GOODS (GENERAL)	PACKAGES	TOTAL WEIGHT	TOTAL VOLUME
	pg platinum coolant	36 DRM	40528.000 KG	53.900 M3

CONTAINER NUMBER	SEAL NUMBER	MODE	TYPE	WEIGHT	VOLUME
TCKU2418747	H092474	FCL	20GP - Twenty foot general purpose	20194.000 KG	26.950 M3
FCIU4913820	4982111	FCL	20GP - Twenty foot general purpose	20334.000 KG	26.950 M3

PRODUCT CODE	DESCRIPTION OF GOODS (ITEMS)	QUANTITY	UNIT PRICE	AMOUNT
CC3608600	PG PLATINUM 1000LTR COOLANT	31KL	2200.00	68,200.00
CC3606100	1000LTR DIESEL EXHAUST FLUID	5KL	843.36	4,216.80

OTHER COSTS	EXCLUDED CHARGES	INCLUDED CHARGES
1. International Freight		3500.00 USD
2. International Insurance	198.00 USD	
3. ExWorks		
4. Inland Freight		
5. Packing		
6. Landing		
7. Dutiable Other		
8. Non-Dutiable Other		
9. Commission		
10. Discount		
TOTALS	198.00 USD	3500.00 USD

TOTAL THIS PAGE: 72,416.80

INVOICE TOTAL (CFR) **72416.80 USD**

EXPORTER'S DECLARATION

I, the authorized signatory hereby declare that I have authority to make and sign this certificate on behalf of the aforesaid supplier, and that I have means of knowing and do hereby certify as follows:-

1. That this invoice is in all respects correct and contains a true and full statement of the price actually paid for the goods, and the actual quantity thereof.
2. That no different invoice of the goods mentioned in the said invoice has been or will be furnished to anyone and that no arrangement or understanding affecting the purchase price of the said goods has been or will be made or entered into between the said exporter and purchaser, or by anyone on behalf of either of them, either by way of discount, rebate, compensation or in any manner whatever other than shown on this invoice as follows:-

EXPORT CLEARANCE NO.	EXPORT DATE	PLACE AND DATE OF ISSUE
ACTFNK9AR	10-APR-17	17-APR-17, Melbourne, Australia
ADDITIONAL INFORMATION		**SIGNATORY'S COMPANY** MEL
		NAME OF SIGNATORY Paul Gallard
		SIGNATURE (FOR AND ON BEHALF OF THE EXPORTER)

图 4-1　商业发票

相关知识
Relevant Knowledge

一、多式联运提单介绍
Multimodal Transport Bill of Lading

多式联运提单（见表 4-1）主要用于成组化的货物，特别是集装箱运输，它把海、陆、空、公路、河流等单一运输有机结合起来，以全程提单来完成一笔跨国进口货物业务的运输。

Multimodal transport bill of lading (as shown in Table 4-1) is mainly used for grouped cargo, especially container transportation, which combines a single transport of sea, land, air, road, river, etc., and completes a transnational import cargo business with a full bill of lading.

表 4-1　　多式联运提单

<table>
<tr><td colspan="3">托运人</td><td colspan="5" rowspan="5">除本合同另有规定外，收到的货物表面状态良好。承运人按照本文件的规定办理。
1）承诺完成或促使完成从货物接收地点到本文件指定交付地点的整个运输；
2）承担本文件规定的运输责任。其中一份提单必须及时背书交回，以换取货物或交货单</td></tr>
<tr><td colspan="3">收货人或指示人</td></tr>
<tr><td colspan="3">通知方地址</td></tr>
<tr><td>前程运输</td><td colspan="2">收货地点</td></tr>
<tr><td>船名航次</td><td colspan="2">装货港</td></tr>
<tr><td>卸货港</td><td colspan="2">交货地</td><td colspan="3">运费付至</td><td colspan="2">正本提单数量</td></tr>
<tr><td colspan="2">集装箱铅封号
或唛头</td><td colspan="2">包装数量和类型</td><td>货物描述</td><td colspan="2">毛重
（千克）</td><td>体积
（立方米）</td></tr>
</table>

续表

<table>
<tr><td rowspan="3">运费和费用</td><td>兹证明上述正本提单数量已签署，其中一份已完成，另一份作废</td></tr>
<tr><td>签发地点及日期</td></tr>
<tr><td>承运人的代理人签字</td></tr>
</table>

Table 4-1　　　Multimodal Transport Bill of Lading

<table>
<tr><td colspan="2">Shipper</td><td colspan="3" rowspan="5">Received the goods in apparent good order and condition as specified below unless otherwise stated herein. The Carrier in accordance with the provisions contained in this document.
1) undertakes to perform or to procure the performance of the entire transport from the place at which the goods are taken in charge to the place designated for delivery in this document.
2) Assumes liability as prescribed in this document for such transport. One of the Bills of Lading must be surrendered duly indorsed in exchange for the goods or delivery order.</td></tr>
<tr><td colspan="2">Consignee or Order</td></tr>
<tr><td colspan="2">Notify Address</td></tr>
<tr><td>Pre-carriage by</td><td>Place of Receipt</td></tr>
<tr><td>Ocean Vessel</td><td>Port of Loading</td></tr>
<tr><td>Port of Discharge</td><td>Place of Delivery</td><td>Freight payable at</td><td colspan="2">Number of Original B/L</td></tr>
<tr><td>Container, Seal No. or Marks and Nos.</td><td>Number and Kind of Packages</td><td>Description of Goods</td><td>Gross weight (KGS)</td><td>Measurement (m^3)</td></tr>
<tr><td colspan="2" rowspan="3">Freight & Charges</td><td colspan="3">In witness where of the number of original Bills of Lading stated above have been signed , one of which being accomplished, the other (s) to be avoid.</td></tr>
<tr><td colspan="3">Place and date of issue</td></tr>
<tr><td colspan="3">Signed for or on behalf of the Carrier</td></tr>
</table>

二、缮制或审核多式联运提单时的注意事项

Precautions for Completing or Reviewing Multimodal Bills of Lading

（1）表面上应注有多式联运经营人或承运人或船长或其代理人的签名。

The signature of multimodal transport operator or carrier or master or their agent shall appear on the surface.

（2）表明货物已发运，接受监管或装船并有装运日期。

Indicate that the goods have been shipped, subject to supervision or shipment, and have a date of shipment.

（3）提交的单据是全套的。

The documents submitted are in full set.

（4）有货物的接受监管地和最后目的地，并与信用证规定相符。

The place of supervision and final destination of the goods is in conformity with the provisions of the letter of credit.

（5）在所有方面均符合信用证规定，并可参照海运提单缮制或审核。

In all respects, it complies with the provisions of the letter of credit and can be controlled or reviewed by reference to the bill of lading.

任务实施

Task Implementation

一、询价及订舱

Enquiry and Booking

向船公司询价。订舱时，货物描述中要添加过境字样“THE GOODS IN TRANSIT TO MONGOLIA VIA XING GANG CHINA”。同时要注意货物重量控制在限重之内。

Make an inquiry at the shipping company. When booking space, the transit words “The GOODS IN TRANSIT TO MONGOLIA VIA XING GANG CHINA” should be added to the cargo description. At the same time, it should be noted that the cargo weight should be controlled within the weight limit.

二、接单及审单（船靠港之前）

Receiving and Reviewing Documents (before the ship arrives)

船开航以后，船代会发出单据：海运提单（见图 4-2）、货代提单装箱单、发票、食品或是其他物品会有原产地证书、植检证、健康证等。

After the ship sails, the shipping agent will issue documents: the shipping bill of lading (and appendix) (as shown in Figure 4-2), the freight forwarding bill of lading, the packing list, the invoice, certificate of origin for the food or other items, plant inspection certificate, health certificate, etc.

多式联运经营人须进行审单，注意 CONSIGNEE，过境字样，件、重、尺及其他信息与单据是否一致。如有不一致，及时与相关负责人（如发出单据和提单的人）联系，

PROFORMA

TLX: 33057 COSCO SHIPPING
FAX: +86(21) 65458984
PORT TO PORT OR COMBINED TRANSPORT BILL OF LADING

1. Shipper Insert Name Address and Phone/Fax FIRST PORT LOGISTICS PTY LTD UNIT 1403 31 SPRING STREET MELBOURNE VIC 3000 AUSTRALIA PHONE: +61 3 9654 9724 FAX: +61 3 8677 3323	Booking No. 6119959950 Bill of Lading No. COSU6119959950 Export References
2. Consignee Insert Name Address and Phone/Fax COSCO TIANJIN INTL. FREIGHT CO LTD ROOM 2102 OCEAN PLAZA, HEIBEI DISTRICT 30010 TIANJIN CHINA ATT MR MA YAN PH +86 22 6670 8155	Forwarding Agent and References FMC/CHB No Point and Country of Origin
3. Notify Party Insert Name Address and Phone/Fax (It is agreed that no responsibility shall attach to the Carrier or his agents for failure to notify) TIANJIN HUAHENG INTL FORWARDING CO LTD RM 713, JINGONG BUILDING, NO 72 JIEFANGBEI ROAD TIANJIN 30010 CHINA ·	Also Notify Party-routing & Instructions · ATT MR WANG HENG PH 86 22 23300529 PHONE: 86 22 23300529 FAX: 86 22 23125406

4. Combined Transport* Pre-Carriage by	5. Combined Transport* Place of Receipt MELBOURNE		
6. Ocean Vessel Voy. No. OOCL LE HAVRE 0082N	7. Port of Loading MELBOURNE	Service Contract No.	Commodity Code
8. Port of Discharge TIANJIN NEW PORT	9. Combined Transport* Place of Delivery XINGANG	Type of Movement FCL / FCL CY-CY	

Marks & Nos Container / Seal No	No. of Container or Packages	Description of Goods (If Dangerous Goods, See Clause 20)	Gross Weight	Measurement
N/M	36 DRUMS	20GP X 2 PG PLATINUM COOLANT CARGO IN TRANSIT TO MONGOLIA VIA XINGANG CHINA IS UNDER THE CONSIGNEE'S ARRANGEMENT, ACCOUNT AND RESPONSIBILITY, CONSIGNEE'S ACCOUNT AND RISKS	40528.000KGS	53.9000CBM
OCEAN FREIGHT PREPAID ON CY-CY TERM SHIPPER'S LOAD STOW COUNT AND SEAL SHIPPED ON BOARD				

图 4-2 提单

确认后再进行更改。

Multimodal transport operators are required to conduct the review, paying attention to CONSIGNEE, transit words, pieces, weights, feet and other information consistent with the documents. If there is any discrepancy, contact the relevant person in charge (such as the person issuing the documents and bills of lading) in time and make changes after confirmation.

三、准备单据

Preparing Documents

（一）单据复印件

Copies of Documents

（1）提单复印三份（一份换单，一份报关，一份做特转）。

Three copies of Bill of Lading (one for exchange, one for customs declaration and one for special transfer).

（2）箱单（如图 4-3 所示）、发票及证书复印两份（一份报关，一份随铁路大票）。

Two copies of the packing list (as shown in Figure 4-3), invoice and certificate (one for customs declaration and one for railway tickets).

（3）D/O 复印件（特转需要 5 份——报关、铁路请车、车队、随车单据、留底；自提需要 4 份，不用给车队）。

D/O copy (5 copies are needed for special transfer, such as customs declaration, railway vehicle request, vehicle team, on-board documents, and keeping the record; 4 copies are needed for self-delivery without giving to the vehicle team).

（二）报关单据

Customs Declaration Documents

提单复印件一份，箱单一份，发票一份（食品类需要证书一份），报关草联一份，转关单（白联）一份，D/O 及 D/O 复印件各一份。

One copy of bill of lading, one copy of packing list, one copy of invoice (one copy of food certificate is required), one copy of customs declaration form, one copy of customs transfer form (blank form), one copy of D/O and D/O.

EXPORT PACKING LIST

EXPORTER	PACKING LIST NO.	PACK DATE	PAGE NO.
CUMMINS FILTRATION 31 GARDEN ST KILSYTH VIC 3137 AUSTRALIA		10-APR-17	1 of 1
	HOUSE BILL: S00001622	OWNER'S REFERENCE:	
	METHOD OF DISPATCH: SEA - Sea Freight	ORDER NUMBER(S): E170227	
CONSIGNEE / BUYER CUMINS MONGOLIA INVESTMENT LLC UNIT 413, LEVEL 4 CENTRAL TOWER 2 SUKHBAATAR SQUARE 8TH KHOROO SUKHBAATAR DISTRICT ULAANBATAR 14200 MONGOLIA	BUYER (IF NOT CONSIGNEE)		

MARKS & NUMBERS	DESCRIPTION OF GOODS (GENERAL)	PACKAGES	TOTAL WEIGHT	TOTAL VOLUME
	pg platinum coolant	36 DRM	40528.000 KG	53.900 M3

INTERNAL USE ONLY

CONTAINER NUMBER	SEAL NUMBER	MODE	TYPE	WEIGHT	VOLUME
TCKU2418747	H092474	FCL	20GP - Twenty foot general purpose	20194.000 KG	26.950 M3
FCIU4913820	4982111	FCL	20GP - Twenty foot general purpose	20334.000 KG	26.950 M3

PRODUCT CODE	DESCRIPTION OF GOODS (ITEMS)	QUANTITY	NET WEIGHT	GROSS WEIGHT	VOLUME
CC3608600	PG PLATINUM 1000LTR COOLANT	31000 L	32612 KG	34758 KG	31000 L
CC3606100	1000LTR DIESEL EXHAUST FLUID	5000 L	5260 KG	5770 KG	5000 L

NAME OF AUTHORISED SIGNATORY	ORIGINAL B/L	SIGNATORY'S COMPANY
Paul Gallard	0	MEL
PLACE AND DATE OF ISSUE: 17-APR-17, Melbourne, Australia		SIGNATURE:

图 4-3 出口箱单

四、制作铁路单据

Making Railway Documents

联系蒙古客户要铁路单据的指令，确认好到站、HS 号码、品名、车站代码等，制作以后发给客户确认。

Contact Inner Mongolian customers for railway shipments, confirm the station, HS number, product name, station code, etc. , and send them to customers for confirmation after production.

箱单、发票、D/O 复印件、转关白联（盖海关放行章）、食品类需要通关单、电子凭条等随车单据与铁路三联订在一起，供外勤向铁路请车。

Packing list, invoice, D/O copy, customs clearance form (with customs release seal), customs clearance for food, electronic vouchers and other accompanying documents are linked together with the railway for field transportation.

若单票分批发运，扫描白联给二连，方便在随附关封的箱子未到口岸的情况下，其他箱子先行办理过境手续。

If the single shipment is transported in batches, scan the blank link to make it convenient for other containers to go through the transit formalities before the attached sealed ones arrive at the port.

五、特转或自送

Special Transfer or Self-delivery

（一）特转

Special Transfer

货物将由车队直接从码头提箱至堆场，一般情况下船靠港 1~3 天。特转需要给堆场发一份特转申请表、两份海运提单复印件。五洲码头需要船靠港前三天做特转，其他码头一般提前一天。日本航线一般周五靠港，最晚周四做特转。注意字迹清楚，核对提单号、箱号及箱型等信息。同一条船、同一船公司的录在一起。

The goods will be picked up by the vehicle team directly from the terminal to the yard. Generally, the vessel will dock for 1 day to 3 days. A special transfer application form and two copies of the ocean bill of lading are required to be sent to the yard. Wuzhou Wharf needs to make special transfers three days before the ship is docked, and other wharfs are generally one day ahead of schedule. Japanese routes usually dock on Fridays and make special transfers on Thursday at the latest. Pay attention to the written words, check the bill of lading number, box number and box type. The same ship or the same shipping company should be recorded together.

（二）自送

Self-delivery

货物放行后，由自有车队送箱至堆场。一般情况下，对于周前期到港的可自送，放行后报码头计划提箱，第二天早上就可以用磅单去申请火车，以免因特转不及时导致无法请车的情况。

After the goods are released, the self-owned vehicle fleet delivers the containers to the yard. Generally speaking, for those who arrive at the port before the week, they can deliver the goods by themselves, and report to the dock to pick up the container after the release. Then, they can use the pound sheet to ask for railway wagon in the morning of the next day, so as to avoid the situation that the train cannot be transferred in time due to the reason of delay.

六、海运跟踪及换单

Maritime Tracking and Order Replacement

根据提单号、箱号登陆相应船公司网站，查询货物的预抵时间。货物快到港之前，每天查询动态，以免货物提前到港。

According to the bill of lading number and the container number, the corresponding shipping company website is landed to inquire about the anticipated time of the cargo. Before the arrival of the goods, check the dynamics every day so as not to advance the arrival of the goods.

日本货物一般周五或周六到港，中外运、中远周五可换单，中海最晚周一换单，应与船公司确定换单时间，并将事先准备好的换单单据交与外勤。操作与外勤要将单据交接好，要清楚每个船公司、每条船的换单数量。外勤换单后要点清 D/O 后交给报关员，以免出现漏换问题。

Japanese cargo usually arrives at port on Friday or Saturday. Sino-foreign shipments and COSCO can exchange documents on Friday. China Shipping can exchange documents on Monday at the latest. The operation will be timely with the shipping company to determine the time for change, and the prepared documents will be handed over to the field. It is necessary to hand over the documents to the operations and the field, and to know about the number of exchanges for each shipping company and each ship. In order to avoid the problem of missing change, the D/O should be clarified and handed over to customs declaration officers after exchanging documents with the field.

七、报关、报检

Customs Declaration and Inspection Submission

（一）报关所需要单据

Documents Required for Customs Declaration

D/O 原件、D/O 复印件、转关白联（5 联）、箱单、发票、报关委托书、食品类需要商检通关单。

D/O original, D/O copy, customs transfer blank sheet (5 couplets), packing list, invoice, customs declaration letter of attorney, commodity inspection customs clearance form for the food.

（二）报关草联

Customs Declaration

（1）注意运输方式和关区代码：二连铁路0702，二连公路0705，新港海关0202，东疆海关0217。

Pay attention to transportation mode and customs code: Erlian Railway 0702, Erlian Highway 0705, Xingang Customs 0202 and Dongjiang Customs 0217.

（2）核对客户提供的箱单、发票的重量、件数和金额。天津报关可使用多币种，蒙古国一般不接受多个币种的发票。

Check the bill of lading, the weight, the number of pieces and the amount on the invoice provided by the customer. Tianjin Customs declaration can use multiple currencies, and Mongolia generally does not accept invoices in multiple currencies.

（3）确定HS. CODE编码，相同种类的货物可以归为一类，但D/O货物描述体现的品名一定要全部体现。

Determine the HS. CODE code. The same type of goods can be classified into one category, but the brand of the description of D/O goods must be fully embodied.

（三）报关流程

Customs Declaration Process

（1）根据报关草联，由电子口岸录入报单系统。

Input the declaration form system by electronic port according to the customs declaration form.

（2）太平洋报关需要保函（盖公章和法人章），其他所有单据盖公章（D/O复印件两份，箱单，发票，海运提单）。

The Pacific Customs requires a letter of guarantee (with official seal and legal person seal), and all other documents are stamped with official seals (two copies of D/O, packing list, invoice, and ocean bill of lading).

（3）船靠港前，刷出转关白联，核对相关信息（船名、航次、提单号、箱号、重量、数量）录入是否有误。

Check whether relevant information (ship name, voyage number, bill of lading number, container number, weight and quantity) is incorrectly recorded before the ship approaches port.

(4) 外勤换回 D/O 后，分单的时候将 D/O 信息（重量、数量）与白联再次核对。

After the field service is replaced with D/O, the D/O information (weight and quantity) will be checked again with the blank sheet.

八、铁路请车

Applying for Railway

偏载分为 X 轴（横向）和 Y 轴（纵向）。若 X 轴偏载 50~60mm，需要向铁路提供保函才能正常发运。60~80mm 按偏载箱装车，需要主任签字。80~100mm 需要装箱照片，超过 100mm 以上需要调偏。

Bias loads are divided into X-axis (horizontal) and Y-axis (vertical). If the X-axis load is off-loaded 50-60mm, it is necessary to provide a letter of guarantee to the railway to be shipped normally. 60 - 80mm is loaded in unbalanced load container, which needs the signature of the director. 80 -100mm needs to be packed with photos, and more than 100mm needs to be adjusted.

20’ GP 限重 24 吨，超过 24 吨<总重<30480KGS，按照加强箱运输。

The 20’ GP has a weight limit of 24 tons, more than 24 tons <total weight <30480KGS, and is transported according to the reinforcement container.

40’ HC 限重 30.48 吨，超重箱需要按照设备运输。首先由内勤操作从网络平台申请铁路计划，待铁路编组站有相应车型后装车及加固，请主任现场验车后，用铁路计划号请计划发运。

The 40’ HC has a weight limit of 30.48 tons, and the overweight container needs to be transported according to the equipment. Firstly, the railway plan is applied for from the network platform by the internal service operation. After the railway marshaling station has the corresponding model, the vehicle is loaded and reinforced. After the on-site inspection, please use the railway plan number to request the planned shipment.

九、动态跟踪及回空

Tracking and Returning

货物发运后，及时录入过境系统，并将发运信息及箱号准确地提供给蒙古国收货人。

After the goods are shipped, they are entered into the transit system promptly. The shipping information and container number will be provided to the Mongolian consignee accurately.

跟踪货物抵达二连浩特的日期和过境日期，若发生滞留问题，及时了解情况并解决。

Track the arrival date and transit date of the goods in Erenhot. If there is any detention problem, keep abreast of the situation and resolve it in time.

按照提供给蒙古客户的免箱期（20~25 天）及时跟踪并提示客户及时安排回空，以免产生滞箱费。蒙古段的用箱期始于扎门乌德，止于二连浩特。

According to the free time period（20-25 days）provided to Mongolian customers, the customer will be promptly tracked and reminded to return the container so as to avoid the demurrage charges. The period of container use in Mongolia began in Zamen Ude and ended in Erenhot.

根据船公司的要求，及时将回空指令提供给蒙古代理。所有箱子必须按照指令进行回空操作，否则产生的费用由过失方承担。

According to the requirement of the shipping company, the instruction for returning containers will be provided to the Mongolian agent in time. All containers must be returned in accordance with the instructions; otherwise the costs incurred shall be borne by the faulty party.

集装箱异地回空，及时跟踪动态并进行核联操作。

Containers are returned to different places, tracking the dynamics in time and conducting joint operation.

集装箱回空天津，及时跟踪到场情况并办理下线，安排司机用入场联进行回空操作。外勤及时取回回空联并到船公司核销。如发生回空堆场押联的情况，应及时确认费用明细，若无问题安排缴费赎联。

Containers are returned to Tianjin, and the arrival situation is tracked in time and offline is handled. Drivers are arranged to use the entrance sheet to carry out the operation. The field promptly takes back the blank sheet and goes to the shipping company for verification. Confirm the cost details in a timely manner, and arrange for the payment and redemption if there is no problem.

办理下线、核联等操作，内勤外勤做好交接记录，以免发生遗漏而产生滞纳金的情况。

Handle offline, check-up and other operations, and make the handover records of the internal and external work, so as to avoid late fees caused by omission.

思考题
Questions

1. 缮制或审核多式联运提单时的注意事项有哪些?

What are the precautions when completing or reviewing multimodal bills of lading?

2. 请说明多式联运业务的流程。

Please explain the process of the multimodal transport business.

参考文献
References

[1] 杨性如．物流人员专业英语［M］．北京：中国劳动社会保障出版社，2004.
Yang Xingru. Logistics English for Logisticians［M］. Beijing: China Labor and Social Security Press, 2009.

[2] 中国国际货运代理协会．新编国际货运代理专业英语［M］．北京：中国商务出版社，2015.
China International Freight Forwarders Association. New English Course for International Freight Forwarders［M］. Beijing: China Commerce and Trade Press, 2015.

[3] 彭娟，郑美琴．国际货运代理实务［M］．西安：西北工业大学出版社，2015.
Peng Juan, Zheng Meiqin. International Freight Forwarders Practic［M］. Xi'an: Northwestern Polytechnical University Press, 2015.

[4] 刘晶璟，程红兰，刘英．物流与货代英语［M］．武汉：武汉大学出版社，2015.
Liu Jingjing, Cheng Honglan, Liu Ying. Logistics and Forwarding English［M］. Wuhan: Wuhan University Press, 2015.

[5] 张明齐，武莉，刘宝森．国际货运代理实务［M］．南京：南京大学出版社，2018.
Zhang Mingqi, Wu Li, Liu Baosen. International Freight Forwarders Practice［M］. Nanjing: Nanjing University Press, 2018.

附录 I
Appendix I

一、术语

Terms

（一）船代

Shipping Agent

Shipping Agent 船舶代理

Handling Agent 操作代理

Booking Agent 订舱代理

Cargo Canvassing 揽货

FFF：Freight Forwarding Fee 货代佣金

Brokerage / Commission 佣金

（二）订舱

Booking

Booking 订舱

Booking Note 订舱单

Booking Number 订舱号

Dock Receipt 场站收据

M/F（Manifest）：a manifest that lists only cargo，without freight and charges 舱单

Cable/Telex Release 电放

A Circular Letter 通告信/通知书

PIC：Person in Charge 具体负责操作人员

The Said Party 所涉及的一方

On Board B/L：A B/L in which a carrier acknowledges that goods have been placed on board a certain vessel. Used to satisfy the requirements of a L/C=On Board 提单

Cancellation 退关箱

（三）港口

Port

BP Base Port 基本港

Prompt Release 即时放行

Transit Time 航程时间 / 中转时间

Cargo availability at destination in 货物运抵目的地

Second Carrier（第）二程船

In Transit 中转

Transportation Hub 中转港

（四）拖车

Trailer

Tractor 牵引车/拖头

Low-bed 低平板车

Trailer 拖车

Transporter 运输车

Trucking Company 车队（汽车运输公司）

Axle load 轴负荷

Tire-load 轮胎负荷

Toll Gate 收费口

（五）保税

Bonded

Bonded Area 保税区

Bonded Goods（ Goods in Bond）保税货物

Bonded Warehouse 保税库

Caged stored at bonded warehouse 进入海关监管

Fork Lift 叉车

Loading Platform 装卸平台

（六）船期

Voyage

A Friday（Tuesday / Thursday）sailing 周五班

A fortnight sailing 双周班

A bi-weekly sailing 周双班

A monthly sailing 每月班

On-schedule arrival / departure 准班抵离

ETA：Estimated （Expected）Time of Arrival 预计到达时间

ETB：Estimated （Expected） Time of Berthing 预计靠泊时间

ETD：Estimated （Expected）Time of Departure 预计离泊时间

The sailing Schedule/Vessels are subject to change without prior notice 船期/船舶如有变更将不事先通知

Closing Date 截止申报时间

Cut-off time 截关日

（七）费用

Freight

Ocean Freight 海运费

Sea Freight 海运费

Freight Rate 海运价

Charge / Fee（收）费

Dead Freight 空舱费

Dead Space：Space in a car，truck，vessel，etc.，that is not utilized 亏舱

Surcharge / Additional Charge 附加费

Toll 桥/境费

Charges that are below a just and reasonable level 低于正当合理的收费

Market Price Level 市场价水平

Special Rate 特价

Rock Bottom Price 最低底价

Best Obtainable Price 市场最好价

Freight to Collect 运费到付

Freight Payable at Destination 运费到付

Back Freight 退货运费

Fixed Price 固定价格

Commission 佣金

Rebate 回扣/折扣

Drayage charge：made for local hauling by dray or truck 拖运费

GRI：General Rate Increase 运价上调

SGRI：Second General Rate Increase 第二次运价上调

GRD：General Rate Decrease 运价下调

TGRD：Temporary General Rate Decrease 临时运价下调

PSS：Peak Season Surcharge 旺季附加费

Wharfage：A charge assessed by a pier against freight handled over the pier 码头附加费

THC：Terminal Handling Charge 码头操作附加费

ORC：Origin Receiving Charge 始发接单费

CUC：Chassis Usage Charge 拖车运费

IAC：Inter-modal Administrative Charge（U. S. Inland Surcharge）内陆运输附加费

DDC：Destination Delivery Charge（目的地卸货费）

OAC：Origin Accessory Charge 始发港杂

MAF：Manifest Amendment Fee 舱单改单费

（八）货物

Cargo

For Prompt Shipment 立即出运

Cargo Supplier（供）货方

Upcoming Shipment 下一载货

Same Assignment 同一批货

Nomination Cargo 指定（指派）货

Indicated / Nominated Cargo 指装货

Shipments under B/L No. ××××××提单货

Cargo Volume 货量

Freight Volume 货量

Reefer Cargo 冷冻货

High-value Cargo（goods）高价货

Miss Description 虚报货名

Agreement Rate 协议运价

D & H：Dangerous and Hazardous 危险品

（九）单证

Document

S/O：Shipping Order 托（运）单

B/L：Bill of Lading 提单

B/L：Copy 提单副本

OBL：Ocean Bill of Lading 海运提单

HBL：House Bill of Lading 无船承运人提单

TBL：Through Bill of Lading 全程提单

Advanced BL：Advanced Bill of Lading 预借提单

Anti-Dated BL：Anti-dated Bill of Lading 倒签提单

Blank BL：Blank Bill of Lading 空白提单

"To Order" B/L 指示提单

Combined Bill 并单（提单）

Separate Bill 拆单（提单）

Straight B/L：A non-negotiable B/L. 记名提单

Shipped B/L：A B/L issued only after the goods have actually been shipped on board the vessel，as distinguished from the received for Shipments B/L 已出运的货物提单（On Board B/L; Shipped B/L 已装船提单）

Received for Shipment B/L 备运提单

Transhipment B/L 转船提单

Through B/L 联运提单

Shipper（Consignee）Box 发（收）货人栏（格）

Arrival Notice 到货通知书

M/F：Manifest Form 舱单

Batch Filing 批量报备

Manifest Discrepancy 舱单数据不符

Acknowledgement of Manifest Receipt 收到舱单回执

Packing List 装箱单

Cargo Receipt 承运货物收据

D/R：Dock Receipt 场站收据

D/O：Delivery Order 交货单（小提单）

Shipper's Export Declaration 货主出口申报单

Shipping Advice 装运通知（似舱单 NVOCC 用）

Manifest information 舱单信息

FCN：Freight Correction Notice 舱单更改单（通知）

Surrender O B/L copies for consignment 交回提单副本

Release Note receipt signed by customer acknowledging delivery of goods 货物收讫单

（十）检验

Inspection

Customs Inspection 海关查验

Commodity Inspection 商品检验

Tally 理货

Tally Report 理货报告

Check 查验/检查/核对

Fumigation 熏蒸

Animal / Plant Inspection 动/植物检验

INSP Inspection / Inspector 检验/检验员

Certificate of Origin（normally issued or signed by a Chamber of Commerce or Embassy）始发地原产地证书

Arbitration 仲裁

ACH：Automated Clearing House（part of ACS）自动清关

AMS：Automated Manifest System（for anti-terrorism）自动舱单（反恐）申报系统

CSS：Cargo Selectivity System 货物抽验

CHB：Customs House Broker 报关行

SED：（EX-DEC）Shipper's Export Declaration 货主出口报关单

Bonded Warehouse 保税库

Bonded Area 保税区

Bonded Goods 保税货物

QUOTAs Quantity of one HTS item allowed to be imported at either higher or lower rate of duties 进口配额

DDP：Delivery Duty Paid 完税

DDU：Delivery Duty Unpaid 未完税

Drawback 退税金额

Customs Fine 海关罚款

Customs Seals 海关关封

Application for Inspection 检验申请

To expedite the Clearance 加快清关

Pilferage 盗窃/偷窃

To be Liable for a Penalty of 受到……处罚

Non-Fraudulent Violation of the Regulation 非故意违反规定

To File Certifications with Customs 向海关申报有效证明

To Follow the Current Procedure 遵循现行程序

To Abide by Rule 遵照……的规定

To Provide Specific Language 提供一定说法

To be not Authorized 不予认可

（十一）集装箱

Container

COC：Carrier's Own Container 船东自有箱

Container Cleaning 洗箱

VEN：Ventilated 通风

FRZ：Frozen 冰冻

HTD：Heated 加热

I. D. ：Inside Dimension 箱内尺码

Inside Measurement 箱内尺码

TW（Tare Weight）：The weight of an empty container 箱子皮重

Container Leasing Co. 租箱公司

Equipment Exchange（Interchange）Receipt 设备交接单

Repositioning 集装箱回空

Container Leasing long-term / short-term lease 集装箱租赁 长期/短期

Leasing Company 租箱公司

Premises for longer period than provided in Tariff 空箱滞箱费

Demurrage 重箱滞箱费

THC. Terminal Handling Charge 集装箱码头装卸作业费

EBS：Emerent Bunker Surcharges 紧急燃油附加费

BAF：Bunker Adjustment Factor 燃油附加费

二、简称

Abbreviation

A/W：All Water 全水路

ANER：Asia North America Eastbound Rate 亚洲北美东行运费协定

B/L：Bill of Lading 提单

B/R：Buying Rate 买价

BAF：Bunker Adjustment Factor 燃油附加费

C&F：Cost and Freight 成本加海运费

C. C：Collect 运费到付

C. S. C：Container Service Charge 货柜服务费

C. Y. ：Container Yard 货柜场

C/（CNEE）：Consignee 收货人

C/O：Certificate of Origin 产地证

CAF：Currency Adjustment Factor 货币汇率附加费

CFS：Container Freight Station 散货仓库

CFS/CFS：散装交货（起点/终点）

CHB：Customs House Broker 报关行

CIF：Cost，Insurance，Fright 成本，保险加海运费

CIP：Carriage and Insurance Paid To 运费、保险费付至目的地

COMM：Commodity 商品

CPT：Carriage Paid To 运费付至目的地

CTNR：Container 柜子

CY/CY：整柜交货（起点/终点）

D/A：Document Against Acceptance 承兑交单

D/O：Delivery Order 到港通知

D/P：Document Against Payment 付款交单

DAF：Delivered at Frontier 边境交货

DDC：Destination Delivery Charge 目的港码头费

DDP：Delivered Duty Paid 完税后交货

DDU：Delivered Duty Unpaid 未完税交货

DEQ：Delivered Ex Quay 目的港码头交货

DES：Delivered Ex Ship 目的港船上交货

Doc#：Document Number 文件号码

EPS：Equipment Position Surcharges 设备位置附加费

Ex：Work/ExFactory 工厂交货

F/F：Freight Forwarder 货运代理

FAF：Fuel Adjustment Factor 燃料附加费

FAK：Freight All Kind 各种货品

FAS：Free Alongside Ship 装运港船边交货

FCA：Free Carrier 货交承运人

FCL：Full Container Load 整柜

FVL Feeder Vessel/Lighter 驳船航次

FEU：Forty-Foot Equivalent Unit 40’ 40’ 柜型

FMC：Federal Maritime Commission 联邦海事委员会

FOB：Free on Board 船上交货

GRI：General Rate Increase 全面涨价

H/C：Handling Charge 代理费

HBL：House B/L 子提单

I/S：Inside Sales 内销售

IA：Independent Action 各别调价

L/C：Letter of Credit 信用证

LB：Land Bridge 陆桥

LCL：Less Than Container Load 拼柜

M/T：Measurement Ton 尺码吨（即货物收费以尺码计费）

MB/L：Master Bill of Loading 主提单

MLB：Mini Land Bridge 小陆桥，自一港到另一港口

MV：Mother Vessel 主线船

MTD：Multimodal Transport Document 多式联运单据

N/F：Notify 通知人

NVOCC：Non Vessel Operating Common Carrier 无船承运人

O/F：Ocean Freight 海运费

OBL：Ocean（or original ）B/L 海运提单

OCP：Overland Continental Point 货主自行安排运到内陆点

OP：Operation 操作

ORC：Origen Receive Charges 本地收货费用（广东省收取）

P. P：Prepaid 预付

PCS：Port Congestion Surcharge 港口拥挤附加费

POD：Port of Destination 目地港

POL：Port of Loading 装运港

PSS：Peak Season Surcharges 旺季附加费

S/（Shpr）：Shipper 发货人

S/C：Sales Contract 售货合同

S/O：Shipping Order 装货指示书

S/R：Selling Rate 卖价

S/S Spread Sheet 棋盘式对照表

SC：Service Contract 服务合同

SSL：Steam Ship Line 船公司

T. O. C：Terminal Operations Option 码头操作费

T. R. C：Terminal Receiving Charge 码头收柜费

T/S：Trans-Ship 转船，转运

T/T：Transit Time 航程

TEU：Twenty-Foot Equivalent Unit 20’20’柜型

THC：Terminal Handling Charges 码头操作费（香港收取）

TTL：Total 总共

TVC/ TVR：Time Volume Contract/ Rate 定期定量合同

VOCC：Vessel Operating Common Carrier 船公司

W/M：Weight or Measurement ton 以重量吨或者尺码吨中从高收费

W/T：Weight Ton 重量吨

YAS：Yard Surcharges 码头附加费

三、与客户谈价格时的30句常用英语口语

30 Frequent English Expressions When Discussing Prices with Customers

1. Let’s get down to business, shall we?

让我们开始谈生意好吗？

2. I’d like to tell you what I think about that.

我想告诉你我的一些想法。

3. Are those prices FOB or CIF?

这些价格是船上交货价还是运费及保险费在内价?

4. Are these prices wholesale or retail?

这些价格是批发价还是零售价?

5. That's too high.

价钱太高了。

6. Oh, no, this is the lowest price.

噢,不,这是最低价。

7. Let us have your rock-bottom price.

我们给你低价。

8. What's the price range?

价格范围是多少?

9. They start at one hundred and fifty yuan and go up to two hundred yuan.

它们以 50 元起价,至多到 200 元。

10. The price is quite reasonable.

这个价格相当合理。

11. The price is unreasonable.

这个价格不合理。

12. Can you make it a little cheaper?

=Can you come down a little?

=Can you reduce the price?

你能不能便宜一点?

13. That sounds very impressive.

那似乎非常好。

14. That sounds reasonable.

那似乎非常好。

15. I'd like to hear your ideas on...

我想听听你关于……的看法

16. You're offering us this product at 1800 yuan per unit, is that right?

你为我们提供的这种产品报价是每台 1800 元,对吗?

17. We'd appreciate it if you could sell it to us for 1350 yuan per unit.

如果你能以每台 1350 元的价格卖给我们,我们将不胜感激。

18. Taking the quality into consideration, I think the price is reasonable.

考虑到产品质量,我认为价格是合理的。

19. There's one problem to be mentioned.

有一个问题要提出来。

20. The price we quoted is quite good for your country.

我们报的价格相当适合贵国。

21. The price you quoted is a little stiff for exporting.

你报的价格对于出口而言，有点偏高。

22. Your price is 15% higher than that of last year.

你们的价格比去年高 15%。

23. I think you misunderstood me on this point.

在这一点上我想你是误会我了。

24. We're in complete agreement.

我们完全同意。

25. I can't make a decision at this time.

我现在无法决定。

26. It's not possible for us to make any sales at this price.

我们无法以这种价格销售。

27. 380 yuan is about as low as we can go.

380 元大约是我们能出的最低价格。

28. I'm afraid I can't agree with you there.

恐怕我不能同意您出的价格。

29. Your price is higher than that of other companies.

你方的价格比其他公司的价格要高。

30. But considering the high quality, our price is very reasonable.

不过鉴于产品的优良质量，我们的价格非常合理。

四、海运业务常用费用英语

Frequent English Expressions on Shipping Business

THC：Terminal Handling Charge 码头操作费

ORC：Receiving Charger at Origin 出运港货运费

ARB：Arbitariec 中转费

BAF：Bunker Adjustment Factor 燃油附加费

CAF：Currency Adjustment Factor 币值附加费

PSC：Peak Season Charge 旺季附加费

STF：Suez Transit Fee 苏伊士运河附加费

PCS：Port Congestion Surcharge 港口拥挤费

NPS：Nigerian Port Surcharge 尼日利亚港口附加费

WRS：War Risk Surcharge 战争风险附加费

DCD：Delivery Charges at Destination 目的港交货费

EBS：Emergency Bunker Surcharge 紧急燃油附加费

R/R：Rate / Restoration 费率恢复费

EBA：Emergency Bunker Additional 应急燃油费

YAS：Yen Appreciation Surcharge 日元币值附加费

GRI：General Rate Increase 正常费率增加

PTF：Panama Canal Transit Fee 巴拿马运河过境费

IFP：Interim Fuel Participation 暂时燃油附加费

ETS：Emergency Trucking Surcharge 应急卡车附加费

DOC：Document Fee 文件费

ERC：Equipment Repositioning Charge 集装箱返回费

CGS：Contingency Surcharge 拥挤附加费

IFA：Interim Fuel Assessment 暂时燃油费

SPS：Shanghai Port Surcharge 上海港口附加费

FRC：Fuel Recovery Charge 燃油恢复费

CUC：Chassis Usage Charge 底盘使用费

MCS：Metal Coil Surcharge 卷钢附加费

RFC：Rail Fuel Recovery Charge 铁路燃油恢复费

CDS：Calcutta Draft Surcharge 加尔各达附加费

TAR：Temporal Additional Risk Surcharge 临时战争风险附加费

CY：Container Yard 集装箱堆场

CFS：Container Fereight Station 集装箱中转站

FAF：Fuel Additional Fee 燃油附加费

CFS：Container Freight Station 集装箱货运站

TEU：Twenty-feet Equivalent Unit 换算箱

五、短语

Words and Phrases

Firm offer 实盘

Official offer 正式报价（报盘）

To make an offer for 对……报盘（报价）

To offer for 对……报价

Wild speculation 漫天要价

The preference of one's offer 优先报盘

Subject to 以……为条件，以……为准

Make headway 有进展

At wide intervals 间隔时间太长

Counter-offer 还盘，还价

附录Ⅱ 对话
AppendixⅡ：Dialogue

任务一：货代业务商讨

背景：A 在 Eagle 货代公司担任客服代表，B 在 Senda 外贸公司工作。

A 在 9 月 1 日接到电话。

A：这里是 Eagle 货代公司，有什么能帮助您的吗？

B：我来自 Senda 外贸公司。最近，我有 10000 件牛仔裤准备从上海装运到鹿特丹，我想询问一下价格。

A：谢谢。首先，我想了解一些细节。您的最晚装期是什么时候？

B：货物需要 9 月 15 日左右装运，在 11 月 10 日之前运达目的地。

A：有两个航次您参考一下。船舶“Pioneer”将会在 9 月 15 日驶离，11 月 6 日到达，运价是每标箱 1,400 美元。船舶“Venture”将会在 9 月 14 日驶离，11 月 4 日到达，运价是每标箱 1,500 美元。您也可以申请额外的费用请求，像内陆运输、港口操作、报关费，等等。

B：我委任你们公司运输，包括内陆运输。我选择 Pioneer 船舶。

A：谢谢。我将在 5 分钟内把代理人的表格传真给您。请您填写一下包括清单、货物数量、集装箱的尺寸和类型、数量、毛重、体积、贸易条款和 CFS/CFS 或者 CY/CY 的选择。请在一个小时内将盖有贵公司章的表格传真给我。

B：好的，为了便于商品审查，需要我发送给你其他的东西吗？

A：好的，需要以下单据：原产地证明、营业执照、外汇价格声明、证明表格和发票。如果需要额外的材料，尽快联系您。

B：谢谢。

A：为了防止紧急事件和问题的发生，请尽早联系我。希望我们能有一个愉快的合作。

B：好的，拜拜。

10,000件牛仔裤已经按时装运了。A在9月16日打电话给B进行了确认。

A：是Senda外贸公司吗？这里是Eagle货代公司。我想告诉您，10,000件牛仔裤昨天已经装上船了。制作海运提单的时候还有要求吗？

B：我需要修改现在海运提单上通知方的名字。

A：我明白了。我将会把修改通知方名称的担保函传真给您，请您填写担保函，谢谢。

B：好的。

Task One：Talking about Forwarding Business

Background：A works in Eagle Freight Forwarding Company, who is responsible for client serve. B works in Senda Foreign Trade Company.

A received a phone call on Sep. 1st.

A：This is Eagle Freight Forwarding Company. What can I do for you?

B：I'm from Senda Foreign Trade Company. Recently, I have 10,000 sets of jeans ready for shipment from Shanghai to Rotterdam, so I'd like to make an inquiry.

A：Thanks for your inquiry. First, I'd like to ask you some details. What's your deadline for shipment?

B：The goods need to be shipped around Sep. 15 th and to be delivered before Nov. 10th.

A：There are 2 voyages for your reference. One is that M. V. "Pioneer" will depart on Sep. 15th and arrive on Nov. 6th, the freight rate is USD1,400 per TEU. The other is that M. V. "Venture" will depart on Sep. 14th and arrive on Nov. 4th , the freight rate is USD 1,500 per TEU. Additional fees apply if you want, like inland transport, port handing, customs fees, and so on.

B：I'd like to appoint your company for the shipment, including inland transport. And I choose M. V. "Pioneer" .

A：Thanks a lot. I will fax you the standard form of power of attorney in five minutes. Please fill in details such as schedule, number of items, type and size of containers, number of containers, gross weight, volume, trade terms and CFS/CFS or CY/CY selection etc. Please fax back the form while your stamp in one hour.

B：OK. In case of commodity inspection, anything else should I send you?

A：Yes, the following things are required, C/O, business license, foreign exchange sales statement, verification form and invoice. We will contact you as soon as possible for materials.

B: Thanks.

A: In case of emergency or problems, please contact me as soon as possible. Looking forward to having a pleasant cooperation.

B: OK, bye.

10,000 sets of jeans were shipped on schedule. A made a phone call to B for further confirmation on Sep. 16th.

A: Is that Senda Foreign Trade Company? This is Eagle Freight Forwarding Company. I'd like to inform you that your 10,000 sets of jeans were shipped on aboard yesterday. Is there any requirements when making the bill(s) of lading?

B: Indeed to revise the name of notified party showed in B/L.

A: I see. I will fax you the standard form of Letter of Indemnity for revising name of notified party showed in the B/L. Please fill in the letter of indemnity. Thanks.

B: OK.

任务二：存储货物沟通

王是物流公司的仓库管理员，史密斯是客户。

王：早上好！很高兴见到你！

史密斯：早上好！很高兴见到你！

王：先生，我能为你做点什么？

史密斯：我想了解一下贵公司的货物存放情况。货物放入仓库后，您能告诉我一些关于您的存储过程的信息吗？

王：管理包括货物的仓储与养护。

史密斯：我明白了。商品的保护是什么？

王：货物保护包括保护和养护管理的技术措施。

史密斯：对于不同的商品，应该使用不同的保护技术？

王：是的。让我举个例子，对于铁制品，应该使用防锈技术，保鲜技术应该用于食品，而使用防潮技术是保护木制品的最佳方法。

史密斯：你们公司呢？

王：我们公司在这方面采用了最先进的技术和管理。

史密斯：谢谢你的详细描述。

王：我很高兴这样做。

史密斯：我对贵公司的特殊服务很感兴趣，期待着我们的合作。

王：我也是。

Task Two：Talking about storage of goods

Wang is a warehouse keeper of the logistics company, Smith is a customer.

Wang：Good morning! Pleased to meet you!

Smith：Good morning ! Pleased to meet you!

Wang：What can I do for you, sir?

Smith：I'd like to know something about the storage of goods of your company. Can you tell me something about your storage process after the goods are put into the warehouse?

Wang：The management includes goods storage and conservation.

Smith：I see. What about conservation of goods?

Wang：Goods protection includes technical measures for protection and conservation management.

Smith：For different goods different conservation techniques should be used?

Wang：Yes. For example, for the iron products, rust-proof technology should be used, and preservation technology should be used for food, while it is the best method to use the moisture-proof technology for wood products.

Smith：What about your company?

Wang：Our company has adopted the most advanced technology and management in this aspect.

Smith：It's very kind of you to give me the detailed description.

Wang：It's my pleasure to do so.

Smith：I am very interested in your company's special service and I am looking forward to our cooperation.

Wang：Me too.

任务三：海运货物保险

卖方（出口商）有一批货要根据 CIF 条件下的销售合同从上海运往伦敦。他正在和货运代理协商海运货物保险的事情。

A 是出口商，B 是货运代理。

A：真是美好的一天，先生。我想和你商量一下海运货物保险的事情。

B：好的。

A：我需要为买方货物购买在海运途中丢失或损坏的保险吗？为什么？

B：是的，因为根据《2010 年国际贸易术语解释通则》，卖方的义务之一是在运输过程中投保买方货物丢失或损坏的风险，而买方没有义务与卖方订立保险合同。

A：保险金额是多少？

B：如果信用证上没有注明要求投保的险别，那么保险金额至少要达到货物到岸价或 CIP 价的 110%。

A：我应该买哪种货物保险？

B：如果保险信用证上没有注明，那就要看保险公司的情况了，根据《海洋运输货物保险条款》和根据《协会货物条款的条款》，你必须投至少符合平安险（FPA）规定的最低保险全额的货物保险。

Task Three：Talking about Marine Cargo Insurance

The seller (the exporter) has one consignment of cargo to be transported from Shanghai to London under the sales contract with CIF terms. He is consulting with the freight forwarder about marine cargo insurance.

A is a Exporter, B is a Freight Forwarder.

A：Good day, Mr. B, I have something to consult with you about marine cargo insurance.

B：Good day, Mr. A, yes, please.

A：Do I need to contract for insurance cover against the buyer's risk of loss of or damage to the goods during the carriage by sea and why?

B：Yes, you need to do so because according to Incoterms 2010, one of the seller's obligations is to contract for insurance cover against the buyer's risk of loss of or damage to the goods during the carriage and the buyer has no obligation to the seller to make a contract of insurance.

A：What is the amount insured?

B：If there is no indication in the credit of the insurance coverage required, the amount of insurance coverage must be at least 110% of the CIF or CIP value of the goods.

A：What type of cargo insurance should I procure?

B：It depends on the L/C, if there is no indication in the credit of the insurance coverage required, you must obtain cargo insurance complying at least with the minimum cover provided by free from Particular Average（FPA）as per Open Marine Cargo Clauses（2009）of the PICC Property and Casualty Company Limited or Clauses（c）of the Institute Cargo Clauses.

任务四：参观配送中心

李是配送中心的管理员，王是物流专业的学生。

李：欢迎来到配送中心。让我先介绍一下我自己，我是这个配送中心的经理，并且我很高兴为您介绍配送中心。

王：谢谢！这里好大啊！是什么类型的配送中心？

李：这是一个药物配送中心。

王：哦，我明白了。这里有所有的药品，但没有其他种类的商品。

李：是的，这个配送中心的设计目的是储存药品，药品需要特定的储存条件。

王：配送中心需要什么样子的储存条件？

李：最重要的条件是控制温度和避免阳光直射，否则药物会变质。所以我们必须保持配送中心的凉爽。有些药物甚至不得不进行冷藏。

王：哦，我明白了。我们还需要注意哪些问题？

李：带有刺激性气味的药品应单独存放以防止串味。并且不同药品的特性可能相互影响，应分开存放。除此之外，我们需要定期检查产品和设施，保持配送中心的清洁和安全，使每项操作标准化并做好信息收集。

王：哦，我知道了。非常感谢你！

李：不客气。

Task Four：Visiting to Distribution Centre

Li is a manager of a distribution center, Wang is a student in logistics major.

Li：Welcome to the distribution center. Let me introduce myself first, I am the manager of this distribution center and I am very glad to give an introduction about the distribution center to you.

Wang：Thank you! How big it is! What kind of distribution center it is?

Li：According to the goods property, this is a pharmaceuticals distribution center.

Wang：Oh I see. There are all pharmaceuticals here but no other kind of goods.

Li: Yes, this distribution center is designed to store pharmaceuticals, pharmaceuticals require a specific storage conditions.

Wang: What kind of storage conditions should a distribution center need?

Li: The most important is to avoid heat and sunlight, pharmaceuticals are more likely to deteriorate in that condition. So we must keep the distribution center cool. Some drugs even have to put in cold storage.

Wang: Oh, I see. What other problems we need to pay attention?

Li: Pharmaceuticals with big smell should be kept separately to prevent odor.. Also, traits of different medicines may affect each other and they should be stored separately. In addition, we need to check the products and facilities regularly, keeping the distribution center clean and safe, standardizing each operation and gathering the information.

Wang: Wow, I got it. Thank you very much!

Li: You are welcome.

附录Ⅲ
Appendix Ⅲ

测试题一

一、单项选择（共 20 分，每小题 2 分，每小题有一个正确答案，请将序号填写在题目前面的括号内）

（　　）1. ______ port is not within the Far East to Europe and Mediterranean route.

A. Napoli　　B. Hamburg　　C. Vancouver　　D. Antwerp

（　　）2. Nowadays, ______ containers are mainly used in international marine cargo transport.

A. ten-foot, twelve-foot　　B. twenty-foot, thirty-foot

C. twenty-foot, forty-foot　　D. thirty-foot, forty-foot

（　　）3. If the shipment date in the L/C is "on or about July 17th, 2019", then the goods can be shipped from ______ .

A. July 7th to July 27th, 2019　　B. July 8th to July 20th , 2019

C. July 13th to July 21st, 2019　　D. July 8th to July 26th, 2019

（　　）4. ______ is one of the international payment methods, it is more widely used for settlement than remittance and collection.

A. Letter of Delivery　　B. Letter of Indemnity

C. Letter of Credit　　D. Letter of Guarantee

（　　）5. ______ risks is not covered in All Risks as per Ocean Marine Cargo clauses of the PICC.

A. Natural calamities　　B. Collision　　C. War　　D. Fire

（　　）6. ______ is the United Nations specialized agency with responsibility for the safety and security of shipping and the prevention of marine pollution by ships.

A. IMO　　B. IATA　　C. CIFA　　D. WCO

(　　) 7. ______ is one of the forms of multimodal transport that combines the economy of sea transport and the speed of air transport.

A. Mini-bridge　　B. Piggyback

C. Road/Air/Road　　D. Sea/Air/Sea

(　　) 8. In marine container liner transportation, the consignee or its forwarding agent has to obtain the ______ .

A. booking note　　B. import cargo manifest

C. delivery order　　D. mate's receipt

(　　) 9. It is usually the ______ who issues relevant documents such as the Forwarder's Certificate of Receipt, the Forwarder's Certificate of Transport etc.

A. ship agent　　B. carrier　　C. consignee　　D. freight forwarder

(　　) 10. In voyage chartering business, the relationship between the parties is governed by the voyage charter party. ______ is one of standards forms of voyage charter party.

A. NYPE　　B. BIMCO　　C. GENCON　　D. BALTIME

二、判断正误（共 20 分，每小题 2 分。答案正确的，在括号打"√"；答案为错误的，在括号打"×"，请将答案正确的序号填写在题目前面的括号内）

(　　) 1. Equipment Interchange Receipt is given by the container operator to the container user.

(　　) 2. The trade association for the word's airlines which representing about 240 airlines or 84% of total air traffic is FIATA.

(　　) 3. The sea waybill serves as same functions as bill of lading.

(　　) 4. The amount of insurance coverage must be at least 110% of the FOB value of the goods if there is no indication in the credit of the insurance coverage required.

(　　) 5. In marine chartering business, the relationships between the shipowner and charterer are governed by the charter party. There are some standard forms of voyage charter party, a typical example is NYPE.

(　　) 6. According to *INCOTERMS 2010*, FOB means that the seller pays the ocean freight.

(　　) 7. The air waybill is the most important document in air cargo transport and can be transferred by endorsement.

(　　) 8. In time charter, the charterer is liable for cost of crew wages.

(　　) 9. Consolidation can not benefit the parties concerned such as shippers, consignees，carriers and forwarders.

(　　) 10. Land transport is typically more affordable than air transport，but more expensivethan sea transport especially in developing countries where inland infrastructure is not efficient.

三、翻译（共 30 分，每小题 3 分）

1. DDP represents the maximum obligation for the seller.

____

____

2. Documents to be presented within 10 days after the date of shipment but within the validity of the credit.

____

____

3. What is your deadline for shipment?

____

____

4. In case of emergency or problems，please contact me as soon as possible.

____

____

5. Please fill in details such as schedule，type and size of containers.

____

____

6. What preparations should be made before the customs declaration?

____

____

7. The customs duty and other relevant charges should be paid before the deadline.

____

____

8. The voyage chartering means that the ship-owner promises to carry on board a specific ship a particular cargo for a single voyage from one or more loading ports to one or more discharging ports.

____

____

9. Please quote me your best offer for 1×40’ GP ex Qingdao to Rotterdam.

10. The seller contracts for insurance and pays the insurance premium.

四、综合题（共 20 分，每小题 10 分）

1. 说明：假定你是张小明，准备参加某公司的面试。请根据下列内容编写英文自我介绍。

（1）个人信息

姓名：张小明　出生地：天津市　年龄：20 岁。

学校：天津海运职业学院　专业：港口与航运管理专业。

（2）学习情况

学习努力，掌握了本专业的基础知识；参加了认知实习，对本行业有所了解。

（3）对公司的认识表达出对工作的热情和自信

（4）自我评价

具有团队意识，能够承受较大的工作压力等。

（5）表达清晰

2. 请用中英文介绍一下作为发货人的国际货运代理人的业务内容（至少 10 点）。

五、单证操作（共 10 分，每小题 10 分）

Shipper BB CORPORATION	B/L NO.:CCLU11038221358
Consignee TO THE ORDER OF BB CORPORATION	CC SHIPPING LINE LTD.
Notify party AA COMPANY	BILL OF LADING

Pre-carriage by		Place of Receipt
Ocean vessel SUNSHINE	Voy.No. V.007E	Port of Loading QINGDAO
Port of Discharge YOKOHAMA		Place of Delivery

Marks& Nos. Container No.Seal No.	No. Of Container or Pkgs	Kinds of packages;Description Of Goods	Gross Weight (KGS)	Measurement (M3)
CXRU1131335/CCL244603K TRIU8943343/CCL213003K	7620CTNS	SHIPPER'S LOAD COUNT AND COUNT 2 × 40' REEFER CONTAINERS SAID TO CONTAIN: FRESH GINGER FREIGHT PREPAID	52,000.00	110.00

TOTAL NUMBER OF CONTAINER OR PACKAGES (IN WORDS)

SAY TOTAL SEVEN YHOURSAND SIX HUNDRED AND TWENTY CTNS ONLY.

Freight & Charge	Revenue Tons	Rate	Per	Prepaid	Collect

Ex.Rate.	Prepaid at QINGDAO	Payable at	Place and Date of Issue QINGDAO SEP/26/2016
	Total Prepaid	No.of Original B(s)/L THREE	Signed for Carrier CC SHIPPING LINE LTD AS CARRIER

LADEN ON BOARD THE VESSEL

DATE

(TERMS PLEASE FIND ON BACK OF ORINGINAL B/L)

1. In this bill of loading, the port of loading is________________________________.

2. In this bill of lading, the port of discharge is ________________________________.

3. In this bill of lading, the notify party is ________________________________.

4. In this bill of lading, the shipper is ________________________________.

5. In this bill of lading, the carrier is ________________________________.

6. If the trade term of the consignment is CIF, the relative marine cargo insurance should be arranged by________________________________.

7. This bill of lading is signed by________________________________.

8. There are ________________________number of original bill of lading issued.

9. The container's numbers are ________________________________.

10. The container's seal number are ________________________________.

测试题一（答案）

一、单项选择（共 20 分，每小题 2 分，每小题有一项正确答案，请将序号填写在题目前面的括号内）

（C）1. ______ port is not within the Far East to Europe and Mediterranean route.

A. Napoli　　B. Hamburg　　C. Vancouver　　D. Antwerp

（C）2. Nowadays, ______ containers are mainly used in international marine cargo transport.

A. ten-foot, twelve-foot　　B. twenty-foot, thirty-foot

C. twenty-foot, forty-foot　　D. thirty-foot, forty-foot

（C）3. If the shipment date in the L/C is "on or about July 17th, 2018", then the goods can be shipped from ______ .

A. July 7th to July 27th, 2019　　B. July 8th to July 20th , 2019

C. July 13th to July 21st, 2019　　D. July 8th to July 26th, 2019

（C）4. ______ is one of the international payment methods, it is more widely used for settlement than remittance and collection.

A. Letter of Delivery　　B. Letter of Indemnity

C. Letter of Credit　　D. Letter of Guarantee

（C）5. ______ risks is not covered in All Risks as per Ocean Marine Cargo clauses of the PICC.

A. Natural calamities　　B. Collision

C. War　　D. Fire

(A) 6. ______ is the United Nations specialized agency with responsibility for the safety and security of shipping and the prevention of marine pollution by ships.

A. IMO B. IATA C. CIFA D. WCO

(B) 7. ______ is one of the forms of multimodal transport that combines the economy of sea transport and the speed of air transport.

A. Mini-bridge B. Piggyback

C. Road/Air/Road D. Sea/Air/Sea

(C) 8. In marine container liner transportation, the consignee or its forwarding has to obtain the ______ .

A. booking note B. import cargo manifest

C. delivery order D. mate's receipt

(D) 9. It is usually the ______ who issues relevant documents such as the Forwarder's Certificate of Receipt, the Forwarder's Certificate of Transport etc.

A. ship agent B. carrier C. consignee D. freight forwarder

(C) 10. In voyage chartering business, the relationship between the parties is governed by the voyage charter party. ______ is one of standards forms of voyage charter party.

A. NYPE B. BIMCO C. GENCON D. BALTIME

二、判断正误(共20分,每小题2分。答案正确的,在括号打"√";答案为错误的,在括号打"×",请将答案正确的序号填写在题目前面的括号内)

(√) 1. Equipment Interchange Receipt is given by the container operator to the container user.

(×) 2. The trade association for the word's airlines which representing about 240 airlines or 84% of total air traffic is FIATA.

(×) 3. The sea waybill serves as same functions as bill of lading.

(×) 4. The amount of insurance coverage must be at least 110% of the FOB value of the goods if there is no indication in the credit of the insurance coverage required.

(×) 5. In marine `chartering business, the relationships between the shipowner and charterer are governed by the charter party. There are some standard forms of voyage charter party, a typical example is NYPE.

(×) 6. According to INCOTERMS 2010, FOB means that the seller pays the ocean freight.

(×) 7. The air waybill is the most important document in air cargo transport and can be transferred by endorsement.

(×) 8. In time charter, the charterer is liable for cost of crew wages.

（×） 9. Consolidation can not benefit the parties concerned such as shippers, consignees, carriers and forwarders.

（√） 10. Land transport is typically more affordable than air transport, but more expensive than sea transport especially in developing countries where inland infrastructure is not efficient.

三、翻译（共 30 分，每小题 3 分）

1. DDP represents the maximum obligation for the seller.

DDP 是卖方承担责任最大的术语。

2. Documents to be presented within 10 days after the date of shipment but within the validity of the credit.

在装运日后的十日内交单，但还必须保证在信用证的有效期内。

3. What is your deadline for shipment?

最晚的装期是什么时候？

4. In case of emergency or problems, please contact me as soon as possible.

为了防止紧急事件和问题的发生，请尽早联系我。

5. Please fill in details such as schedule, type and size of containers.

请填写船期、集装箱种类和尺寸的详细信息。

6. What preparations should be made before the customs declaration?

通关前需要做什么准备工作？

7. The customs duty and other relevant charges should be paid before the deadline.

最后期限前关税和其他有关费用都应予以交齐。

8. The voyage chartering means that the shipowner promises to carry on board a specific ship a particular cargo for a single voyage from one or more loading ports to one or more discharging ports.

航次租船是指船东承诺按一个单程航次装运约定的货物，从一个或多个港口运至另一个或多个港口。

9. Please quote me your best offer for 1×40’ GP ex Qingdao to Rotterdam.

请报给我青岛到鹿特丹一个 40 尺的最低价格。

10. The seller contracts for insurance and pays the insurance premium.

由卖方签订保险合同并且支付保险费用。

四、综合题（共 20 分，每小题 10 分）

1. 说明：假定你是张小明，准备参加某公司的面试。请根据下列内容编写英文自我介绍。

（1）个人信息

姓名：张小明　出生地：天津市　年龄：20 岁。

学校：天津海运职业学院　专业：港口与航运管理专业。

（2）学习情况

学习努力，掌握了本专业的基础知识；参加了认知实习，对本行业有所了解。

（3）对公司的认识表达出对工作的热情和自信

（4）自我评价

具有团队意识，能够承受较大的工作压力等。

（5）表达清晰

My name is Zhang Xiaoming. It is really my honor to have this opportunity for this interview, I hope I can make a good performance today. I'm confident that I can succeed. Now I will introduce myself briefly. I am 20 years old, born in Tianjin. I will graduate from Tianjin Maritime College. My major is management of Port and Shipping. I spend most of my time on study, and I have acquired basic knowledge of my major during my school time. Besides, I have taken a tour to some relevant companies. Through this I have a deep understanding of the industry.

I'd like to find a job which is full of challenges. AAA is a global company, so I feel I can gain the most from working in this kind of company environment. That is the reason why I am here to compete for this position. I think I'm a good team player and I'm a person of great honesty to others. Also I am able to work under great pressure. That's all. Thank you for giving me the chance.

2. 请用中英文介绍一下作为发货人的国际货运代理人的业务内容。（至少 10 点）

■ Choose the route, mode of transport and a suitable carrier. 选择路线、运输方式和承运人。

■ Book space with the selected carrier. 订舱

■ Take delivery of the goods and issue relevant documents such as the Forwarders' Certificate of Receipt,（FCR 收货凭证）the Forwarders' Certificate of Transport,（FCT 运输凭证）etc. 提取货物并签发 FCT、FCR

■ Study the provisions of the letter of credit. 研究信用证条款

■ Pack the goods, taking into account the route, the mode of transport, the nature of the goods and applicable regulations. 包装货物

■ Arrange warehousing of the goods. 安排仓储

■ Weight and measure the goods. 货物的称重与测量

■ Draw the consignor's attention to the need for insurance and arrange for the insurance of goods. 办理保险

■ Transport the goods to the port. 运送至港口

■ Arrange for customs clearance. 安排清关

■ Deliver the goods to the carrier. 货交承运人

■ Attend to foreign exchange transactions, if any. 兑换外汇

■ Pay fees and other charges including freight. 支付运费

■ Obtain the signed bills of lading from the carrier. 获取已签发的单证

■ Arrange for transshipment en route if necessary. 安排转运

■ Monitor the movement of goods all the way to the consignee. 监管货物

■ Note（记录） damages to or losses of the goods. 记录货损

■ Assist the consignor in pursuing claims. 协助发货人进行索赔

五、单证操作（共 10 分，每小题 10 分）

1. In this bill of loading, the port of loading is Qingdao.

2. In this bill of lading, the port of discharge is Yokohama.

3. In this bill of lading, the notify party is AA Company.

4. In this bill of lading, the shipper is BB corporation.

5. In this bill of lading, the carrier is CC Shipping Line LTD.

6. If the trade term of the consignment is CIF, the relative marine cargo insurance should be arranged by BB corporation/shipper.

7. This bill of lading is signed by CC Shipping Line LTD/carrier.

8. There are three number of original bill of lading issued.

9. The container's numbers are CXRU1131335 and TRIU8943343.

10. The container's seal number are CCL213003k and CCL244603k.

测试题二

一、单项选择（共 20 分，每小题 2 分，每小题有一项正确答案，请将序号填写在题目前面的括号内）

（　　）1. Import Licenses

A. 进口关税　　B. 出口许可证

C. 进口许可证　　D. 进口配额

（　　）2. Insurance Premium

A. 保险单　　B. 保险合同

C. 保险费　　D. 保险批单

(　　) 3. Bilateral trade

A 国际贸易　　B. 国内贸易

C. 双边贸易　　D. 多边贸易

(　　) 4. Reefer Container

A. 框架集装箱　　B. 超高集装箱

C. 冷藏集装箱　　D. 敞顶集装箱

(　　) 5. NVOCC

A. 合并运输人　　B. 货运代理人

C. 无船承运人　　D. 船舶所有人

(　　) 6. 航空货运单

A. Master Air Waybill　　B. House Air Waybill

C. Master Bill of Lading　　D. House Bill of Lading

(　　) 7. 散装舱容

A. Bale Capacity　　B. Grain Capacity

C. Dead Weight Tonnage　　D. Carrying Capacity

(　　) 8. 救助费用

A. Port Charges　　B. Emergency Charges

C. Salvage Charges　　D. Insurance Premium

(　　) 9. 收货待运提单

A. Shipped B/L　　B. Straight B/L

C. Direct B/L　　D. Received for Shipment B/L

(　　) 10. 原产地证书

A. Commercial Invoice　　B. Packing List

C. Certificate of Origin　　D. Forwarder's Cargo Receipts

二、完形填空题（共 20 分，每小题 2 分。每小题有一项正确答案，请将序号填写在题目前面的括号内）

Marine cargo insurance is one of the most important parts in international trade. The three (1) as per Ocean Marine Cargo Clauses of the PICC are FPA, WA and All Risks. Among them, (2) is the most widely used in the transport of marine cargo because it provides the best coverage among the three but does not cover risks of war, strike and (3). The only difference between WA and FPA is that WA provides larger cover than FPA, since (4) is recoverable from the insurer from (5).

(　　) 1. A. general additional risks　　B. special additional risks

C. basic coverage D. additional risks

( ) 2. A. WA B. FPA

C. all Risks D. additional risks

( ) 3. A. special additional risks B. rain damage risks

C. general additional risks D. external risks

( ) 4. A. total loss B. constructive total loss

C. partial loss and damage D. particular average

( ) 5. A. intentional act or of the assured B. external causes In the transport

C. natural calamities D. fortuitous accidents

A letter of credit is one of the international payment methods. It can be defined as a written promise of the (6) acting at the request and on the instructions of the (7) to make a payment to the beneficiary. The L/C is based on the (8) while the remittance and collection are based on the commercial credit which is generally considered less creditable.

The L/C is issued on the basis of the sales contract but independent of it. Under a L/C, the banks deal with (9) rather than (10), the banks have to pay if the documents presented to them are complied with the terms and conditions.

( ) 6. A. issuing bank B. negotiating bank

C. advising bank D. confirming bank

( ) 7. A. beneficiary B. applicant

C. shipper D. consignee

( ) 8. A. commercial credit B. state credit

C. bank's credit D. international credit

( ) 9. A. goods B. ship

C. people D. document

( ) 10. A. people B. documents

C. goods D. ship

三、英译汉（共30分，每小题3分）

1. Have you found the agent for this ***vessel***?

____

____

2. If you have any requirement, please call me.

____

____

3. Port Control answering.

____

____

4. Call me back half an hour before arrival.

____

____

5. Did you take any brochures with you?

____

____

6. There is no dangerous cargo on board.

____

____

7. How about the payment for overtime work?

____

____

8. We hope to establish long business relationship with you.

____

____

9. We should cooperate to ensure the safety of the ship.

____

____

10. This file contains all the necessary documents.

____

____

四、问答题（共 10 分）

假如你在 DDD（TIANJIN）INT'L SHIPPING & TRADING CO.，LTD.（公司）担任货代销售，请根据以下要点编订中英文公司介绍，从而为拓展公司业务。

内容：（1）公司业务主要包括集装箱运输等全方位物流服务；

（2）公司能够提供海上出口和航空出口服务；

（3）在某些航线上具有优势；

（4）具备强大的代理网络；

（5）能够为客户提供优质的服务和有竞争力的价格。

五、信函写作（共10分）

说明：假定你是王明，根据下列信息写一封信。

写信日期：2019年5月4日

收信人：Mr. John Brown

内容：（1）感谢对方订购了你公司的最新产品；

声音隔板规格 Partition Dimension	每只常规价 Regular Price Each Special	每只特别价（12 及以上） Price Each（12 or more）
4×4’	US $ 112. 75 FOB Bern	US $ 98. 20 FOB Bern
4×5’	US $ 132	US $ 115. 50
5×5’	US $ 152. 75	US $ 129. 85

（2）所订购的货物为 M-S 声音隔板（M-S Acoustical Partitions），订单号是 TG0633 该订单已于 5 月 2 日收到；

（3）货物已装船，大约一周后到达；

（4）收到货物后请回复。

____

六、翻译对话（共 10 分）

说明：请将下列对话按照角色顺序翻译成中文。

Owner：Good morning sir，we are from “Sunlight Shipping Company” . My name is Peter. On this visit today we’d like to discuss our long-term agency agreement with you.

Agent：Hello！Peter，good morning，a warm welcome to you from our company，please sit down. Yes，since both of us have contacted for a period of time and laid a good foundation for mutual cooperation，I hope that this meeting today will be very pleasant and fruitful.

Owner：I think so，thank you.

Agent：Well，how about the draft of the agreement? We sent you last week，anything to be corrected further?

Owner：Yes，I would say that most of the terms are acceptable. There are only two points which need to be discussed between us this time. One is the discount percentage of the agency fee，the other is the time for us to remit you the ship disbursement.

Owner：____

____

____

Agent：____

____

____

Owner：____

____

____

Agent: ______________________________________

____

____

Owner: ______________________________________

____

____

测试题二（答案）

一、单项选择（共20分，每小题2分，每小题有一项正确答案，请将序号填写在题目前面的括号内）

（C） 1. Import Licenses

A. 进口关税　　B. 出口许可证

C. 进口许可证　　D. 进口配额

（C） 2. Insurance Premium

A. 保险单　　B. 保险合同

C. 保险费　　D. 保险批单

（C） 3. Bilateral trade

A. 国际贸易　　B. 国内贸易

C. 双边贸易　　D. 多边贸易

（C） 4. Reefer Container

A. 框架集装箱　　B. 超高集装箱

C. 冷藏集装箱　　D. 敞顶集装箱

（C） 5. NVOCC

A. 合并运输人　　B. 货运代理人

C. 无船承运人　　D. 船舶所有人

（A） 6. 航空货运单

A. Master Air Waybill　　B. House Air Waybill

C. Master Bill of Lading　　D. House Bill of Lading

（B） 7. 散装舱容

A. Bale Capacity　　B. Grain Capacity

C. Dead Weight Tonnage　　D. Carrying Capacity

（C）8. 救助费用

A. Port Charges　　B. Emergency Charges

C. Salvage Charges　　D. Insurance Premium

（D）9. 收货待运提单

A. Shipped B/L　　B. Straight B/L

C. Direct B/L　　D. Received for Shipment B/L

（C）10. 原产地证书

A. Commercial Invoice　　B. Packing List

C. Certificate of Origin　　D. Forwarder's Cargo Receipts

二、完形填空题（共20分，每小题2分。每小题有一项正确答案，请将序号填写在题目前面的括号内）

Marine cargo insurance is one of the most important parts in international trade. The three （1） as per Ocean Marine Cargo Clauses of the PICC are FPA, WA and All Risks. Among them, （2） is the most widely used in the transport of marine cargo because it provides the best coverage among the three but does not cover risks of war, strike and （3）. The only difference between WA and FPA is that WA provides larger cover than FPA, since （4） is recoverable from the insurer from （5）.

（C）1. A. general additional risks　　B. special additional risks

C. basic coverage　　D. additional risks

（C）2. A. WA　　B. FPA

C. All Risks　　D. additional risks

（C）3. A. special additional risks　　B. rain damage risks

C. general additional risks　　D. external risks

（C）4. A. total loss　　B. constructive total loss

C. partial loss and damage　　D. particular average

（C）5. A. intentional act or of the assured　　B. external causes in the transport

C. natural calamities　　D. fortuitous accidents

A letter of credit is one of the international payment methods. It can be defined as a written promise of the （6） acting at the request and on the instructions of the （7） to make a payment to the beneficiary. The L/C is based on the （8） while the remittance and collection are based on the commercial credit which is generally considered less creditable.

The L/C is issued on the basis of the sales contract but independent of it. Under a L/C, the banks deal with （9） rather than （10）, the banks have to pay if the documents presented to them are complied with the terms and conditions.

（A） 6. A. issuing bank　　B. negotiating bank
　　C. advising bank　　D. confirming bank

（B） 7. A. beneficiary　　B. applicant
　　C. shipper　　D. consignee

（C） 8. A. commercial credit　　B. state credit
　　C. bank's credit　　D. international credit

（D） 9. A. goods　　B. ship
　　C. people　　D. documents

（C） 10. A. people　　B. documents
　　C. goods　　D. ship

三、英译汉（共 30 分，每小题 3 分）

1. Have you found the agent for this vessel?

你为这条船找到代理了吗?

2. If you have any requirement, please call me.

如果你有任何需求，请给我打电话。

3. Port Control answering.

港口控制站收到。

4. Call me back half an hour before arrival.

到达前半小时回复我。

5. Did you take any brochures with you?

你带你们公司的宣传册了吗?

6. There is no dangerous cargo on board.

船上没有危险品货物。

7. How about the payment for overtime work?

加班费用是多少?

8. We hope to establish long business relationship with you.

我希望同你建立长久的商业关系。

9. We should cooperate to ensure the safety of the ship.

我们必须合作以确保船舶的安全。

10. This file contains all the necessary documents.

这个文件中装了所有必要的单据。

四、问答题（共 10 分，每小题 2 分）

假如你在 DDD（TIANJIN）INT' L SHIPPING & TRADING CO.，LTD. 担任货代销售，请根据以下要点编订中英文公司介绍，以拓展公司业务。

内容：（1）公司业务主要包括集装箱运输等全方位物流服务；

（2）公司能够提供海上出口和航空出口服务；

（3）在某些航线上具有优势；

（4）具备强大的代理网络；

（5）能够为客户提供优质的服务和有竞争力的价格。

（每点两分）

As one of the top-ranking forwarders, DDD（TIANJIN）INT'L SHIPPING & TRADING CO., LTD. specialize in logistics and freight transportation. Our business mainly covers container transportation and other logistics services at full range. We provide ocean export and air export services which including space booking, distribution, warehousing, transshipment, containers' consolidation, customs declaration, quarantine and insurance. We also provide various of ship movement service, freight rate, maritime information as well as consultation service. We keep the advantages on the lines to the Middle East, India & Pakistan, Europe & America, Central & South America and Southeast Asia. We have a great number of clients from all over China including many factories and trading company agents. We also have overseas agents from many countries of the world. This strong network enables us to provide a safe transportation to your cargo and helps us to provide our clients with quality service and competitive price.

作为一家一流的代理公司，DDD（TIANJIN）INT' L SHIPPING & TRADING CO.，LTD. 专门从事物流和货运业务。业务主要包括集装箱运输等全方位物流服务。我们提供海上出口和航空出口服务：包括订舱、分销、仓储、中转、集装箱的整合、报关、检疫、保险等。我们还提供各种船舶服务，运费率、海事信息咨询服务。我们保持优势的航线有中东、印度和巴基斯坦、欧洲和美国、中美洲和南美洲和东南亚。我们有很多客户来自全国各地包括许多工厂和贸易公司代理。我们也有许多来自世界各国的海外代理。这个强大的网络使我们能够提供一个安全的运输服务，有助于我们为客户提供优质的服务和有竞争力的价格。

五、信函写作（共 10 分）

说明：假定你是王明，根据下列信息写一封信。

写信日期：2019 年 5 月 4 日。

收信人：Mr. John Brown。

内容：（1）感谢对方订购了你公司的最新产品；

（2）所订购的货物为 M－S 声音隔板（M－S Acoustical Partitions），订单号是 TG0633；该订单已于 5 月 2 日收到；

（3）货物已装船，大约一周后到达；

（4）收到货物后请回复。

声音隔板规格	每只常规价	每只特别价（12 及以上）
4×4’	US $ 112.75 FOB Bern	US $ 98.20 FOB Bern
4×5’	US $ 132	US $ 115.50
5×5’	US $ 152.75	US $ 129.85

May 4，2019

评分标准：书信格式（3 分，其中日期 1 分，称谓 1 分，署名 1 分）；内容完整（4 分）；表达清晰（2 分）；拼写正确（1 分）。

六、翻译对话（共 10 分）

说明：请将下列对话按照角色顺序翻译成中文。

Owner：Good morning Sir，we are from “Sunlight Shipping Company”. My name is Peter. On this visit today we’d like to discuss our long-term agency agreement with you.

Agent：Hello！Peter，good morning，a warm welcome to you from our company，please sit down. Yes，since both of us have contacted for a period of time and laid a good foundation for mutual cooperation，I hope that this meeting today will be very pleasant and fruitful.

Owner：I think so，thank you.

Agent：Well，how about the draft of the agreement？We sent you last week，anything to be corrected further？

Owner：Yes，I would say that most of the terms are acceptable. There are only two points which need to be discussed between us this time. One is the discount percentage of the agency fee，the other is the time for us to remit you the ship disbursement.

Owner：早上好。我是皮特，来自阳光货运公司，今天的这次会谈就是想和你讨论一下我们长期的代理协议。（2 分）

Agent：你好，皮特，早上好！非常欢迎你来到我们的公司，请坐。是的，我们长时间的联系为我们的这次合作打下了基础，我希望我们今天的会谈是愉快和有成果的。（2 分）

Owner：我也这样认为的，谢谢。（1 分）

Agent：很好，协议内容怎么样？协议的草稿我上周发给你了，还需要进一步改进吗？（2分）

Owner：是的，我想说大部分的条款都是可接受的，这次我们需要讨论的只有两点。一个是关于代理费的折扣，另一个是关于船舶支出的费用我们什么时候给你汇过去。（3分）

附录Ⅳ
Appendix Ⅳ

一、场站收据
D/R

集装箱货物托运单（货主留底）（B/N）
十联单第一联

托运人	场站收据编号	抬头
收货人	集装箱货物托运单	
通知方	货主留底	第一联
由收货地××××前程运输		
船舶　航次		
装货港		

卸货港	交货地点	最终的目的地

集装箱号	铅封号	集装箱或 包装数量	包装种类： 货物描述	毛重	尺寸

续表

集装箱或包裹总数（大写）	

货运费用	运费吨	费率	每	预付	到付

<table>
<tr><td rowspan="2">货币汇率</td><td>预付地</td><td>运费支付地</td><td>签发地</td></tr>
<tr><td>预付总额</td><td>正本提单数量</td><td></td></tr>
</table>

收货服务类型	交货服务类型	冷藏温度要求	

<table>
<tr><td rowspan="2">货物种类</td><td>□普通货
□冷藏货
□危险品</td><td rowspan="2">危险品</td><td rowspan="2">等级：
性质：
《国际海运危险货物规则》所在页码：
UN 编号</td></tr>
<tr><td>□液体
□活动物
□散货</td></tr>
</table>

<table>
<tr><td>可否转船</td><td>可否分批</td><td rowspan="4"></td></tr>
<tr><td>装期</td><td>效期</td></tr>
<tr><td colspan="2">金额：</td></tr>
<tr><td colspan="2">制单日期</td></tr>
</table>

Container Cargo Consignment Note（Reserved by Cargo Owner）

the First Copy

<table>
<tr><td colspan="3">SHIPPER</td><td colspan="2">D/R NO.</td><td colspan="3">HEADLINE</td></tr>
<tr><td colspan="3">CONSIGNEE</td><td colspan="5">CONTAINER CARGO CONSIGNMENT NOTE</td></tr>
<tr><td colspan="3">NOTIFY PARTY</td><td colspan="4">RESERVED BY CARGO OWNER</td><td>THE FIRST COPY</td></tr>
<tr><td colspan="3">PRE-CARRIAGE BY××××
PLACE OF RECEIPT××××</td><td colspan="5" rowspan="3"></td></tr>
<tr><td colspan="3">OCEAN VESSEL　VOY. NO.</td></tr>
<tr><td colspan="3">PORT OF LOADING</td></tr>
<tr><td colspan="3">PORT OF DISCHARGE</td><td colspan="2">PLACE OF DELIVERY</td><td colspan="3">FINAL DESTINATION FOR THE MERCHANT'S REFERENCE</td></tr>
<tr><td>CONTAINER NO.</td><td>SEAL NO.</td><td>NO. OF CONTAINERS OR PKGS</td><td colspan="2">KIND OF PACKAGES DESCRIPTION OF GOODS</td><td>GROSS WEIGHT</td><td colspan="2">MEASUREMENT</td></tr>
<tr><td colspan="2">TOTAL NUMBER OF CONTAINERS OR PACKAGES（IN WORDS）</td><td colspan="6"></td></tr>
<tr><td colspan="2">FREIGHT & CHARGES</td><td>REVENUE TONS</td><td>RATE</td><td>PRE</td><td>PRE-PAID</td><td colspan="2">COLLECT</td></tr>
</table>

Continued

EX. RATE	PREPAID AT	PAYABLE AT	PLACE OF ISSUE
	TOTAL PREPAID	NO. OF ORIGINA B/L	

SERVICE TYPE ON RECEIVE	SERVICE TYPE ON DELIVERY	REETER TEMPERATURE REQUIREDL		

TYPE OF GOODS	☐ ORDINARY ☐ REETER ☐ DANGEROUS	DANGEROUS	CLASS: PROPERTY: IMDG CODE: PAGEUN NO. :
	☐ LIQUIDLIVE ☐ ANIMAL ☐ BULK		

TRANSSHIPMENT	PARTIAL	
DATE OF SHIPMENT	EXPIRY DATE	
AMOUNT OF MONEY		
DATE OF FILLING		

集装箱货物托运单（船代留底）（B/N）

十联单第二联

<table>
<tr><td colspan="3">托运人</td><td colspan="2">场站收据编号</td><td colspan="2">抬头</td></tr>
<tr><td colspan="3">收货人</td><td colspan="4">集装箱货物托运单</td></tr>
<tr><td colspan="3">通知方</td><td colspan="3">船代留底</td><td>第二联</td></tr>
<tr><td colspan="3">由收货地××××前程运输</td><td colspan="4" rowspan="3"></td></tr>
<tr><td colspan="3">船舶　航次</td></tr>
<tr><td colspan="3">装货港</td></tr>
<tr><td colspan="2">卸货港</td><td colspan="2">交货地点</td><td colspan="3">最终的目的地</td></tr>
<tr><td>集装箱号</td><td>铅封号</td><td>集装箱或包装数量</td><td colspan="2">包装种类
货物描述</td><td>毛重</td><td>尺寸</td></tr>
<tr><td colspan="2">集装箱或包裹总数（大写）</td><td colspan="5"></td></tr>
<tr><td colspan="2">货运费用</td><td>运费吨</td><td>费率</td><td>每</td><td>预付</td><td>到付</td></tr>
</table>

续表

<table>
<tr><td rowspan="2">货币汇率</td><td>预付地</td><td>运费支付地</td><td>签发地</td></tr>
<tr><td>预付总额</td><td>正本提单数量</td><td></td></tr>
</table>

<table>
<tr><td>收货服务类型</td><td>交货服务类型</td><td>冷藏温度要求</td><td></td><td></td></tr>
</table>

<table>
<tr><td rowspan="2">货物种类</td><td>□普通货
□冷藏货
□危险品</td><td rowspan="2">危险品</td><td rowspan="2">等级：
性质：
《国际海运危险货物规则》所在页码：
UN 编号</td></tr>
<tr><td>□液体
□活动物
□散货</td></tr>
</table>

<table>
<tr><td>可否转船</td><td>可否分批</td><td rowspan="4"></td></tr>
<tr><td>装期</td><td>效期</td></tr>
<tr><td colspan="2">金额</td></tr>
<tr><td colspan="2">制单日期</td></tr>
</table>

<table>
<tr><td>卸货港</td><td>交货地点</td><td>最终的目的地</td></tr>
</table>

CONTAINER CARGO CONSIGNMENT NOTE (RESERVED BY FREIGHT FORWARDER) DUPLICATE

SHIPPER	D/R NO.	HEADLINE
CONSIGNEE	CONTAINER CARGO CONSIGNMENT NOTE	
NOTIFY PARTY	RESERVED BY FREIGHT FORWAR-DER	DUPLICATE
PRE-CARRIAGE BY ×××× PLACE OF RECEIPT××××		
OCEAN VESSEL VOY. NO.		
PORT OF LOADING		

PORT OF DISCHARGE	PLACE OF DELIVERY	FINAL DESTINATION FOR THE MERCHANT'S REFERENCE

CONTAINER NO.	SEAL NO.	NO. OF CONTAINERS OR PKGS	KIND OF PACKAGES DESCRIPTION OF GOODS	GROSS WEIGHT	MEASUREMENT

TOTAL NUMBER OF CONTAINERS OR PAC-KAGES (IN WORDS)	

FREIGHT & CHARGES	REVENUE TONS	RATE	PRE	PRE-PAID	COLLECT

Continued

<table>
<tr><td rowspan="2">EX. RATE</td><td>PREPAID AT</td><td>PAYABLE AT</td><td>PLACE OF ISSUE</td></tr>
<tr><td>TOTAL PREPAID</td><td>NO. OF ORIGINAL B/L</td><td></td></tr>
</table>

<table>
<tr><td>SERVICE TYPE ON RECEIVE</td><td>SERVICE TYPE ON DELIVERY</td><td>REETER TEMPERATURE REQUIRED</td><td></td><td></td></tr>
</table>

<table>
<tr><td rowspan="2">TYPE OF GOODS</td><td>☐ ORDINARY
☐ REETER
☐ DANGEROUS</td><td rowspan="2">DANGEROUS</td><td rowspan="2">CLASS:
PROPERTY:
IMDG CODE PAGE:
UN NO.</td></tr>
<tr><td>☐ LIQUID
☐ LIVE ANIMAL
☐ BULK</td></tr>
</table>

<table>
<tr><td>TRANSSHIPMENT</td><td>PARTIAL</td><td rowspan="4"></td></tr>
<tr><td>DATE OF SHIPMENT</td><td>EXPIRY DATE</td></tr>
<tr><td colspan="2">AMOUNT OF MONEY</td></tr>
<tr><td colspan="2">DATE OF FILLING</td></tr>
</table>

<table>
<tr><td>PORT OF DISCHARGE</td><td>PLACE OF DELIVERY</td><td>FINAL DESTINATION FOR THE MERCHANT'S REFERENCE</td></tr>
</table>

运费通知（1）

十联单第三联

托运人	场站收据编号	抬头
收货人	集装箱货物托运单	
通知方	运费通知（1）	第三联
由收货地××××前程运输		
船舶　航次	装货港	

卸货港	交货地点	最终的目的地

集装箱号	铅封号	集装箱或包装数量	包装种类：货物描述	毛重	尺寸

集装箱或包裹总数（大写）	声明只有________________

货运费用	运费吨	费率	每	预付	到付

货币汇率	预付地	运费支付地	签发地	
	预付总额	正本提单数量		

Freight Notice
Triplicate

<table>
<tr><td colspan="3">SHIPPER</td><td colspan="3">D/R NO.</td><td colspan="3">HEADLINE</td></tr>
<tr><td colspan="3">CONSIGNEE</td><td colspan="6">CONTAINER CARGO CONSIGNMENT NOTE</td></tr>
<tr><td colspan="3">NOTIFY PARTY</td><td colspan="3" rowspan="2">FREIGHT NOTICE</td><td colspan="3" rowspan="2">TRIPLICATE</td></tr>
<tr><td colspan="3">PRE-CARRIAGE BY ××××
PLACE OF RECEIPT</td></tr>
<tr><td colspan="3">OCEAN VESSEL VOY. NO.</td><td colspan="6">PORT OF LOADING</td></tr>
<tr><td colspan="2">PORT OF DISCHARGE</td><td colspan="2">PLACE OF DELIVERY</td><td colspan="5">FINAL DESTINATION FOR THE MERCHANT'S REFERENCE</td></tr>
<tr><td>CONTAINER NO.</td><td>SEAL NO.</td><td>NO. OF CONTAINERS OR PKGS</td><td colspan="2">KIND OF PACKAGES; DESCRIPTION OF GOODS</td><td colspan="3">GROSS WEIGHT</td><td>MEAS-URE-MENT</td></tr>
<tr><td colspan="2">TOTAL NUMBER OF CONTAINERS OR PACKAGES (IN WORDS)</td><td colspan="7">SAY ______________ ONLY</td></tr>
<tr><td colspan="2">FREIGHT & CHARGES</td><td>REVENUE TONS</td><td>RATE</td><td>PRE</td><td colspan="2">PREPAID</td><td colspan="2">COLLECT</td></tr>
<tr><td rowspan="2">EX. RATE</td><td colspan="2">PREPAID AT</td><td colspan="3">PAYABLE AT</td><td colspan="2">PLACE OF ISSUE</td><td></td></tr>
<tr><td colspan="2">TOTAL PRE-PAID</td><td colspan="3">NO. OF ORIGINAL B/L</td><td colspan="2"></td><td></td></tr>
</table>

运费通知（2）

十联单第四联

<table>
<tr><td>托运人</td><td>场站收据编号</td><td>抬头</td></tr>
<tr><td>收货人</td><td rowspan="3">运费通知（2）</td><td rowspan="3">第四联</td></tr>
<tr><td>通知方</td></tr>
<tr><td>由收货地××××前程运输</td></tr>
<tr><td>船舶　航次</td><td colspan="2">装货港</td></tr>
</table>

卸货港	交货地点	最终的目的地

集装箱号	铅封号	集装箱或包装数量	包装种类：货物描述	毛重	尺寸

集装箱或包裹总数（大写）	声明只有________________

货运费用	运费吨	费率	每	预付	到付

<table>
<tr><td rowspan="2">货币汇率</td><td>预付地</td><td>运费支付地</td><td>签发地</td></tr>
<tr><td>预付总额</td><td>正本提单数量</td><td></td></tr>
</table>

Freight Notice
Quadruplicate

<table>
<tr><td>SHIPPER</td><td>D/R NO.</td><td>HEADLINE</td></tr>
<tr><td>CONSIGNEE</td><td rowspan="3">FREIGHT NOTICE</td><td rowspan="3">QUADRUPLICATE</td></tr>
<tr><td>NOTIFY PARTY</td></tr>
<tr><td>PRE-CARRIAGE BY ××××
PLACE OF RECEIPT</td></tr>
<tr><td>OCEAN VESSEL VOY. NO.</td><td colspan="2">PORT OF LOADING</td></tr>
</table>

PORT OF DISCHARGE	PLACE OF DELIVERY	FINAL DESTINATION FOR THE MERCHANT'S REFERENCE

CONTAINER NO.	SEAL NO.	NO. OF CONTAINERS OR PKGS	KIND OF PACKAGES: DESCRIPTION OF GOODS	GROSS WEIGHT	MEAS-URE-MENT

TOTAL NUMBER OF CONTAINERS OR PACKAGES (IN WORDS)	SAY ______________ ONLY

FREIGHT & CHARGES	REVENUE TONS	RATE	PRE	PREPAID	COL-LECT

<table>
<tr><td rowspan="2">EX. RATE</td><td>PREPAID AT</td><td>PAYABLE AT</td><td>PLACE OF ISSUE</td></tr>
<tr><td>TOTAL PREPAID</td><td>NO. OF ORIGINAL B/L</td><td></td></tr>
</table>

场站收据（装货单）

十联单第五联

<table>
<tr><td colspan="3">托运人</td><td colspan="2">场站收据编号</td><td>抬头</td></tr>
<tr><td colspan="3">收货人</td><td colspan="2" rowspan="2">装货单</td><td rowspan="2">第五联</td></tr>
<tr><td colspan="3">通知方</td></tr>
<tr><td colspan="3">由收货地××××前程运输</td><td colspan="3"></td></tr>
<tr><td colspan="3">船舶　航次</td><td colspan="3">装货港</td></tr>
<tr><td colspan="2">卸货港</td><td colspan="2">交货地点</td><td colspan="2">最终的目的地</td></tr>
<tr><td>集装箱号</td><td>铅封号</td><td>集装箱或包装数量</td><td>包装种类：货物描述</td><td>毛重</td><td></td></tr>
<tr><td colspan="2">集装箱或包裹总数（大写）</td><td colspan="4">声明只有________________</td></tr>
<tr><td rowspan="2">货币汇率</td><td>预付地</td><td colspan="2">运费支付地</td><td colspan="2">签发地</td></tr>
<tr><td>预付总额</td><td colspan="2">正本提单数量</td><td colspan="2"></td></tr>
</table>

(S/O) Dock Receipt (Loading List)
the Fifth Copy

<table>
<tr><td colspan="3">SHIPPER</td><td colspan="2">D/R NO.</td><td colspan="2">HEADLINE</td></tr>
<tr><td colspan="3">CONSIGNEE</td><td colspan="2" rowspan="2">LOADING LIST</td><td colspan="2" rowspan="2">THE FIFTH COPY</td></tr>
<tr><td colspan="3">NOTIFY PARTY</td></tr>
<tr><td colspan="3">PRE-CARRIAGE BY ×××× PLACE OF RECEIPT</td><td colspan="4"></td></tr>
<tr><td colspan="3">OCEAN VESSEL VOY. NO.</td><td colspan="4">PORT OF LOADING</td></tr>
<tr><td colspan="2">PORT OF DISCHARGE</td><td colspan="3">PLACE OF DELIVERY</td><td colspan="2">FINAL DESTINATION FOR THE MERCHANT'S REFERENCE</td></tr>
<tr><td>CONTAINER NO.</td><td>SEAL NO.</td><td>NO. OF CONTAINERS OR PKGS</td><td colspan="2">KIND OF PACKAGES DESCRIPTION OF GOODS</td><td>GROSS WEIGHT</td><td>MEASUREMENT</td></tr>
<tr><td colspan="2">TOTAL NUMBER OF CONTAINERS OR PACKAGES (IN WORDS)</td><td colspan="5">SAY ________________ ONLY</td></tr>
<tr><td rowspan="2">EX. RATE</td><td>PREPAID AT</td><td colspan="3">PAYABLE AT</td><td colspan="2">PLACE OF ISSUE</td></tr>
<tr><td>TOTAL PREPAID</td><td colspan="3">NO. OF ORIGINAL B/L</td><td colspan="2"></td></tr>
</table>

大副联（场站收据副本）
十联单第六联

<table>
<tr><td colspan="4">托运人</td><td colspan="3">场站收据编号</td><td colspan="3">抬头</td></tr>
<tr><td colspan="4">收货人</td><td colspan="3">场站收据副本</td><td colspan="3" rowspan="2">第六联</td></tr>
<tr><td colspan="4">通知方</td><td colspan="3">大副联</td></tr>
<tr><td colspan="4">由收货地××××前程运输</td><td colspan="6"></td></tr>
<tr><td colspan="4">船舶　航次</td><td colspan="6">装货港</td></tr>
<tr><td colspan="3">卸货港</td><td colspan="3">交货地点</td><td colspan="3">最终的目的地</td><td></td></tr>
<tr><td colspan="2">集装箱号</td><td>铅封号</td><td colspan="2">集装箱或包装数量</td><td>包装种类：货物描述</td><td colspan="3">毛重</td><td>尺寸</td></tr>
<tr><td colspan="3">集装箱或包裹总数（大写）</td><td colspan="7">声明只有________________</td></tr>
<tr><td rowspan="2">货币汇率</td><td colspan="2">预付地</td><td colspan="5">运费支付地</td><td colspan="2">签发地</td></tr>
<tr><td colspan="2">预付总额</td><td colspan="5">正本提单数量</td><td colspan="2"></td></tr>
</table>

FOR CHIEF OFFICE

(COPY OF DOCK RECEIPT)

<table>
<tr><td colspan="4">SHIPPER</td><td colspan="4">D/R NO.</td><td colspan="3">HEADLINE</td></tr>
<tr><td colspan="4">CONSIGNEE</td><td colspan="4">COPY OF DOCK RECEIPT</td><td colspan="3" rowspan="2">THE SIXTH COPY</td></tr>
<tr><td colspan="4">NOTIFY PARTY</td><td colspan="4">(FOR CHIEF OFFICE)</td></tr>
<tr><td colspan="4">PRE-CARRIAGE BY ××××
PLACE OF RECEIPT</td><td colspan="7"></td></tr>
<tr><td colspan="4">OCEAN VESSEL VOY. NO.</td><td colspan="7">PORT OF LOADING</td></tr>
<tr><td colspan="3">PORT OF DISCHARGE</td><td colspan="3">PLACE OF DELIVERY</td><td colspan="5">FINAL DESTINATION FOR THE MERCHANT'S REFERENCE</td></tr>
<tr><td colspan="2">CONTAINER NO.</td><td>SEAL NO.</td><td colspan="2">NO. OF CONTAINERS ORPKGS</td><td colspan="2">KIND OF PACKAGES DESCRIPTION OF GOODS</td><td colspan="3">GROSS WEIGHT</td><td>MEASUREMENT</td></tr>
<tr><td colspan="3">TOTAL NUMBER OF CONTAINERS OR PACKAGES (IN WORDS)</td><td colspan="8">SAY ________________ ONLY</td></tr>
<tr><td rowspan="2">EX. RATE</td><td colspan="2">PREPAID AT</td><td colspan="6">PAYABLE AT</td><td colspan="2">PLACE OF ISSUE</td></tr>
<tr><td colspan="2">TOTAL PREPAID</td><td colspan="6">NO. OF ORIGINAL B/L</td><td colspan="2"></td></tr>
</table>

场站收据（D/R）
十联单第七联

<table>
<tr><td colspan="4">托运人</td><td colspan="4">场站收据编号</td><td colspan="3">抬头</td></tr>
<tr><td colspan="4">收货人</td><td colspan="4" rowspan="2">场站收据</td><td colspan="3" rowspan="2">第七联</td></tr>
<tr><td colspan="4">通知方</td></tr>
<tr><td colspan="4">由收货地××××前程运输</td><td colspan="7"></td></tr>
<tr><td colspan="4">船舶　航次</td><td colspan="7">装货港</td></tr>
<tr><td colspan="3">卸货港</td><td colspan="3">交货地点</td><td colspan="4">最终的目的地</td><td></td></tr>
<tr><td colspan="2">集装箱号</td><td>铅封号</td><td colspan="2">集装箱或包装数量</td><td colspan="2">包装种类：货物描述</td><td colspan="3">毛重</td><td>尺寸</td></tr>
<tr><td colspan="3">集装箱或包裹总数（大写）</td><td colspan="8">声明只有________________</td></tr>
<tr><td rowspan="2">货币汇率</td><td colspan="2">预付地</td><td colspan="6">运费支付地</td><td colspan="2">签发地</td></tr>
<tr><td colspan="2">预付总额</td><td colspan="6">正本提单数量</td><td colspan="2"></td></tr>
</table>

Dock Receipt (the Seventh Copy)

<table>
<tr><td colspan="3">SHIPPER</td><td colspan="2">D/R NO.</td><td colspan="2">HEADLINE</td></tr>
<tr><td colspan="3">CONSIGNEE</td><td colspan="2" rowspan="2">DOCK RECEIPT</td><td colspan="2" rowspan="2">THE SEVENTH COPY</td></tr>
<tr><td colspan="3">NOTIFY PARTY</td></tr>
<tr><td colspan="3">PRE-CARRIAGE BY ×××× PLACE OF RECEIPT</td><td colspan="4"></td></tr>
<tr><td colspan="3">OCEAN VESSEL VOY. NO.</td><td colspan="4">PORT OF LOADING</td></tr>
<tr><td colspan="2">PORT OF DISCHARGE</td><td colspan="3">PLACE OF DELIVERY</td><td colspan="2">FINAL DESTINATION FOR THE MERCHANT'S REFERENCE</td></tr>
<tr><td>CONTAINER NO.</td><td>SEAL NO.</td><td>NO. OF CONTAINERS OR PKGS</td><td colspan="2">KIND OF PACKAGES DESCRIPTION OF GOODS</td><td>GROSS WEIGHT</td><td>MEASUREMENT</td></tr>
<tr><td colspan="2">TOTAL NUMBER OF CONTAINERS OR PACKAGES (IN WORDS)</td><td colspan="5">SAY ________________ ONLY</td></tr>
<tr><td rowspan="2">EX. RATE</td><td>PREPAID AT</td><td colspan="3">PAYABLE AT</td><td colspan="2">PLACE OF ISSUE</td></tr>
<tr><td>TOTAL PREPAID</td><td colspan="3">NO. OF ORIGINAL B/L</td><td colspan="2"></td></tr>
</table>

货代留底
十联单第八联

<table>
<tr><td colspan="3">托运人</td><td colspan="2">场站收据编号</td><td>抬头</td></tr>
<tr><td colspan="3">收货人</td><td colspan="2" rowspan="2">货代留底</td><td rowspan="2">第八联</td></tr>
<tr><td colspan="3">通知方</td></tr>
<tr><td colspan="3">由收货地××××前程运输</td><td colspan="3"></td></tr>
<tr><td colspan="3">船舶　航次</td><td colspan="3">装货港</td></tr>
<tr><td colspan="2">卸货港</td><td colspan="2">交货地点</td><td colspan="2">最终的目的地</td></tr>
<tr><td>集装箱号</td><td>铅封号</td><td>集装箱或包装数量</td><td>包装种类：货物描述</td><td>毛重</td><td>尺寸</td></tr>
<tr><td colspan="2">集装箱或包裹总数（大写）</td><td colspan="4">声明只有________________</td></tr>
<tr><td rowspan="2">货币汇率</td><td>预付地</td><td colspan="2">运费支付地</td><td colspan="2">签发地</td></tr>
<tr><td>预付总额</td><td colspan="2">正本提单数量</td><td colspan="2"></td></tr>
</table>

Reserved by Freight Forwarder
(the Eighth Copy)

<table>
<tr><td colspan="4">SHIPPER</td><td colspan="4">D/R NO.</td><td colspan="3">HEADLINE</td></tr>
<tr><td colspan="4">CONSIGNEE</td><td colspan="4" rowspan="2">RESERVED
BY FREIGHT
FORWARDER</td><td colspan="3" rowspan="2">THE EIGHTH COPY</td></tr>
<tr><td colspan="4">NOTIFY PARTY</td></tr>
<tr><td colspan="4">PRE-CARRIAGE BY ××××
PLACE OF RECEIPT</td><td colspan="7"></td></tr>
<tr><td colspan="4">OCEAN VESSEL VOY. NO.</td><td colspan="7">PORT OF LOADING</td></tr>
<tr><td colspan="3">PORT OF DISCHARGE</td><td colspan="3">PLACE OF DELIVERY</td><td colspan="5">FINAL DESTINATION FOR THE MERCHANT'S REFERENCE</td></tr>
<tr><td colspan="2">CONTAINER NO.</td><td>SEAL NO.</td><td colspan="2">NO. OF CONTAINERS OR PKGS</td><td colspan="2">KIND OF PACKAGES DESCRIPTION OF GOODS</td><td colspan="3">GROSS WEIGHT</td><td>MEASUREMENT</td></tr>
<tr><td colspan="3">TOTAL NUMBER OF CONTAINERS OR PACKAGES (IN WORDS)</td><td colspan="8">SAY ________________ ONLY</td></tr>
<tr><td rowspan="2">EX. RATE</td><td colspan="2">PREPAID AT</td><td colspan="6">PAYABLE AT</td><td colspan="2">PLACE OF ISSUE</td></tr>
<tr><td colspan="2">TOTAL PREPAID</td><td colspan="6">NO. OF ORIGINAL B/L</td><td colspan="2"></td></tr>
</table>

货代负责的单证之出口
十联单——第九联

<table>
<tr><td colspan="3">上海××国际货运有限公司</td><td>出场</td></tr>
<tr><td colspan="4">集装箱发放/设备交接单</td></tr>
<tr><td colspan="4">编号</td></tr>
<tr><td colspan="3">用箱人/运箱人</td><td>提箱地点</td></tr>
<tr><td colspan="3"></td><td></td></tr>
<tr><td>发往地点</td><td colspan="3">返回/收箱地点</td></tr>
<tr><td></td><td colspan="3"></td></tr>
<tr><td>船名/航次</td><td>集装箱号</td><td>尺寸/类型</td><td>营运人</td></tr>
<tr><td></td><td></td><td></td><td></td></tr>
<tr><td>提单号</td><td>铅封号</td><td>免费期限</td><td>运载工具牌号</td></tr>
<tr><td></td><td></td><td></td><td></td></tr>
<tr><td colspan="2">出场目的</td><td>进场目的/状态</td><td>出场日期</td></tr>
<tr><td colspan="2"></td><td></td><td></td></tr>
<tr><td colspan="4">出场检查记录</td></tr>
<tr><td>普通集装箱</td><td>冷藏集装箱</td><td>特种集装箱</td><td>发电机</td></tr>
<tr><td>正常</td><td>正常
异常</td><td>正常
异常</td><td>正常
异常</td></tr>
</table>

除列明者外，集装箱及集装箱设备交接单时完好无损，铅封完好无损。

用箱人/运箱人签署

码头/堆场值班员签署

Export Certificate for Freight Forwarding

(the Ninth Copy)

<table>
<tr><td colspan="3">×× SHANGHAI INTERNATIONAL FREIGHT CO. , LTD.</td><td>OUT</td></tr>
<tr><td colspan="4">EQUIPMENT INTERCHANGE RECEIPT</td></tr>
<tr><td colspan="4">NO.</td></tr>
<tr><td colspan="3">CONTAINER USER/HAULIER</td><td>PLACE OF DELIVERY</td></tr>
<tr><td colspan="3"></td><td></td></tr>
<tr><td>DELIVERED TO</td><td colspan="3">PLACE OF RETURN</td></tr>
<tr><td></td><td colspan="3"></td></tr>
<tr><td>VESSEL/VOYAGE NO.</td><td>CONTAINER NO.</td><td>SIZE/TYPE</td><td>CNTR. OPRT.</td></tr>
<tr><td></td><td></td><td></td><td></td></tr>
<tr><td>B/L NO.</td><td>SEAL NO.</td><td>FREE TIME PERIOD</td><td>TRUCK, WAGON, BARGE NO.</td></tr>
<tr><td></td><td></td><td></td><td></td></tr>
<tr><td colspan="2">PPS OF GATE-OUT/STATUS</td><td>PPS OF GATE-INSTATUS</td><td>TIME-OUT</td></tr>
<tr><td colspan="2"></td><td></td><td></td></tr>
<tr><td colspan="4">INSPECTION AT THE TIME OF INTERCHANGE</td></tr>
<tr><td>GP CONTAINER</td><td>RF CONTAINER</td><td>SPERCIAL CONTAINER</td><td>GEN SET</td></tr>
<tr><td>SOUND
DEFECTIVE</td><td>SOUND
DEFECTIVE</td><td>SOUND
DEFECTIVE</td><td>SOUND
DEFECTIVE</td></tr>
</table>

The container/associated equipment interchanged in sound condition and seal intact unless otherwise stated.

Container User/Hauliers Signature

Terminal/Depotclerk's Signature

货代负责的单证之出口

十联单——第十联

<table>
<tr><td colspan="3">托运人</td><td colspan="4">场站收据编号</td><td colspan="3">抬头</td></tr>
<tr><td colspan="3">收货人</td><td colspan="4" rowspan="2">配舱回单</td><td colspan="3" rowspan="2">第十联</td></tr>
<tr><td colspan="3">通知方</td></tr>
<tr><td colspan="3">由收货地××××前程运输</td><td colspan="7" rowspan="3"></td></tr>
<tr><td colspan="3">船舶　航次</td></tr>
<tr><td colspan="3">装货港</td></tr>
<tr><td colspan="2">卸货港</td><td colspan="4">交货地点</td><td colspan="4">最终的目的地</td></tr>
<tr><td>集装箱号</td><td>铅封号</td><td>集装箱或包装数量</td><td colspan="3">包装种类：
货物描述</td><td colspan="2">毛重</td><td colspan="2">尺寸</td></tr>
<tr><td colspan="2">集装箱或包裹总数（大写）</td><td colspan="8"></td></tr>
<tr><td colspan="2">货运费用</td><td>运费吨</td><td>费率</td><td>每</td><td>预付</td><td colspan="4">到付</td></tr>
<tr><td rowspan="2">货币汇率</td><td colspan="2">预付地</td><td colspan="3">运费支付地</td><td colspan="4">签发地</td></tr>
<tr><td colspan="2">预付总额</td><td colspan="3">正本提单数量</td><td colspan="4"></td></tr>
<tr><td>收货服务类型</td><td colspan="2">交货服务类型</td><td colspan="3">冷藏温度要求</td><td colspan="2"></td><td colspan="2"></td></tr>
<tr><td colspan="2" rowspan="2">货物种类</td><td colspan="2">□普通货
□冷藏货
□危险品</td><td colspan="3" rowspan="2">危险品</td><td colspan="3" rowspan="2">等级：
性质：
《国际海运危险货物规则》所在页码：
UN 编号</td></tr>
<tr><td colspan="2">□液体
□活动物
□散货</td></tr>
<tr><td colspan="2">可否转船</td><td>可否分批</td><td colspan="7" rowspan="4"></td></tr>
<tr><td colspan="2">装期</td><td>效期</td></tr>
<tr><td colspan="3">金额</td></tr>
<tr><td colspan="3">制单日期</td></tr>
</table>

Export Certificate for Freight Forwarding

(the Tenth Copy)

SHIPPER	D/R NO.	HEADLINE
CONSIGNEE		THE TENTH COPY
NOTIFY PARTY		
PRE - CARRIAGE BY ×××× PLACE OF RECEIPT		
OCEAN VESSEL VOY. NO.		
PORT OF LOADING		

PORT OF DISCHARGE	PLACE OF DELIVERY	FINAL DESTINATION FOR THE MERCHANT'S REFERENCE

CONTAINER NO.	SEAL NO.	NO. OF CONTAINERS OR PKGS	KIND OF PACKAGES DESCRIPTION OF GOODS	GROSS WEIGHT	MEASUREMENT
TOTAL NUMBER OF CONTAINERS OR PACKAGES (IN WORDS)					

FREIGHT &CHARGES	REVENUE TONS	RATE	PRE	PRE-PAID	COLLECT

EX. RATE	PREPAID AT	PAYABLE AT	PLACE OF ISSUE
	TOTAL PREPAID	NO. OF ORIGINAL B/L	

SERVICE TYPE ON RECEIVE	SERVICE TYPE ON DELIVERY	REETER TEMPERATURE REQUIRED		

TYPE OF GOODS	☐ ORDINARY ☐ REETER ☐ DANGEROUS ☐ LIQUID ☐ LIVE ANIMAL ☐ BULK	DANGEROUS	CLASS: PROPERTY: IMDG CODE PAGE: UN NO.)

TRANSSHIPMENT	PARTIAL	
DATE OF SHIPMENT	EXPIRY DATE	
AMOUNT OF MONEY		
DATE OF FILLING		

二、装箱单
Packing List

中国××××进出口公司

唛头：　　　　　　　　　　　发票号：

合同号：

装箱单

提单号：　　　　　　日期：

船名：　　　　　　　单号：　　　　　　　从：　　　　　　至：

卖给：

唛头及标记	商品	数量	净重	毛重	尺寸

装箱单

1）收件人：

2）运单号：____________公司名称：____________承运人：____________地址：____________重量：____________城市/地区号：____________体积：____________州名/国家：____________电话/传真：____________

3）详细的商品名称：

4）生产厂商：

5）数量：

6）本人认为以上提供的资料属实和正确，货物原产地是____________

7）出口理由：

签名：

公章：

CHINA×××× IMPORT AND EXPORT COMPANY

Shippingmark: Invoice No:

Contract No. :

Packing List

B/L No. : Date:

Name of Vessel: B/L No. From: To:

Sold To Messrs:

Marks & Nos	Commodity	Quantity	NW	GW	Measurement

PACKING LIST

1) Consignor:

2) Consignee: ______________ Airbill No: ______________ Company Name: ______________ Carrier: ______________ Address: ______________ Weight: ______________ Town/Area Code: ______________ Dimensions: ______________ State/Country: ______________ Phone/Fax No. ______________

3) The Name of Goods:

4) Manufacturers:

5) Full Description of Manufacturer No. of Items Goods:

6) ______________ I declare that the above information is true and correct to the

best of my knowledge and that the goods are of ______________________ origin.

7）Reason for Export：

Signature：

Stamp：

装箱单是发票的补充单据，它列明了信用证（或合同）中买卖双方约定的有关包装事宜的细节，便于国外买方在货物到达目的港时供海关检查和核对货物，通常可以将其有关内容加列在商业发票上，但是在信用证有明确要求时，就必须严格按信用证约定制作。类似的单据还有：重量单、规格单、尺码单等。其中重量单是用来列明每件货物的毛、净重；规格单是用来列明包装的规格；尺码单用于列明货物每件尺码和总尺码，或用来列明每批货物的逐件花色搭配。装箱单名称应按照信用证规定使用。通常用“PACKING LIST”“PACKING SPECIFICATION”或“DETAILED PACKING LIST”。如果来证要求用“中性包装单”（NEUTRAL PACKING），则包装单名称打“PACKING LIST”，但包装单内不打卖方名称，不能签章。出单方（Issuer）出单人的名称与地址，应与发票的出单方相同。在信用证支付方式下，此栏应与信用证受益人的名称和地址一致。受单方（To）受单方的名称与地址，与发票的受单方相同。多数情况下填写进口商的名称和地址，并与信用证开证申请人的名称和地址保持一致。在某些情况下也可不填，或填写“To whom it may concern”（致有关人）。发票号（Invoice No.）与发票号码一致。日期（Date）装箱单缮制日期。应与发票日期一致，不能迟于信用证的有效期及提单日期。唛头及件数编号（Marks and Numbers）与发票一致，有的注实际唛头，有时也可以只注“as per invoice No. ×××”。包装种类和件数、货物描述（Number and kind of packages，description of goods）要求与发票一致。货名如有总称，应先注总称，然后逐项列明每一包装件的货名、规格、品种等内容。外包装件数（PACKAGE）填写每种货物的包装件数，最后在合计栏处注外包装总件数。毛重（G. W）注明每个包装件的毛重和此包装件内不同规格、品种、花色货物各自的总毛重，最后在合计栏处注总毛重。信用证或合同未要求，不注亦可。如：2588. 36 KGS。净重（N. W）注明每个包装件的净重和此包装件内不同规格、品种、花色货物各自的总净重，最后在合计栏处注总净重。信用证或合同未要求，不注亦可。如：760 KGS。箱外尺寸（Meas.）注明每个包装件的体积，最后在合计栏处注总体积。信用证或合同未要求，不注亦可。如：1623. 548 CBM。SAY TOTAL 以大写文字写明总包装数量，必须与数字表示的包装数量一致。如：FOUR THOUSAND FOUR HUNDRED CARTONS ONLY。签名（Signature）由出口公司的法人代表或者经办制单人员代表公司在装箱单右下方签名，上方空白栏填写公司英文名称，下方则填写公司法人英文名称。

三、设备交接单
Equipment Interchange Receipt

集装箱及设备交接单

出场

日期（DATE）: 0016582

用箱人/运箱人	提箱地

箱号	尺寸/类	铅封号	船名/航次 营运人 提单号 免费期限

出场时间	出场目的/状态	返场时间	返场目的/状态

出场检查记录

普通箱	冷藏箱	特种箱	发电机
□正常 □异常	□正常 □异常	□正常 □异常	□正常 □异常

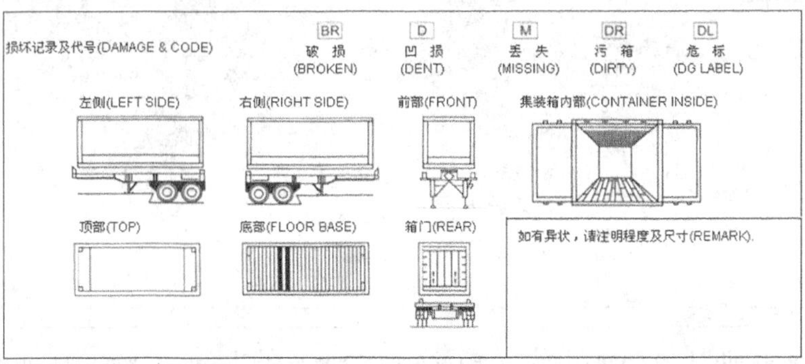

除列明者外，集装箱及设备交接是完好无损，铅封完好无损。

用箱人/运箱人签　　　　箱管员签　　　　场站值班签

EQUIPMENT INTERCHANGE RECEIPT

OUT

Date:　　　　　　　　　　　　0016582

Container User/Haulier			Place of Delivery
Container No.	Size/Type	Seal No.	Vessel/Voyage No. Cntr Optr B/L No. Free Time Period

Time Out	Pps of Gate-Out/Status	Time In	Pps of Gate-in /Status

INSPECTION AT THE TIME OF INTERCHANGE			
GP Container	RF Container	SP Container	GEN Set
□Sound □Defective	□Sound □Defective	□Sound □Defective	□Sound □Defective

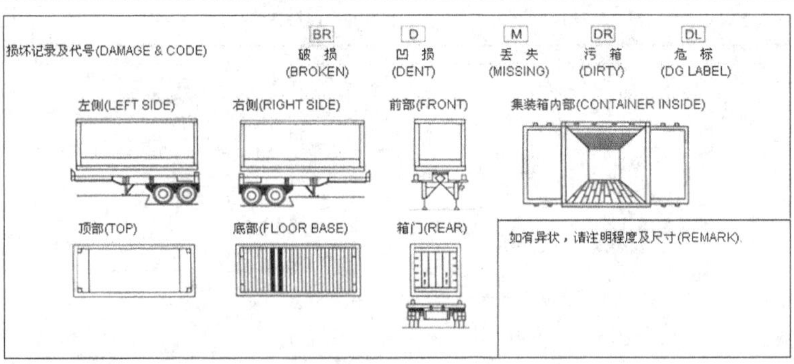

Unless otherwise specified, the containers and equipment are handed over in good condition and the lead seals are intact.

Container User/Hauliers' Signture)　　　　(Container Manager' Signture)　　　　(Clerk' Signture)

四、装货单
Shipping Order

装货单

托运人

编号　　　　　　　　　　　　　　船名

目的港

兹将下列完好状况之货物装船后签署收货单

标记及号码	件数	货名	重量公斤
			净

共计件数（大写）

日期

时间

装入何舱

实收

理货员签名

经办员

SHIPPING ORDER

Shipper

No. S/S

For

Receive on board the undermentioned goods apparent in good order and condition and sign the accompanying receipt for the same

Marks &No. s	Quantity	Description of Goods	Weight Kilos
			Net

Total Number of Packages in Writing

Date

Time

Stowed

Received

Tally Man

Operator

五、海运出口货物投保单
Insurance Policy For Export Goods By Sea

海运出口货物投保单

保险人		被保险人	
标记	包装及数量	保险货物项目	保险货物金额
总保险金额：（大写）			
运输工具（船名）（航次）			
装运港		目的港	
投保险别		货物起运日期	
投保日期		投保人签字	

Insurance Policy for Marine Export Goods

<table>
<tr><td colspan="2">Insurer</td><td colspan="2">Insured</td></tr>
<tr><td colspan="2"></td><td colspan="2"></td></tr>
<tr><td>Sign</td><td>Packaging and Quantity</td><td>Cargo Items</td><td>Amount</td></tr>
<tr><td></td><td></td><td></td><td></td></tr>
<tr><td colspan="4">Total Insurance Amount</td></tr>
<tr><td colspan="4"></td></tr>
<tr><td colspan="2">Means of Transportation：(Vessel name)
(voyage number)</td><td colspan="2"></td></tr>
<tr><td>Port of Shipment</td><td></td><td colspan="2">Port of Destination</td></tr>
<tr><td>Insurance Type</td><td></td><td colspan="2">Date of Shipment</td></tr>
<tr><td>Date of Insurance</td><td></td><td colspan="2">Signature of Policyholder</td></tr>
</table>

六、商检换证提供资料表格
Commodity Inspection Certificate Information Form

商检换证提供资料表格

<table>
<tr><td colspan="8">收货人（英文）：</td></tr>
<tr><td colspan="8">发货人（核销单公司名）：</td></tr>
<tr><td colspan="8">商检注册号（报检号）：</td></tr>
<tr><td>品名</td><td>编码</td><td>数量</td><td>箱 数</td><td>单 价</td><td>总金额</td><td>毛重</td><td>净重</td></tr>
<tr><td></td><td></td><td></td><td></td><td></td><td></td><td></td><td></td></tr>
<tr><td></td><td></td><td></td><td></td><td></td><td></td><td></td><td></td></tr>
<tr><td></td><td></td><td></td><td></td><td></td><td></td><td></td><td></td></tr>
<tr><td></td><td></td><td></td><td></td><td></td><td></td><td></td><td></td></tr>
<tr><td colspan="3">出口口岸（启运地或者仓库）：</td><td colspan="5">到达国家（中文）：</td></tr>
<tr><td colspan="3">包装形式：</td><td colspan="5">集装箱规格：</td></tr>
<tr><td colspan="3">合同号：</td><td colspan="5">运输方式：</td></tr>
<tr><td colspan="8">唛头：</td></tr>
<tr><td colspan="8">请注意：请逐一确认所填数据，商检一旦安排后，不得改单，不得删单，不得退单，否则后果自负
填写联系人：
联系电话（手机和电话）：</td></tr>
</table>

Commodity Inspection Certificate Information Form

<table>
<tr><td colspan="8">Consignee:</td></tr>
<tr><td colspan="8">Consignor:</td></tr>
<tr><td colspan="8">Commodity Inspection Registration Number:</td></tr>
<tr><td>Product Name</td><td>H. S H. S Encoding</td><td>Quantity</td><td>Number of Container</td><td>Unit Price</td><td>Total Amount</td><td>Gross Weight</td><td>Net Weight</td></tr>
<tr><td></td><td></td><td></td><td></td><td></td><td></td><td></td><td></td></tr>
<tr><td></td><td></td><td></td><td></td><td></td><td></td><td></td><td></td></tr>
<tr><td></td><td></td><td></td><td></td><td></td><td></td><td></td><td></td></tr>
<tr><td></td><td></td><td></td><td></td><td></td><td></td><td></td><td></td></tr>
<tr><td colspan="3">Export Port (place of departure or warehouse):</td><td colspan="5">Country of Arrival (Chinese):</td></tr>
<tr><td colspan="3">Package Style:</td><td colspan="5">Container Specification:</td></tr>
<tr><td colspan="3">Contract Number:</td><td colspan="5">Mode of Transportation:</td></tr>
<tr><td colspan="8">Marks:</td></tr>
<tr><td colspan="8">Please confirm the data filled in one by one. Once the commodity inspection is arranged, it is not allowed to change, delete or return the order. Otherwise, the consequences will be borne by yourself.
Contact person:
Contact number (mobile and telephone):</td></tr>
</table>

七、订舱委托书
Booking Note

订舱委托书

公司编号　　　　　　　　　　　　　　　　　　　　　　　　日期

<table>
<tr><td rowspan="4">1）发货人</td><td colspan="2">4）信用证号码</td></tr>
<tr><td colspan="2">5）开证银行</td></tr>
<tr><td>6）合同号码</td><td>7）成交金额</td></tr>
<tr><td>8）装运口岸</td><td>9）目的港</td></tr>
<tr><td rowspan="4">2）收货人</td><td>10）转船运输</td><td>11）分批装运</td></tr>
<tr><td>12）信用证效期</td><td>13）装船期限</td></tr>
<tr><td>14）运费</td><td>15）成交条件</td></tr>
<tr><td>16）公司联系人</td><td>17）电话/传真</td></tr>
<tr><td rowspan="2">3）通知人</td><td>18）公司开户行</td><td>19）银行账号</td></tr>
<tr><td colspan="2">20）特别要求</td></tr>
<tr><td colspan="3">21）标记唛码　　22）货号规格
23）包装件数　　24）毛重
25）净重　　26）数量
27）单价　　28）总价
29）总件数　　30）总毛重
31）总净重　　32）总尺码
33）总金额</td></tr>
<tr><td colspan="3">34）备注</td></tr>
</table>

Booking Note

Company Number　　　　　　　　　　　　　　　　　　　　Specific Date

<table>
<tr><td rowspan="4">1) Consignor</td><td colspan="2">4) L / C Number</td></tr>
<tr><td colspan="2">5) Issuing Bank</td></tr>
<tr><td>6) Contract Number</td><td>7) Transaction Amount</td></tr>
<tr><td>8) Shipping Port</td><td>9) Port of Destination</td></tr>
<tr><td rowspan="4">2) Consignee</td><td>10) Transshipment</td><td>11) Partial Shipment</td></tr>
<tr><td>12) Validity of L / C</td><td>13) Shipping Period</td></tr>
<tr><td>14) Freight</td><td>15) Transaction Conditions</td></tr>
<tr><td>16) Company Contact</td><td>17) Telephone / Fax Number</td></tr>
<tr><td rowspan="2">3) Notifier</td><td>18) Opening Bank</td><td>19) Account Number</td></tr>
<tr><td colspan="2">20) Special Requirements</td></tr>
<tr><td colspan="3">21) Mark Code　22) Number and Specification
23) Number of Packages　24) Gross Weight
25) Net Weight　26) Quantity
27) Unit Price　28) Total Price
29) Total Number of Pieces　30) Total Gross Weight
31) Total Net Weight　32) Total Size
33) Total Amount</td></tr>
<tr><td colspan="3">34) Remarks</td></tr>
</table>

八、中华人民共和国检验检疫局出境商品检验申请单

Application Form for Outbound Commodity Inspection by the Inspection and Quarantine Bureau of the People's Republic of China

中华人民共和国检验检疫局出境商品检验申请单

<table>
<tr><td colspan="7">报检单位（加盖公章）：
＊编号____________</td></tr>
<tr><td colspan="7">报检单位登记号：　　　　　　联系人：
电话：　　　　　　报检日期：</td></tr>
<tr><td rowspan="2">发货人</td><td colspan="6">（中文）</td></tr>
<tr><td colspan="6">（外文）</td></tr>
<tr><td rowspan="2">收货人</td><td colspan="6">（中文）</td></tr>
<tr><td colspan="6">（外文）</td></tr>
<tr><td>货物名称（中/外文）</td><td>编号</td><td>产地</td><td>数/重量</td><td>货物总值</td><td colspan="2">包装种类及数量</td></tr>
<tr><td></td><td></td><td></td><td></td><td></td><td colspan="2"></td></tr>
<tr><td>运输工具名称号码</td><td></td><td>贸易方式</td><td></td><td>存放地点</td><td colspan="2"></td></tr>
<tr><td>合同号</td><td></td><td>信用证号</td><td colspan="2"></td><td>用途</td><td></td></tr>
<tr><td>发货日期</td><td></td><td>输往国家（地区）</td><td></td><td colspan="2">许可证/审批号</td><td></td></tr>
<tr><td>启运地</td><td></td><td>到达口岸</td><td></td><td colspan="2">生产单位注册号</td><td></td></tr>
<tr><td colspan="2">集装箱规格、数量及号码</td><td colspan="5"></td></tr>
</table>

续表

<table>
<tr><td>合同、信用证定力的检验检疫条款或特殊要求</td><td>标记及号码</td><td colspan="2">随附单据（划“✓”或补填）</td></tr>
<tr><td rowspan="4"></td><td rowspan="4"></td><td>□合同</td><td>□集装箱</td></tr>
<tr><td>□信用证</td><td>□厂检单</td></tr>
<tr><td>□发票</td><td>□包装性能结果单</td></tr>
<tr><td>□换证凭单</td><td>□许可/审批文件</td></tr>
</table>

<table>
<tr><td colspan="3">需要证单名称（划“✓”或补填）</td><td colspan="2">＊检验检疫费</td></tr>
<tr><td>□□品质证书</td><td>____正____副</td><td>□卫生证书____正____副</td><td rowspan="2">总金额
（人民币元）</td><td rowspan="2"></td></tr>
<tr><td>□重量证书</td><td>____正____副</td><td>□动物卫生证书
____正____副植物</td></tr>
<tr><td>□数量证书</td><td>____正____副</td><td>□检疫证书____正____副</td><td rowspan="2">计费人</td><td rowspan="2"></td></tr>
<tr><td>□兽医卫生证书</td><td>____正____副</td><td>□熏蒸/消毒证书____正____副</td></tr>
<tr><td>□健康证书</td><td>____正____副</td><td>□出境货物换证凭单</td><td>收费人</td><td></td></tr>
</table>

<table>
<tr><td rowspan="3">保荐人郑重声明：
1. 本人被授权报检。
2. 上列填写内容正确属实，货物无伪造或冒用他人的厂名、标志、认证标志、并承担货物质量责任。
签名：________________</td><td colspan="2">领取单证</td></tr>
<tr><td>日期</td><td></td></tr>
<tr><td>签名</td><td></td></tr>
</table>

Application Form for Outbound Commodity Inspection by the Inspection and Quarantine Bureau of the People'S Republic of China

<table>
<tr><td colspan="7">Inspection Applicant (with official seal):
No. ____________</td></tr>
<tr><td colspan="3">Registration Number:
Telephone Number:</td><td colspan="4">Contact:
Inspection Date:</td></tr>
<tr><td rowspan="2">Consignor</td><td colspan="6">Chinese</td></tr>
<tr><td colspan="6">English</td></tr>
<tr><td rowspan="2">Consignee</td><td colspan="6">Chinese</td></tr>
<tr><td colspan="6">English</td></tr>
<tr><td>Cargo Name (Chinese/English)</td><td>H. S. H. S. Encoding</td><td>Place of Origin</td><td>Quantity/ Weight</td><td>Total Value</td><td colspan="2">Packaging Type and Quantity</td></tr>
<tr><td></td><td></td><td></td><td></td><td></td><td colspan="2"></td></tr>
<tr><td>Means of Transport</td><td></td><td>Trade Mode</td><td></td><td>Storage Location</td><td colspan="2"></td></tr>
<tr><td>Contract Number</td><td></td><td>Letter of Credit No.</td><td colspan="2"></td><td>Usage</td><td></td></tr>
<tr><td>Shipping Date</td><td></td><td>Countries (regions)</td><td></td><td colspan="2">License / Approval Number</td><td></td></tr>
<tr><td>Place of Departure</td><td></td><td>Port of Arrival</td><td></td><td colspan="2">Company Registration Number</td><td></td></tr>
<tr><td colspan="2">Container Specification, Quantity and Number</td><td colspan="5"></td></tr>
<tr><td colspan="2">Inspection and Quarantine Clauses or Special Requirements Stipulated in the Contract or Letter of Credit</td><td>Marks and Numbers</td><td colspan="4">Attached Documents (marked "✓" or filled in)</td></tr>
</table>

Continued

<table>
<tr><td colspan="2" rowspan="4"></td><td rowspan="4"></td><td>☐Contract</td><td colspan="2">☐Container</td></tr>
<tr><td>☐Letter of credit</td><td colspan="2">☐Factory Inspection List</td></tr>
<tr><td>☐Invoice</td><td colspan="2">☐Packing Sheet</td></tr>
<tr><td>☐Exchange Voucher</td><td colspan="2">☐Permission/Approval Documents</td></tr>
<tr><td colspan="4">Required Documents (marked "✓" or filled in)</td><td colspan="2">Inspection and Quarantine Fees</td></tr>
<tr><td>☐Quality Certificate</td><td>(Original and Duplicate)</td><td colspan="2">☐Health Certificate (Original and Duplicate)</td><td rowspan="2">Total Amount (RMB yuan)</td><td rowspan="2"></td></tr>
<tr><td>☐Weight Certificate</td><td>(Original and duplicate)</td><td colspan="2">☐Animal/Plant Health Certificate (original and duplicate)</td></tr>
<tr><td>☐Quantity Certificate</td><td>(Original and Duplicate)</td><td colspan="2">☐Quarantine Certificate (original and duplicate)</td><td rowspan="2">Biller</td><td rowspan="2"></td></tr>
<tr><td>☐Veterinary Health Certificate</td><td>(Original and Duplicate)</td><td colspan="2">☐Fumigation / Disinfection Certificate (original and duplicate)</td></tr>
<tr><td>☐Health Certificate</td><td>(Original and Duplicate)</td><td colspan="2">☐Voucher for Outbound Cargo</td><td>Charger</td><td></td></tr>
<tr><td colspan="3" rowspan="3">The sponsor solemnly declares that:
1. I am authorized to apply for inspection.
2. The contents listed above are correct and true, and the goods are free from forgery or false use of other factory names, signs, certification marks. I bear the responsibility for the quality of goods.

Signature: ____________</td><td colspan="3">Documents</td></tr>
<tr><td>Date</td><td colspan="2"></td></tr>
<tr><td>Signature</td><td colspan="2"></td></tr>
</table>

九、提货单
Delivery Order

提货单

<table>
<tr><td colspan="4">海关编号</td><td colspan="4"></td></tr>
<tr><td>电话</td><td colspan="3"></td><td colspan="4" rowspan="2">下列货物已办妥手续，运费结清，准予交付收货人</td></tr>
<tr><td>传真</td><td colspan="3"></td></tr>
<tr><td>船名</td><td></td><td>航次</td><td></td><td>起运港</td><td></td><td>目的港</td><td></td></tr>
<tr><td>提单号</td><td></td><td>交付条款</td><td></td><td>第一程运输</td><td colspan="3"></td></tr>
<tr><td>集装箱号</td><td></td><td>箱数</td><td></td><td>换单日期</td><td></td><td>卸货地点</td><td></td></tr>
<tr><td colspan="2">集装箱号，铅封号</td><td colspan="2">货物名称</td><td>件数与包装</td><td>重量</td><td colspan="2">体积</td></tr>
<tr><td colspan="2"></td><td colspan="2"></td><td></td><td></td><td colspan="2"></td></tr>
<tr><td colspan="5">收货人章：</td><td colspan="3">海关单：</td></tr>
<tr><td colspan="2"></td><td colspan="2"></td><td colspan="2"></td><td colspan="2"></td></tr>
<tr><td colspan="8">注意事项：
1. 本提货单需要有船单（船公司）放货章和海关放行章后方始有效。凡属法定检验，检疫的进口商品，必须向检验检疫机构申报。
2. 货物超过港存取，码头公司可以按有关规定处理。在规定期间无人提取的货物，按《海关法》和国家有关规定处理。</td></tr>
</table>

Delivery Order

<table>
<tr><td colspan="6">Customs Number</td><td colspan="2"></td></tr>
<tr><td>Tel</td><td colspan="4"></td><td colspan="3" rowspan="2">The following goods have gone through the formalities, the freight has been settled, and it is allowed to deliver them to the consignee.</td></tr>
<tr><td>Fax</td><td colspan="4"></td></tr>
<tr><td>Vessel Name</td><td></td><td>Voyage Number</td><td></td><td>Port of Departure</td><td></td><td>Port of Destination</td><td></td></tr>
<tr><td>Bill of Lading</td><td></td><td>Terms of Delivery</td><td></td><td>First Transportation</td><td colspan="3"></td></tr>
<tr><td>Container Number</td><td></td><td>Number of Containers</td><td></td><td>Replacement Date</td><td></td><td>Place of Discharge</td><td></td></tr>
<tr><td colspan="2">Container Number, Seal Number</td><td colspan="2">Cargo Number</td><td>Number of Pieces and Packaging</td><td>Weight (KGS)</td><td colspan="2">Volume</td></tr>
<tr><td colspan="2"></td><td colspan="2"></td><td></td><td></td><td colspan="2"></td></tr>
<tr><td colspan="2">Consignee' s Seal</td><td colspan="6">Customs Form</td></tr>
<tr><td colspan="2"></td><td colspan="2"></td><td colspan="2"></td><td colspan="2"></td></tr>
<tr><td colspan="8">Precautions:
1. This bill of lading shall be valid only after it has the shipping company release seal and customs release seal. All imported commodities subject to statutory inspection and quarantine must be declared to the inspection and quarantine institutions.
2. The terminal company may handle the goods according to the relevant regulations when they exceed the port of deposit and withdrawal. Goods that are not picked up during the prescribed period shall be handled in accordance with the Customs Law and relevant state regulations.</td></tr>
</table>